PRAISE FOR DEER HUNTING IN PARIS

"Paula Young Lee's memoir, *Deer Hunting in Paris*, bursts with wit, recipes, and unexpected juxtapositions. I grew up Korean American in Alabama, but Paula grew up Korean American in Maine, which is even stranger. I did not go on to explore Paris and moose hunting like Paula did, but her memoir, which is unexpectedly moving, makes me wish I had. A truly extraordinary life and a truly unique voice. More than any other book I know, *Deer Hunting in Paris* explores the tendons and gristle of life."
— Michael Chwe, author of *Jane Austen, Game Theorist*

"From the rugged backwoods of Maine to the streets of Paris, Paula Young Lee takes you on an unexpected journey. Through deep insight, arresting imagery, and deft turns of phrase, she reveals the meat, blood, and bone of our hungers, dark and true."
— Tara Austen Weaver, author of *The Butcher & The Vegetarian*

"Not many narratives have you laughing, wincing, and weeping at the same time. *Deer Hunting in Paris* is pure prose genius. Smart and smart-alecky, a delight on every page."
— Gary Buslik, author of *A Rotten Person Travels the Caribbean* and *Akhmed and the Atomic Matzo Balls*

"Paula Young Lee is M.F.K. Fisher with a gun, Julia Child prepping roadkill."
— Marcy Gordon, editor, *Leave the Lipstick, Take the Iguana*, author, comeforthewine.com

"*Deer Hunting in Paris* is a story of hunger and faith, and faith in hunger. But there's more to it than that: a frenetic electricity, a stumbling toward an illusion of arrival that's hard to put a finger on. Paula Young Lee's memoir is the stuff of sumptuous and bloodthirsty parable, a story at once new and strange, and yet engrained, guiding us with searing wit through the chambers of our lives. In her commentary on contemporary culture, her catalogue of references that shift from ancient to pop in the blink of an eye, this is a memoir that proves and interrogates the wild interconnectedness of things, especially those that may at first seem glaringly dissimilar. Lee moves us from Maine to France and back again, whirls us among Jesus and Kafka, IKEA and The Big Buck Club, love, shotguns, longing, and death. 'The dying,' she tells us, 'have epiphanies and enemas.' Rarely has such a spectrum of quirky meditations been so funny, and so true. The result is a tale that makes you laugh, scratch your head, rock your heart back from the breaking, and ultimately, exhale, exhilarated, having just learned that the weirdest arenas in our lives are often the most beautiful."
— Matthew Gavin Frank, author of *Prepar̶ ̶ ̶Pot Farm*, and *Barolo*

"I have a new favorite writer—I love thi
her, Paula Young Lee has written an end
cleaver-sharp, side-splitting storytelling. '
J. Maarten Troost, Tahir Shah) that conta
I read aloud to friends, but *Deer Huntin.*

moments. I phoned friends and family and stopped strangers to read aloud some of Paula's moments: her nose nestled between her boyfriend's butt cheeks as they train for the wife-carrying competition, her childhood dream that Turkish delight is 100% giblets, trying on a camouflage bikini (while ammo shopping) that turns her into both a wallflower and a butterball, a wedding day pig roast with a guy nicknamed Smeg, short for smegma. What I wasn't expecting in this witty romp was a wisdom and way of looking at life and death that would make this the most personally profound book I've ever read. My life-long all-consuming terror of death was bizarrely put out of its misery with Lee's rational portrait of the inevitable for all of us creatures as she deftly handles flesh for feasting."

—*Kirsten Koza,* author of *Lost in Moscow: A Brat in the USSR*

"Paula Young Lee takes us on an intriguing whirl through a Paris most of us have never seen—a Paris of Republicans, rifle-toting New Englanders, and riotous tales of hunting. Your stomach will ache from laughter and hunger at the same time."

—David Farley, author of *An Irreverent Curiosity*

Praise for Paula Young Lee

On *Meat, Modernity, and the Rise of the Slaughterhouse*:

"An unexpectedly fascinating collection of essays by historians, geographers, economists, and even an architectural historian (who is the general editor), covering France, Germany, Britain, the United States, and Mexico. The subjects range from technology to sanitation to humanitarian concerns, with rich material on the culture and traditions of the abbatoir."

—*Kitchen Arts & Letters*

"A unique compilation that chronicles the transition of the meat processing industry in the nineteenth century. The collection illustrates the change from individual, community-based butchering to a centralized, municipally controlled process. Readers who enjoyed the popular books of Michael Pollan, Erich Schlosser, or Peter Singer would be drawn to this."

—*The Social Science Journal*

On *How To Be a Homeless Frenchman*:

"Intelligent without snobbery, poignant without sappiness, and hilarious without end, the novel serves up delights and surprises like a many-layered candy egg with a secret center."

—Ron Cooper, author of the critically acclaimed novel, *Purple Jesus*

DEER HUNTING IN PARIS

TRAVELERS' TALES

DEER HUNTING IN PARIS

A Memoir of God, Guns, and Game Meat

PAULA YOUNG LEE

Solas House
Palo Alto

Travelers' Tales and *Solas House* are trademarks of Solas House, Inc. 2320 Bowdoin Street, Palo Alto, California 94306. www.travelerstales.com

Production Editor: Natalie Baszile
Page layout and photo editing: Scribe Inc. using the fonts Granjon, Nicolas Cochin and Ex Ponto
Cover design: Kimberly N. Coombs
Author photographs: snowshoeing with campfire, Arthur Jackson; carousel, John Feeney
Interior design: Melanie Haage

Distributed by Publishers Group West, 1700 Fourth Street, Berkeley, CA 94710

Library of Congress Cataloguing-in-Publication Data Pending

ISBN 10: 1-60952-080-7
ISBN 13: 978-160952080-9

First Edition
Printed in the United States
10 9 8 7 6 5 4 3 2 1

To my parents

Contents

17. HAM SUPPER FOR 227   271

    EPILOGUE   299

    ACKNOWLEDGMENTS   303

    ABOUT THE AUTHOR   305

Prologue

"Keaton always said, 'I don't believe in God, but
I'm afraid of him.' Well I believe in God, and the
only thing that scares me is Big Bird."
– *Verbal Kint, in* The Usual Suspects, *1995*

*P*arishioners believed he could heal them with his hands.
As a kid, I knew my father was different, and it had
nothing to do with the fact that he was a preacher. His legs
were shriveled down to bone and he walked funny, sometimes with a cane. His face beamed. He forgot to eat. He liked
Maine, because the rocky terrain reminded him of home. He
and my mother came to the U.S. from Korea after the war.
At first, there were four of us, and then there were five: my
father, my mother, my brother, my sister, and me in the middle. My older brother and I fought mean and hard, locked in
a death match from the day I was born. Oblivious to the slug-
fest, my baby sister sat back and let the adults admire her. She
was the pretty one, and could never figure out why I was so
furious all the time. She was born with grace. Predictably, her
Korean name, Young-Mi, means "flower." Mine is Young-
Nan. It means "egg."

Together, the three of us practiced our musical instruments,
spoke English at home, and got straight A's in school. We
grew up ringing church bells every Sunday, pulling down the
ropes and flying up into the belfry. My sister and I sang in the
choir as my brother pummeled toccatas and fugues out of the
organ. There was Sunday school, bible study, and neighborly

visits to the nursing home, but the part I liked about church was Christmas, and the fancy food.

I could cook before I could read. I could read before I was four, because I was mad that my older brother was Sacred Cow Oldest Number One Son, and he got to do everything first. From birth, I knew the weight of karmic injustice, and I knew what that meant thanks to those theological discussions at dinner. Not only would I never be older than him, he would always be smarter. And a boy. His Korean name began with "Ho," which in English means "Great." Humph. What's so great about *him*? "How come he gets to be a Ho?" I would howl, a pudgy ball of rage stamping angrily on tabletops. "It's not fair! *I* want to be a Ho!" Sure, he could make electric generators out of Tinker Toy sets, but I could make layer cakes, and I had friends. So there. Cakes win.

With "Auntie" Ima the babysitter, I baked coffee cakes and apple pies. With my mother, I made *mondu* (dumplings) and *nangmyun* (noodles). The church ladies taught me how to knead dough and whip cream. I didn't eat the goodies that I made. Nothing about me was sweet, including my teeth. My great food love was meat, the kind of meat that demands a sharp knife and a taste for blood. We never seemed to have much. I suppose we were dirt poor, but so was everyone else. Poor was normal. Poverty was too. Instead of plastic reindeer glowing on front yards, winter meant gutted deer hanging off porch roofs, hovering lightly in the blue air, black noses sniffing the ground. I'd extend a searching hand, flicking away flakes, and stick my nose in where it didn't belong. Like magic, the deer's length and heft became food and it was Good, the body and blood of Amen, a serving of flesh tying the community together through the violence of hunger.

Deer and hunter walked the same paths through the woods. I wanted to follow them.

Sunday dinners at the parsonage, guests would discard the gristle, the cartilage, the marrow, and the rind, all the stuff that pale priests and thickening colonels refused to touch in mixed company. I'd serve and clear the table, acting the perfect hostess as my baby sister sat quietly, basking in her cuteness, and my savant brother played young Christ before the Elders. Back in the kitchen where no one would see me, I'd grab bones off dirtied plates and gnaw off that bulbous white knob at the end, my favorite part, a tasty tidbit that only appeared after the commonplace had been excavated. Lollipops for carnivores. It wasn't meat that I really craved. I loved liver and heart, along with the tangled tissues that connected the big sheets of muscle together. The offal fed to animals was the stuff I wanted to chew, because I was more contrary than Mary, not Mary mother of God but the stubborn one that ruled Scotland before she lost her head.

So, Mistress Mary, how does your garden grow?

Oh, very well, thanks to the corpse of my murdered husband fertilizing the marigolds.

Nursery rhymes mask vicious politics. So does a well-cooked meal.

A giblet was a meat pacifier, rubbery and melting at the same time. It resisted. It put up a fight. I cherished its toughness as I gnawed and glowered in the kitchen, a fat feral gnome surrounded by the aromas of love and yeast and holy ghosts I did not believe in.

"It does not matter if you believe in God," my father said with infuriating patience. "Because God believes in you."

"But I'm an *iconoclast*," I protested loudly, trying out my interesting new word.

"So was Martin Luther," my father responded placidly. "You're a Protestant through and through."

"No, I'm not!"

"Yes, you are."

And so I was boxed into a corner.

At bedtime, my mom tucked me and my sister into our respective twin beds with matching quilts that she and the quilting bee ladies had made. Then she'd make me say my prayers. "Dear God," I'd start obediently. And stop. Patiently, my mother waited while I struggled to free my arms from the leaden weight of white sheets so I could clasp my hands in the correct form, shaping them into a steeple pointing toward heaven. "Dear God," I'd start again, with a heavy sigh. "Thank you for my mom, my dad, my baby sister,"—at which point, my baby sister would look like she just won a puppy—"and my brother who is the worst brother ever but I'm not supposed to say that so I'M NOT, and thank you for the really good turkey that we had for dinner tonight. Amen." Satisfied, my mother would return my struggling arms back under the covers and re-tuck the sheets so tightly that I felt like a PEZ dispenser ready to poop out little turds of peppermint candy. Carefully, she'd turn out the light, plunging the room into darkness, and close the bedroom door behind her as she left to repeat the ritual with my brother, who got his own room, just like he got his own bike and his own underwear. Clutching her beloved stuffed animal to her chest, my sister would immediately close her eyes, fall asleep, and start drooling, not necessarily in that order. I would wait one, two, three seconds for her adenoids to be fully charged, and then I'd struggle free of my swaddling, grab the flashlight hidden beneath my pillow, reach for the books I'd stashed under my bed, duck under the covers, and start reading.

I slept on books too. To this day, I prefer a very hard mattress.

After regular services at our church, we'd sometimes drive out to visit the Bahá'ís because it was the neighborly thing to do. Who were the Bahá'ís? In 1900, a Maine woman named Sarah Jane Farmer had gone to Palestine by herself. When she returned, she established a religious retreat in Eliot, Maine, for the Baháʼí Faith. It's the religious equivalent of cricket, the most popular professional sport in the world, but one that most Americans have never heard of and have no idea how to play. Baháʼís believe in God, but their version has no gender. It's basically what Christianity would look like if the Vatican hadn't taken over the God business. Sarah Jane's childhood home in Eliot, Maine, had been a mecca for the most progressive minds of the period, including Harriet Beecher Stowe and Sojourner Truth. Her father, Moses Farmer, invented the fire box pull and 99 other useful things including a useless toy called the "light bulb." Along came this other guy named Thomas Edison, who had a genius for taking lame inventions and tweaking them so they could be mass produced and sold for a profit. This is what Edison did with the incandescent bulb, and he died a very rich man. Farmer believed that his gifts were God-given, and thus it was a sin to profit from them. Today, nobody's heard of him.

What do we learn from this? Successful businessmen believe they are God's gift to the world. They are correct.

To the great disappointment of my four-year-old self, the Baháʼí Faith congregation was made up of nice white folks with heavy Maine accents, same as the people who went to the Methodist church where my dad preached every Sunday. The grounds of the Baháʼí Faith retreat were magically beautiful, leading me to think that "Baháʼí" was the secret code word for "Narnia." I was very disappointed when Mr. Tumnus the Faun did not appear, welcoming us with a turban on his head and a platter of Turkish delight in his hands. Apart from the fact that Edmund Pevensie liked to eat it very much, I had no idea what Turkish delight was, but it sounded very Turkish, and therefore I was keen to try it. I was hoping it was 100 percent giblets.

Even today, Turkish delight isn't widely available in the U.S. I had to go all the way to France to discover that Turkish delight is a nut bomb of death disguised with a heavy dusting of confectioner's sugar. By then, I was also old enough to have learned that C.S. Lewis, the Irish author of the Narnia chronicles, had been professor of English at Oxford University, and he'd nicknamed himself after his dead dog, Jack. He was also a theologian who'd infused the entire *Narnia* series with a Christian agenda aimed straight at convincing sweet, innocent children to believe in the Way and the Truth and the Life after Death for a large talking lion named Aslan. In case you've never noticed, "Aslan" is an anagram of "nasal," which is another way of saying "nose," which is to say, He who "knows" all. Oh . . . my . . . GOD. It's a conspiracy! C.S. Lewis wrote a bunch of other books too, but those were for grownups. I'll bet you can't name one. Which just proves that the conspiracy theorists are correct, and God favors those who write fantasy books in His name.

"Aslan" is the Turkish word for "lion." There is no lion meat in Turkish delight. There is no Turkish delight in the Aslan.

I read and re-read the Narnia books about a hundred times, because a set was in the library of just about every church my dad served. It was a lot. In small towns in Maine, churches are like Dunkin' Donuts: there's one on every corner, and they each have a membership of about a dozen. Because many of these churches were too small to support a full-time minister, some of my dad's assignments turned him into a circuit preacher. I literally grew up in the church, but in my head, "church" was a collective set of white clapboard buildings that would have pitchers of red Kool-Aid and stale vanilla finger cookies in the kitchen refrigerators. As a little kid, I'd run around the vestry, hide in the pulpit, and stretch out and nap in the pews. Of course I knew I wasn't supposed to, but God never reached down and smote me, even though I dared Him to. I took this as a sign He approved. The church was God's house, but it was also my dad's office and a building with a reliably flushing toilet. When dragged to visit the Catholics, usually because my dad had meetings with them, I'd grab a book and settle into an empty confessional. They were supposed to be locked when not in use, to prevent sinners from confessing to an empty box, but there's that pesky road to hell separating the best of intentions from skeletons in the closet. Eventually, nuns would figure out where I was, and they always had this perplexed look on their faces, as if they couldn't decide what I was really doing, sitting mostly in the dark with that musty old book about the Pilgrim's progress on my lap. (Unacceptable answer: "Looking for Narnia.")

These little escapades convinced me that nuns came with sagging stockings and wimples, which struck me as extremely appealing. I made up my mind to become one. This impulse didn't last very long, because there was a war going on. There was also a war between the U.S. and Vietnam, and it was on the news every night.

"I'm going to become President of the United States!" I announced.

"Stop blocking the TV," my brother complained.

"Make me," I dared.

"Get out of the way," my brother menaced. "Or else . . ."

"Nyah nyah!"

At which point, my baby sister would start crying, and I'd be sent to my room until my tantrum subsided. If I was the President, I reasoned darkly as I threw Barbie dolls across the room, no one could stop me from blowing up my brother. He was standing between me and my plans for world domination. To thwart me, he'd started booby-trapping the house so a loud buzzer would go off when I hit a hidden tripwire. BBBBBBBRRRRRRRGGG! Sometimes, for extra fun, the booby traps would zap me, so I'd shriek like a howler monkey and then hit the roof. He thought this was hilarious. I was not amused.

This is what happens when you have a mad scientist for an older brother. The adults admired him for being so clever, and I was ready to kill him.

It was just as well that my parents scuttled my political ambitions. I'm too short to win presidential elections. Plus, I'd never make it through vetting, because my mom's name is wrong on the birth certificate. Being dead and all, she can't sign a notarized affidavit stating that she'd given birth to me, no matter how many times the bureaucrats insisted that I drag her to city hall and make her deal with the paperwork. Since I don't know any spells to raise the dead, I was left with the interesting proposition that, legally, I'm the child of a woman who didn't exist.

With every passing year, I'm becoming more and more like her.

My father became a pastor because he'd been a Private First Class in the 9th Division of the Republic of Korea (ROK) Army, and he'd seen what the artillery fire had done to the land. The bombs ate everything green, and left nothing behind but ashes. The war was doing the same to the soldiers' souls. My dad wasn't a military chaplain, but he was a Christian, and soldiers who'd just lost their buddies in battle would ask him if he believed in life after death. If he did believe in the afterlife, what happens then? He responded by praying with them, and singing hymns, and studying the Bible, and resolving that he needed to deepen his understanding of God's holy word. He followed his faith, and it brought him all the way from the Hermit Kingdom to Vacationland, USA.

Still walking on two legs, he traveled to the U.S. in order to study at a small Methodist university in Lincoln, Nebraska. Shortly after he arrived, he was invited to preach the gospel at a church in a town called Cozad. He didn't have a car, so another student volunteered to drive him down that lonesome rural road on a frosty Sunday morning. By the time they saw the other car pulling out of an intersection that came out of nowhere, it was too late. The cars collided.

His friend escaped with a few cuts and scratches. My dad sailed out the front windshield and traveled fifty whole feet before landing. He was in a coma for a long time. When he woke up, the doctors told him he was a paraplegic, because his spinal cord was severed at the waist.

Despite the physical therapy, his legs shriveled due to muscle atrophy. He was in terrible pain. The morphine turned him into an addict. He wanted to kill himself but failed, because he couldn't move without help. He became angry with God, protesting with rage. The hospital put him on suicide watch, and removed everything from arm's reach that could be turned into a weapon.

He became even angrier and lost the will to live.

He was in the hospital for a year. It was a long, hard road, but eventually, for reasons that are his to tell, he made his peace with God, and now my father walks through the strength of that renewed faith. His physician said that my father's recovery was beyond the reach of medical science, and his only explanation was some sort of divine intervention. The doctor was not a religious man. He didn't believe in miracles, but what else was he supposed to call it? Me, I don't think the miracle was the fact that my father regained the use of his legs, but that a young Korean man was spiritually adopted by the whitest bunch of white people that anyone could imagine in 1950s America, and they took him in, cared for him, and helped pay his medical bills. Students gave blood. Strangers pitched in. The entire community helped with his rehabilitation, as he went from mechanical bed, to wheelchair, to metal braces, to crutches, to a cane and finally to special boots that he still wears. If there was racism or bigotry in Nebraska, my father doesn't recall it. That's God working in mysterious ways. That, and a metal plate in his head.

He went on to study for the ministry at Boston University, where he met my mother, a Korean doctor's daughter who'd come to BU to study nursing. She was pious, naïve, and problematically beautiful. They married in a traditional American white-dress ceremony, for she was Christian too, and carried on as stereotypical Asian graduate students. After a respectable amount of time had passed, they were blessed with my brother. He was the Only Begotten Son, a gift from the Heavenly Father, the answer to their heartfelt wishes and nightly prayers. Not only did he have all of his fingers and all of his toes, but he had an IQ so high that he was awake and aware straight out of the womb. Sort of like a cross between Chucky the Doll and Damien in *The Omen*.

About a year later, my mother knew she was pregnant again when she felt something kicking inside her belly with the fury of a trapped beast. Even as a fetus, I abhorred being stuck in one place, and I wasn't going to let a partially formed brainstem interfere with my quest to be free.

For those who enjoy splitting hairs, I was neither born nor conceived in Eliot, but I can truthfully say I was gestated in that teeny town where my dad answered the call to serve the Lord. After being ordained in Boston, he accepted an appointment to a church that none of the other ministers wanted because even religious men have ambitions, and Maine is really cold in the winter. When he and my mother arrived in Eliot, they were an eager family of three. I was merely a pesky case of indigestion that, a few months later, popped out as a pesky case of indigestion with hair on its head.

Some of the congregation objected to my father being appointed to lead their church. Mind you, they were not racists. They had nothing against chinks, gooks, or slant-eyes, excepting, of course, the commie ones in 'Nam. Without them

Chinamen over there in Japan, MacArthur would have had to make do with fighting Russians, and they're not nearly as much fun to shoot. They welcomed immigrants, just as long as they comes here legal and speaks good English. No, they objected to my dad's . . . uh . . . his interpretation of the liturgy! They didn't like the way he planned to run the service. Too many hymns. Not enough scriptural readings, plus he was using the Revised Standard Version of the Bible instead of King James. What are we, Unitarians?

Rather than compromise their religious principles, the objecting faction traipsed off, firm in their moral rectitude and taking their best church supper recipes for glazed ham. I imagine they started their own church, something like the "Rhythm Methodists," because that would be a very American thing to do, starting your own denomination when the old one doesn't suit you, and then making as many miracle babies as possible to fill up those pews. My father felt bad that some parishioners felt that way, but Jesus still loves you, and them, and as long as they were worshipping the Almighty, he had no cause to complain. He'd already been through an unpopular war, and had no interest in fueling another. God has a plan. It is not our place to judge His ways.

My mother, however, had her own feelings on the subject. She tended to get resentful. She talked to herself, and I have dog ears. I heard everything until I stopped listening. I still heard too much.

After my baby sister was born, Auntie Ima started helping my mother manage us kids. We were each a little over one year apart, and my brother was a state-certified genius who required full-time monitoring lest he dismantle the record player and build a satellite out of the parts. Because she could sit on him if necessary, Auntie Ima took charge of my brother, my mother watched my baby sister, my dad tended to his flock, and I was left to my druthers. In nearly every frame

DEER HUNTING IN PARIS

of my parents' home movies, I'm the heel of a patent-leather shoe, a hem of a corduroy jumper, or just not in the picture at all. But when I came back from the twilight woods, I'd head to Auntie Ima's house and launch myself into her bulk. She was very fat. Invariably, I'd find her and my brother planted in spindle chairs at the kitchen table, where he'd be munching a slice of homemade blueberry pie and working through equations. She'd be playing solitaire, keeping one eye on the cards and the other on his motorized doodads. She smelled like old lady lavender and her flesh was fresh bread dough, powdery soft and fluffy, as if pumped full of air. She didn't mind that I'd pet her arm and play with the batwings as if they were kittens. She was over sixty, and had no use for vanity.

"I knew you before you were born," she'd say to me. There is something very weird about that.

She and my Uncle Loren were German Protestants from Ohio. They were a childless couple and good church people, as my dad would say. My Uncle Loren was a bespectacled, retired GE man who was older than his wife. He'd been some kind of engineer, and he spent hours helping my brother perfect his sister-torturing devices. Not only did I end up harboring a visceral dislike of anything with an electrical current, I was banished from my brother's basement laboratory after that time I tiptoed downstairs to peek, and all his gizmos exploded. This only served to increase my resentment, because he got new stuff for his lab, and I got in trouble even though I'd done nothing but stand on the steps and glare politely at him.

Still, despite the fact that I was hopelessly bereft of mechanical ability and quite possibly haunted by a poltergeist, I was Uncle Loren's favorite, and he was mine. We were alike in our crabby natures and dislike of children. He didn't want any, and neither did I. He was dour in the manner of a summertime Santa on a day when the elves were playing hooky, and he knew that I knew it and didn't expect him to change. We were two grumpy old men sitting on the porch, drinking our glasses of ice water and watching the chickadees at the birdfeeder. It never really occurred to me that he was old. For that matter, it didn't occur to me that he was a "he." My Uncle Loren was the closest thing I had to a cat. I was four and he was bald, and we were best friends. I adored my Uncle Loren, because he never expected me to do anything. I didn't even have to cook for him. He had Auntie Ima for that, and she was very good at it.

One day, he went to sleep and never woke up.

He'd died of a heart attack. I suppose he died without knowing he was dead. The adults were tiptoeing around the subject, trying to shield us kids, but of course I knew what death was. All kids do. On cartoons and television, people die by the dozens every day. I'd stared at paintings of crucifixions and martyred saints my whole life. I'd just never seen an actual human corpse. It was my first wake. He was lying in an open casket and I climbed up to inspect him. He was wearing an ill-fitting suit that struck me as being oddly formal for bedtime. There was a small smile on his face. He looked happy, which was not his usual expression, and that really confused me.

"He's gone to Heaven," my dad explained reassuringly, as my Auntie Ima sobbed loudly into a large embroidered hanky.

"No, he didn't. He's right here," I complained. "If he's gone to Heaven, shouldn't he be Assumptioned?"

"That's Catholic," my brother corrected me, because he was a genius, and I was always getting my theological dogma wrong. "Protestants don't believe in that."

There's a soul, and there's a body. Unless you're Mary, Mother of Our Lord Jesus Christ, or Christ the Savior himself, your body sticks around and gets stuffed full of embalming fluid so little kids can stare at you and wonder why you smell funny. I didn't cry, because I wasn't sad that my Uncle

Loren had died. I was too angry at him. It was one more reminder that every positive comes with a negative, and every life demands death as its price. Uncle Loren was the one person I could count on to take my side. So God killed him, as if to say, "Defend yourself, already! What, you think being a little kid earns you a pass? A century ago, you'd be working full time in a factory and dead of dysentery by age six. So whine all you want. Boo hoo!" My dad had lived through two great tragedies, the Korean War and the car accident that destroyed his legs, which turned his life into *Madame Butterfly* meets *The Sun Also Rises*. I just had stupid allergies and an annoying older brother, whose very existence seemed to be God's way of letting me know, "Yes, Little Egg, there *is* a Hell!" And then He cracks me on the head.

"He's in Heaven," my father repeated solemnly. "He was a good man."

My Auntie Ima blew her nose loudly, and resumed blubbering.

The problem isn't death. It's the horrible feeling that something has been taken away. It's Lucy van Pelt convincing Charlie Brown to kick the football, then—"AAUGH!"—she whisks it away. "You shouldn't have trusted me, Charlie Brown," she tells him smugly as he lands with a hard thump on the ground, mentally kicking himself for being such a chump. The joke is that he never learns. Again and again she persuades him with a sweet smile, "Kick the football, Charlie Brown!" and he keeps hoping that this time it will be different, and the ball will soar through the unseen goalposts, earning him cheers from the crowd and kisses from the Little Red-Haired Girl. He falls for the line no less than forty-two times. "You shouldn't have trusted me," Lucy reminds us. We know the outcome and yet, a teeny part of us still hopes that maybe, just maybe, forty-three is the charm . . .

AAUGH!

Sometimes I wonder how I would have turned out if my parents had raised me in Nebraska, a state that grimly warns you: "Equality before the Law." This doesn't mean equality in the *eyes* of Ms. Law, because she's blind and therefore handicapped. Nope. It's all about Procrustean justice, Tarantino-style, and if you don't like it—go ahead, make my day: I'll blow the head right off your oversized corn dog. Because my dad is a saint, his response to war was to pray for men's souls. Me, if I was on a battlefield and my friends were being killed, I'd figure out an attack strategy, grab the best sharpshooters, and save my troops. I'd also be court-martialed for breaking chain of command and having my period, but, like, whatever. A girl's got to do what a girl's got to do.

My father says I focus on the flesh because I already know what happens to the soul after death, and so, it bores me. But he also thinks that in a previous life, I was General George Patton. Even at age four, I thought Heaven seemed suspiciously like the Emerald City in the *Wizard of Oz* series. Now that I'm sprouting gray hairs on my head, I still don't believe in reports of "Heaven" because I've yet to read one of these "I've been to Heaven!"-type books that isn't describing a Renaissance painting full of white people riding unicorns. Logically, Heaven ought to be a place where humanoids are conspicuously absent, not flitting around on butterfly wings as their golden hair flutters in the wind. I don't believe in reports of alien abductions for the same reason, because the aliens from Planet Enema always look like Steven Tyler with a shaved head. An omnipotent, omnipresent, infallible God ought to be able to do better than cough up the judging panel for *American Idol* to populate the infinite Universe.

If Hell, as philosopher Jean-Paul Sartre famously declared, "is other people," then all those authors who died on the table, went to Heaven, ran into grandma and grandpa, and got shoved out so they could return to Earth and tell us lesser mortals about it, are profoundly delusional. Hint: it's not Heaven they visited.

After the funeral, I ran outside and lost myself in the woods while my parents tended to the mourners. I wasn't some kind of feral child communing with the beetles. The basic point was to get away from humans. This would have suited my Uncle Loren just fine. He would have run away from all those soggy people too. Since he believed in Heaven, they should be glad, because his soul has achieved the perfect Eternal. Which means that all those weepers, sitting around snotting up their handkerchiefs, are mostly feeling sorry for themselves. Why? The guy in the coffin's the one who got himself dead. You should be happy it's not you.

Or maybe not.

We can't talk about that. Let's change the subject!

So I fled.

Here is the thing about my Uncle Loren that I wasn't supposed to know: he'd been one of the loudest voices in the faction that got all riled up about the changes to the, ahem, liturgy. Deeply offended by the prospect of excessive hymn singing, he came to services because Auntie Ima made him. He sat, arms crossed and pouting in the pews. He stalked out after the services. He hated going to church when he could be comfortably napping. He scowled as he volunteered to shovel the church sidewalks. He frowned as he handed out programs to the new members at Sunday services. He glowered as he stood at the pulpit and read the extra scriptures he insisted upon choosing from Leviticus, the Old Testament book that fundamentalist Christians love, because it commands humans not to lie, spread malicious gossip, or wear cotton-polyester blends. More and more people started joining my dad's congregation, and my Uncle Loren complained about that too, grumbling that maybe we needed to build a bigger church to hold all the new families, and what could he do to help?

In the end, he practically adopted us because he was, indeed, a good man, and Leviticus also commands: "The stranger that dwells with you shall be to you as one born among you, and you shall love him as yourself." Yes, this verse is from Leviticus. It's also from the New Testament Book of Matthew the Nice, because the Bible plagiarizes itself.

This is why my dad believes the Lord works in mysterious ways. It is also why my mother knew that the Devil does too.

Then we moved.

The Methodist Church moves its pastors around every few years. We ended up living all over the state, from the southernmost border to the northernmost expanses where the U.S. blurs into Canada. So when I say I'm from Maine, that's about as specific as I can get. It's also because I'm very bad at geography. Dyslexics can't distinguish hither from yon. My other deficiencies include no sense of direction—a sense that, I will soapbox here, needs to be added to the other six (sight, smell, taste, touch, hearing, and ESP), then inspected and PASSED at the body factory before the manufacturer can make shipment. On top of everything else, I'm a statistical rarity: a female with color blindness. Color gives me real problems. For a long time, I had no idea I couldn't see them, and neither did the grownups. They just thought I liked wearing mismatched socks. Eventually, I learned that the rest of the world didn't see things like I do, and thought it normal to sort things according to their hue. What was wrong with me? The answer was simple. Frankenstein stuck Abby Normal's rotten brain in my head. So I said: "Ixnay on the ottenray! Normal is overrated." Atchoo!

Maine is full of interesting towns, such as Rome, Mexico, Oxford, Poland, Norway, Moscow—and, of course, Paris. It's the globe in a nutshell, and it's full of snow too! But our moves always took us to dying little towns with dreary names like

"Brownville Junction," not to be confused with "Brownville," even though they're two sides of the same town on the wrong side of the tracks. The state of Maine has a Greenville, but it's brown too. Which makes it Maine's version of Greenland: it's not really green, but somebody insisted that it was, and the name stuck. In Greenland's case, that "somebody" was a Viking named Erik the Red, who was probably blue but nobody is going to correct a very large man on the run for murdering a whole lot of non-colorblind people. I liked these drab towns where nothing much happened. I spent a lot of time staring intently at dirt, and this kept me plenty busy for years.

"Nothing" is still my best speed. It's remarkable how much trouble a kid doing nothing can get into.

Around the age of eight, I ran across one of those lists that whittled down all the literature in the world into one hundred Great Books. I figured I should read them all and make up my own mind if they were any good, so off I trundled to the town library with my little red wagon, tracked down ten titles off my list, and hauled them to the front desk. "Hi Mrs. Lindner! I'd like to check these books out, please!" She opened up each book to the DUE DATE slip glued to the inside back cover, whacked down the stamper on the book, and sometimes, just for fun, she'd stamp my hand too. With my books piled in my wagon, I trundled back home, where I parked my books in the living room and started in on my chores. These included doing the laundry, making dinner, and pummeling my brother for control over the upright piano we were all three supposed to practice for at least an hour each day. Every once in a while, my mother would break up the fist fight and make us practice the dreaded four-handed piano pieces, which meant sitting next to my brother on the bench while my baby sister worked the pedals. At the sound of the music, my father would come out of his office, thrilled to the core at the sight of his prodigies draped on the piano as if it was an orca trained to give rides to Carnegie Hall. Then he'd turn around, go back into his office, and resume his conversations with God.

When I turned my gaze upwards, mine eyes did not behold His glory in the heavenly kingdom above. I saw the metronome parked on top of the piano, ticking like a time bomb next to the white floaty bustheads of Chopin, Beethoven, and Schubert. Mutely, they stared reproachfully at my square hands stamped with DUE DATE hitting all the wrong keys.

Tick . . . tick . . . tick. The metronome arm swung as stiffly as a pendulum in Wonderland.

One hour. Twenty minutes. Only ten minutes to go!

"Stop rushing!" my brother would howl in disgust. "You're messing up the tempo!"

Then he'd shove me bodily off the bench and settle into the center, claiming the piano as his personal exercise equipment. Rubbing my offended bum, I'd hurtle upstairs and start sawing loudly on my violin just to drown out his interpretation of Chopin's Mazurka in E Minor. Does he not understand the meaning of *Lento, ma non troppo?* We learned that *years* ago, I'd grumble to myself. Stupid brother!

Somewhat obviously, we never listened to pop music on the radio, because my brother had taken it apart and made it into a rocket launcher.

Thanks to the list of Great Books, I quickly developed the vocabulary of a fin-de-siècle aesthete obsessed with art and turtles. I also developed breasts. I don't think the reading part was causative, or even correlative. It was just a coincidence that I was going through the Awful Eights and adolescence at the same time. However, the list does explain why I prematurely waded through *Anna Karenina*, the greatest novel ever written about a French-speaking Russian adulteress. I didn't grasp the big themes but somehow, the story of her tragic affair put me off meat for almost two decades. It didn't make any sense, but why does anyone expect that it should? Let's just say that my sudden aversion to meat had something to do with the fact that all the women seemed to spend their time heaving their bosoms at innocent bystanders. The bystanders dined well on their free meal. All the women died.

I had a bosom in third grade. It seemed prudent to keep it to myself.

My parents did not understand my decision to become a vegetarian, especially since the fresh flesh of animals was the only food group I could safely eat. From almonds to zucchini, just about everything else produced unfortunate effects, ranging from discordant fits of sneezing to bouts of hyperactive screaming. Some of my earliest memories are of intense itching and being swaddled so I wouldn't claw myself to bits. Using an old-fashioned washboard and wringer, my parents rinsed out daily dozens of cloth diapers dripping with diarrhea and frowned in confusion when my perpetual rash got infected because I was allergic to detergents. Fish? Allergic! Cats? Allergic! Sunshine? Allergic! Etc. For all that I was a surprisingly functional little kid, but being allergic to just about everything sets up a relationship to the world that is inescapably adversarial. You cannot take anything for granted, including God's purported benevolence as he watches over the (hmmm . . . tasty?) sparrows. Me, I was being eyeballed by the Almighty of Abraham, the judgmental Old Testament God that was busy smiting sinners and turning unworthy women into pillars of salt. Sulkily sucking my thumb (*not* allergic. Safe!), I used to imagine that I was Lot's wife reincarnated, which explained both my liking for salt as well as my instinctive aversion to marriage. It pissed me off that she was "Lot's wife" instead of, say, Veronica or Betty. These things register when you come from a culture that keeps the family unit sorted by calling you "Oldest Daughter."

Koreans don't understand "vegetarian." In general, people who've experienced starvation due to war find it odd when a willful child rejects a perfectly acceptable food group just because. What, no Spam with your eggs? But you love Spam! Dried squid is good! American chop suey is good! *Aigu, aigu*, my mother wailed. What is wrong with Oldest Daughter?

No eight-year-old has a food philosophy. Refusing to eat meat was just something I had to do. In retrospect, I am glad that my father was assigned to churches in tiny towns where psychiatrists did not practice, because in rural America, food allergies are still namby-pamby liberal myths, setting me up for exceedingly vexed relationships with human authority figures who insisted on making me eat home-grown tomatoes and hand-caught lobsters and did not connect the dots when I began crossly exploding into hives. Adding insult to injury, most of my allergies weren't fatal. *That* would have been interesting. No, mine were the kind that merely damned me to the perpetual motions of misery: wiping snot off my nose, knobbling watery eyes, watching my tongue swell, lather, rinse, repeat. Boring!

My dream was to get away from grownups telling me to stop sneezing. My mantra was self-sufficiency, and I started going after it as soon as I was able to crawl. The faster I could learn to fend for myself, the sooner I could set out on my own. I started by running the back roads of Maine, observing the quirks of the local ecology: fiddleheads to eat, pine cones for weapons, and beer cans worth money if you redeemed them. I ran to get out of the house. I ran because I was jumping out of my skin. I ran so I could be alone, running on restless legs that walked in and out of homerooms, kicking bullies in the schoolyard and slamming my brother in the shins. My sister just sat back and watched me fight, blinking bewildered black eyes and sucking contentedly on cookies.

By the following year, we moved again, this time very far
north to a town full of snow plows. Not only was Houlton the
first town we'd lived in that had shops, it had a real down-
town with a shoe store and a movie theater that showed *Star
Wars*. I didn't live there for very long, because school officials quickly decided that my brother's brain was turning
into a black hole, threatening to become a portal to another
dimension. I thought this was super. I couldn't wait for his
cranium to become my own personal TARDIS. To prevent
the impending rupture of the space-time continuum, school
officials recommended "boarding school." This was a peculiar
institution that my parents had never heard of, but one that
might kill a second bird—me—with one stone. My brother
would attend Phillips Academy at Exeter, and I would attend
the sister school, Phillips Academy at Andover. Insofar as I
had no idea what boarding school was—the best approxima-
tion I could come up with was "orphanage," in the manner
of *Oliver Twist*—it never occurred to me that I wouldn't be
admitted. In fact, I was sure I'd fit right in, what with my
thrift-shop clothes and constant begging for gruel.

Off I went, content in my mediocrity, thrilled that I was no
longer going to show up in class and hear, "How come she's
so bad at math? Her brother is so good at it!" From now on,
I would hear, "How come she's so bad at math? Aren't all
Asian kids good at it?" No longer a specific failure, I was a
generic one. Huzzah! If I was a dunderhead with numbers,
however, I excelled at being ornery. Wherefore, I planned to
use my excellent schooling to become an artist. To my parents,
I might as well have declared: "When I grow up, I want to
be homeless!" They hoped it was just a phase, like my sister's
purple hair or my brother's garage rock band. But I wanted to
do what I wanted to do, and figured that I had no claim unless
I was paying my own bills.

This was my father's influence. He loved cowboy west-
erns, so what little television we watched tended to have

dialogue such as: "I got two bits and a buffalo hide. That enough to buy me South Dakota?" In the black-and-white world of my childhood, a "bit" was enough to make small-town dreams come true, and a dime could feed a family of five for a week. "God watches over . . . ," "loaves and the fishes . . . ," "manna from heaven . . . ," etc. What can I say? My dad was plugged into the God hotline; miracles worked for him. He also drew a straight line between education and getting money to pay for . . . more education. One summer back home from boarding school, I'd been hoping to work as an agricultural laborer, because that's how kids in Maine used to earn their allowances. To no one's surprise except for mine, I was a lousy farm hand, because my wheezing scared the milk cows, and my hives scared everybody else. I was left with the next best option: auditioning for the role of Window Girl at the Dairy Queen. Solemnly, my father offered me the choice: I could work for minimum wage and end up with a few dozen dollars after taxes. Or, I could earn terrific grades and get academic scholarships for thousands. I was trapped by the implacable logic of numbers. For me, there was no escaping their maddening grasp: as a full-fledged member of the *lumpenproletariat*, I could barely handle addition, let alone offer a counterargument to Marxist theories of the labor-based marketplace. As a result, I ended up forever unable to make a perfect swirly cone, for some skills require a lifetime of practice, like producing flaky pie crusts or forging metal for swords. Amazingly, however, my dad's plan worked and I ended up winning essay contests where scholarships were the prizes.

This is why Asian kids are good at school, because their parents trick them into believing that it's a slot machine guaranteed to pay off if you keep feeding it. Where do they get such insane ideas? Along with just about every other cultural belief, the explanation can be found in the storyline of a fairytale. The Chinese ones go like this:

There once was a man named Wu Ch'in, who studied hard and became very learned but no woman would marry him, because he stank of fish. A soothsayer had predicted that Wu Ch'in would become a great man, yet he lived in poverty and drowned his sorrows in drink. Decades dragged on, and all the people who'd heard the soothsayer's prophecy were dead of old age. Now, as it happened, the southern provinces were being plagued by a dragon. The Emperor issued a proclamation, calling on his people to help solve this problem. "Maybe Ch'in knows the answer?" the villagers mocked him. Roused out of his stupor by their kicks, Wu Ch'in realized that he *did* know the answer. So he got to his feet, bowed to the startled bullies, and staggered off to see the Emperor, taking advantage of the long walk to get sober. At the palace, he impressed everyone with his great learning. Conveyed into the Emperor's presence, he shared the information that quelled the dragon and cured the Emperor's bunions. In gratitude, the Emperor named him Imperial physician and gave him three beautiful wives plus a most valuable singing canary. Thus the soothsayer's prediction came true, and Wu Ch'in became a great man.

Thanks to the Confucian tradition, the crabby intellectual saves the day and gets the girls. Here's the part that counts: these girls couldn't care less about the beefcake warriors who carried out the Emperor's orders, because they're just dragon fodder. It's a good reminder that the game of love is rigged: if you want to win, you have to bribe the soothsayer.

No surprise, then, that Asian families like to have at least one scholar in the family, the same way that Irish families like one son to be a priest: they're handy to have around in case there's a supernatural emergency involving a soothsayer with a lisp. I enjoyed the studying part, and frankly I was temperamentally inclined to be a drunken bum, but my every attempt at the lush life was promptly smacked down by the better angels of my nature, otherwise known as "allergies." Name a vice, and I'm allergic to it. In my defense, I'm also allergic to most virtues. Every time I tried to break the rules in the predictable adolescent ways—smoking cigarettes, drinking beer, attempting to inhale—I ended up with some weird side effect that made strangers scream at the sight of me.

Eventually, though not as quickly as you might think, I learned that I did not possess the skills to become an amiable pothead. My incompetence at behaving like a normal American teenager did not improve my mood. Making matters worse, my freakishly omniscient dorm mother failed to be bamboozled by clever ruses to throw parties in my room. Not only did Ms. Amster know exactly what I'd been up to, she figured that as soon as I sampled contraband substance X and extracted all the relevant data from the experience, I'd lose all interest in it, because what I was really doing was conducting a dorky science experiment on myself. Take, for example, cigarettes. I was allowed to smoke smugly for exactly one week, after which point my dorm mother informed my parents that I'd developed a few very bad habits, including failing physics, snorting hot chocolate mix straight from the packet, and smoking a pack a day of Marlboro cigarettes. My parents responded by giving me permission to smoke in my room. However, I was to stop with the hot chocolate business *immediately*. So I responded exactly as they expected, and studied until my eyes fell out of my head.

I passed the class by reading every physics book I could get my hands on and memorizing all the solutions to the sample equations, which made me the human equivalent of a parrot squawking "one plus one equals two!" (Don't tell anyone, but the parrot can't really add.) It was a perfect example of how a dyslexic kid can succeed spectacularly in school by learning all the wrong things, but none of the people in charge seemed to care as long as I gave them the answer they wanted. In Sunday school, for example, my takeaway from the story of Nebuchadnezzar, the king of Babylon, who threw Meshach, Shadrach, and Abednego into a burning pit of fire for defying his will, was that 1) a vegetarian diet makes you fireproof, and 2) to be a proper biblical villain, your name must be unpronounceable. I did not, however, correctly internalize that great piety is a virtue rewarded by God, and that I should practice praying fervently, just in case I too ended up tossed in a fire pit by an angry potentate—a fate that, given my congenital inability to worship rich people, was not as far-fetched as it might seem. When a strange man came by my all-girls dorm at Andover and started giving out sexist, possibly feminist, but indisputably ugly t-shirts saying "Vote for Bush," I asked him nicely to state his purpose. His name was George Bush, he said; he'd come by to visit the daughter of a family friend, and he was running for president. (Of what? The Rotary?) It never occurred to me to genuflect, because I was too busy mistrusting him, eyeballing him warily until Katie sauntered into the Clement House common room and drawled delightedly at the stranger, "Y'all are so nice to come and see me!" dispensing beauty-queen air kisses and pacifying "Uncle George" sufficiently that he forgot to sic the Secret Service on me.

This would have been a better story if George had accepted the cigarette I'd offered him while we were waiting for Katie to appear, but no. For several weeks, however, I wore the BUSH button he gave me, because I was too lazy to remove it from my sweatshirt. Meeting the future AAAUGH! didn't inspire me to become a Republican, but shortly thereafter it dawned on me that puffing on cigarettes had turned me into a remarkable facsimile of him, shriveling my skin and stiffening my joints as well as killing off what few spare brain cells I possessed. (I later learned that, yes, I was allergic to tobacco, wherefore smoking it was a bad idea, and eating it was even worse.) So I was stuck with a conundrum. Should I quit smoking and make the adults think they'd won? Should I keep smoking, just for the pleasure of thumbing my nose at authority? My parents were horrified by my habit, but by giving me permission, they were counting on the fact that I'd be so dismayed by their approval that I'd immediately stop. The truly aggravating part was that I'd already decided to quit, but I didn't want to give them the satisfaction of believing their ploy had worked. In the end, I decided that it made no sense to cut off my nose to spite my face, so I crossed cigarettes off the list and carried on with my science experiment on myself.

By the time I graduated high school, I'd managed to sample quite an assortment of youthful indiscretions, but in the manner of nibbling off a corner of all the pieces of chocolate in a Valentine's Day box and putting each one back in their paper-lined spot with an airy look of innocence. Given that adults were always pushing foods on me that made me sick, I had no confidence that forbidden fruits were any worse for my system than, say, avocados or crab cakes. To my teenage self, ingesting beer-in-a-can was fraught with the same mixture of fear, hope, and anticipation that I felt before trying the fish eggs-in-a-tube that Anja from Norway received in a care package: even though it was ninety-nine percent likely that I was allergic, how would I know unless I tried it? Same went for Vegemite, Marmite, and Nutella®, exotic spreads that WASPs seemed to love but which landed me in the Infirmary, where I convalesced dyspeptically on a regimen of ginger tea and Saltines.

In the same spirit of doomed experimentation, my plan was to earn my high school diploma and be done with formal education forever, because I'd tried it, didn't have much use for it, and decided that it was not for me. It irked me that adults were under the impression that I was of a cheerful temperament, whereas in reality I was a misanthropic ball of peevishness. It was almost as if I was two people in one body. I used to think that I'd been a twin in the womb, and I'd eaten the other one while it was still underdone. It would explain a lot, really.

So what's a surly teenager to do? For lack of a better plan, I went to college. This was where the trouble really started, because my antisocial, colorblind self still really wanted to be an artist.

"Foolish human!" the angels giggled as they threw cold water on my dreams. And lo! I was drenched with new allergies—to ink, clay, and paint. I was a sex-change operation away from being a Bubble Boy, the doctors warned, because making art was extremely bad for my health. Unless I was prepared to move to Antarctica and make ice sculptures for penguins, I had some unpleasant realities to face.

Slowly, and rather against my will, I was turning into a scholar named Double Ch'in. Now all I needed was a dragon to slay. So I decided to go looking for the monster of my dreams. By the time I'd finished my undergraduate degree and started on a Ph.D., I'd begun waddling around small continents in sensible shoes, carting around my precious packet of toilet paper, sunscreen, and a jar of antihistamines. Disappearing for months and years, I burrowed into cities such as Florence, London, and Seoul, but mostly Paris, a place that bears remarkably little resemblance to the romantic fantasies spun about it. This was fine with me. I wasn't looking for love, drugs, yoga classes or any other "girl" narratives attached to stories about free spirits bravely traveling alone. When your trips abroad are being paid for by your father/divorce settlement/publisher, you're not free. You're expensive. Besides which, I grew up foreign in a native country. From birth, you're an alien being, a world traveler by default: dropped down the chimney by migratory storks.

In cities called Cosmopolitan, everyone is born of a bird. We are all the same kind, fine in our feathers but naked in our skins. Not all birds fly. Not all birds can. My mother prayed I'd run into a nice Korean boy and start making legally wedded babies. My father hoped my peregrinations would put me on the road to Damascus, where I'd see God's truth and start preaching His word, writing letters to the Corinthians and voting Republican. I was Saint Paul's namesake, after all. My parents had been expecting a boy, because apparently I'd been one in the womb. That's what the baby doctors told them. I chose to disagree. Given my conversion when I saw the light, my destiny was to become an apostle. Failing that, my father was thinking accountant. A good career choice for girls. Ah, but in Latin, Paul also means "little," which is what I ended up being. Or rather, very short. Sometimes wee, mostly Weeble. The wobble was incontestable.

I knew my mind, and it was strange. It disagreed with my body, and my body struggled to get away. Amazingly, wherever my body went, my brain went too, barking, "No meat for you!" Forced to obey, my flesh got its revenge by growing sea monkeys under my skin and refusing to get out of bed. I was living pallid in Paris when my mother surprised everyone by dying first. After that, I got sick of being sick. So I quit being vegetarian and started chomping down chickens with a cheerful "fuck you!" to the medical establishment. I lost twenty pounds in three months eating roasted birds, making up for twenty years of tofu, broccoli, and brown rice, "healthy" foods that, against all logic, made me sickly and obese.

And I was happy as I laughed without mirth, a laugh filling a body exulting as it animated flesh not of my flesh, the body and blood of the animal, a communion that transmutes water into wine and makes hot dogs, pork rinds, and buffalo wings a refuge of the sacred. *Give thanks. It died for you.* I was the killer of the sacred lamb, a sticker of the devil's spawn, a milker of cows and the executioner's song. I was a creature living in a damaged world that I could not heal. *Why not?* Let us not mince words: when we eat, we kill. Nothing lives in the stomach except death and fear.

This I learned after traveling the world, by myself, a girl with fallen arches and no sense of direction.

This I understood after my physician grandfather and his Middle of Five Daughters sickened with cancer in their stomachs.

Elderly, he did not resist. His end was peaceful. My mother was younger than most who will read these words. She got angry. It didn't change the outcome. My death, when it comes, will be different. Because they both really died of regret, "if only . . ." gnawing away at their souls until finally, it consumed their bodies too.

"If" is the most dangerous word in the English language. It is the portal to lost dreams.

I studied the carcasses exposed by my teeth, mulled the pathways that brought them to my plate, and asked myself, could I take a life to serve my needs? But of course. It is childish to pretend otherwise. With every step we take, we destroy a universe. To ants, we are Beelzebub and Kali rolled into one: a towering free-range demon dancing on their graves. To flies, we are the Brave Little Tailor, capable of flattening seven in one blow. To wildlife, we are the Great Exterminator, eradicating untold billions of grain-stealing sparrows so vegetarians can boast that they're not cruel to animals. Each exhalation of breath releases a hallelujah of poisons into the air. Every poopy diaper injects lush microbes into waters drunk by babes in the woods. Only dead things don't kill on purpose. They only kill by accident.

Contrary-wise, I now insist on eating birds and mammals, preferably wild ones shot by the man I love but won't marry, their bodies made into meat by our hands joined together. I don't feel guilty about it, sez the girl for whom a bee sting is lethal. Death is the promise. It is an ineluctable truth, for Nature is a murderous mother offering food everywhere we look. I can't pretend to be one with Her as I tromp up bleak mountains, tracking deer in hopes of filling the winter's larder. Instead, I look at the sheltering sky and think, humbly and with gladness, I stand beneath the heavenly roof of God's yawning mouth. When it closes, *if* it closes, it becomes the maw of Hell. When? Today? Tomorrow? Oh, but Apocalypse Now was thirty years ago. The fear rises. The hymns swell. I am hungry. Such is the human condition. We hope and despair, rejoice and revile, celebrate and curse the profane absurdity of being apes rigged up in angel's wings.

Angels don't eat. Apes covet meat.

I'm no angel. Not before, and not after. For I can walk, and run, and go places my father cannot on shriveled legs made of bone as he sits, peaceably, letting the light of God shine from his face.

He is a spiritual man.

I am neither.

CHAPTER ONE

❧ ❧ ❧

A Kormic Explanation

"How is my grammar?" asked the yellow
hen, anxiously. "Do I speak quite properly,
in your judgment?"
– *Billina the Yellow Hen, from*
Frank L. Baum, Ozma of Oz, *1907*

This is a love story for grownups. There is sex, death, and snoring. A happy ending is not guaranteed. And so, it is a story about hunting. The real kind that starts with hunger and ends with guts being spilled.

Let's start at the beginning.

The first year that I'd spent in the capital city of France, I was conducting dissertation research on a dutifully obscure topic interesting to five people in the world, all of whom enjoy arguing a great deal about it. Along with all the other university students, I was living in the 5th *arrondissement* on the kind of money that turns up under the couch cushions. Fellowships from private institutions paid for these trips, but the sums were barely enough to support a cat, let alone cover rent and food for a human being. I didn't care. Still in my twenties, I was young enough that starving in attics seemed a perfectly reasonable way to live. I was Mimi in *La Bohème*! George Orwell in *Down and Out in London and Paris*! How lucky could I be? Not only was I living in the actual attic of a five-story walkup, but my neighbor wore a black beret and slunk around with a Gaulois dangling from his scowling lips, just like the evil French henchmen in the *Flint* movies.

Lest you think that I am exaggerating my delight, consider these interesting details about my building. When I opened my door, I greeted a tubby, sparkling-white, pink-nosed cat. Every day, rain or shine, she came and waited quietly on my doorstep until I let her in. She'd march ponderously around the perimeter of the entire room, look at me, meow loudly just once, settle onto the bed, and go to sleep. I'd get dressed, toss Mimi back out the door, and head out for the day. No one knew who owned her. I had no idea why she insisted on visiting me every day.

On the wall between the stairwell and my doormat, there was a small locked door about the size of a fuse box. One day, as I trudged up the stairs, I was surprised to find a queue of workmen lining up in front of this miniature portal, then leaning over and disappearing into it, one by one. When my turn came to go through, I held back and peeked: inside, there was a staircase snaking up to a storage space beneath the rafters. The workmen were turning this triangular wedge into an apartment. A few weeks later, a new tenant moved in: she was a Japanese student half my height and unnervingly silent.

The pup tent had no bathroom or plumbing. At the top of the staircase, there was a chemical toilet.

As the months wore on, I realized that the old ladies who lived in the building couldn't tell me apart from the midget camping in the rafters. It was as if my imagination had vomited up the fetal twin of my subconscious and turned her into a pigeon pooping on my pretensions. It was a real-life version of the filthy joke about the rented outhouse and the television (if you don't know it, I'm not going to tell you), but it all boils down to this: when the conversations literally go over your head, be grateful that the joke isn't on you.

Every evening, after I'd finished chasing down documents in the archives, I'd go for my daily constitutional in the Jardin des Plantes across the street. To the great amusement of the gardeners, I would run in large circles, treating the plant beds as if they were an outdoor racetrack. They could not understand why anyone would want to go around and around through life, repeating the same route and getting nowhere at the same time, but it became a nightly ritual: me, jouncing past the roses, and them, waving affably at me, *la chinoise* (sigh) who obviously misunderstood the purpose of exercise since I ran without smoking a cigarette. Depending on my research agenda for the day, I also cut through the Jardin des Plantes to get to the Métro station, and it was on one of these bumblebee excursions that I was approached by a fidgeting little girl, maybe six or seven years old, in the pleated skirt and white blouse of a traditional school uniform.

"*Excusez-moi, mademoiselle,*" she nervously asked her shoes, "but do you speak French?"

"Yes," I affirmed, wondering if she was lost. "What's this about?"

"I'm on a scavenger hunt!" she told me. "See?" she exclaimed, thrusting a laminated list in my face. I took the list from her hands and skimmed it quickly. It requested the usual items, such as a four-leaf clover, a pure white feather, and a letter with a stamp from a foreign country. She pointed a chubby pink finger at the upper part of the page. "I have to get a foreigner to sing a song in her native language."

Yes, there it was, item 32 on the 100-item list.

She fidgeted some more, and then blurted, "Would you most kindly sing for me?"

Who could refuse such politeness? "Sure," I agreed. What the heck. It was for a school project.

She jumped up and clapped her hands, overjoyed.

"Do I start singing now?" I asked.

"No," she replied firmly. "I must get the teacher."

That made sense. Otherwise how does she prove that she really got a foreigner to sing for her?

Retrieving her list, she started to head off, then turned and eyed me doubtfully. "You aren't going to go away?"

"Don't worry," I nodded reassuringly, "I'll stay right here." I sat down on one of the wooden benches at the head of the garden. As she disappeared, I started rustling around in my tote bag for a stray song I might have tossed in there.

"*Arirang*"? "*Doraji*"? These are Korean folk songs my mother used as lullabies. Bad idea, because they'll put me to sleep.

"Three Blind Mice"? It's a round. That requires coordination. No good.

"Joy to the World"? It's the wrong season for Christmas carols.

Hymns? Pop songs? "Happy Birthday to You"?

When I finally emerged from the murky depths of my bag, where I'd turned up a bottle of antihistamines, a bottle of water, a copy of *Plan de Paris par arrondissement*, three broken mechanical pencils, a cough drop, a skeleton key, a dozen library cards, a crumpled brochure from the Hôtel des Arènes, and the all-important packet of toilet paper but no lyric sheets or karaoke cassettes, I was greeted by the terrifying sight of twenty uniformed girls heading straight for me. In seven minutes, one French schoolgirl had multiplied like a rabbit, and a warren of warm and fuzzy creatures was determinedly hopping my way.

This was not in the plan. I'd agreed to sing for one person. Now I was singing to an entire crèche.

The original girl came running over to me, pulling me off the bench, and dragging me over to meet her classmates. She was clearly the Girl of the Moment, having bravely asked a total stranger to sing and getting a positive response. "See!

Here she is!" my little friend declared, gesturing dramatically towards me as if I was a unicorn she'd discovered lurking under her bed. "She's going to sing for us!" More clapping and hopping ensued.

The exhausted teacher greeted me with as much enthusiasm as she could muster. "What will you sing for us?" she asked tiredly, shushing the giggling girls who'd surrounded me, trapping me inside a straightjacket made of sugar and spice. Grubby fingers intertwined and patent-leather feet thumped away in anticipation. Who knew such cuddly creatures could be so scary? Run away, run away . . .

Up until then, I hadn't known what song I would sing. At that moment, I was inspired. "I'm going to sing 'Do Re Mi,'" I announced triumphantly. "You know, from *The Sound of Music*."

The teacher gave me a puzzled look. "Isn't that an American song?"

"Yes, but you said native language, and I was raised speaking English."

Ooohs and ahhs of surprise from the girls.

"Well, it doesn't really matter," the teacher sighed. "The main point is that you're a foreigner."

"True," I agreed. "I'm not French."

More ooohing and ahhing from big-eyed girls. The teacher shushed them again.

I took a deep breath and started the song:

> Do, a deer, a female deer,
> Re, some stuff about the sun
> Mi, a girl who likes to run
> Fa, La, Ti, etc.

By the time the second stanza landed back on "Do," the girls started singing along on cue. The weirdness of the situation

hit me between Mi and Fa the second time around. Here
I was, a Korean-American graduate student, singing an
English song from an American movie set in wartime Sal-
zburg to twenty French six-year-olds and their teacher in
the Jardin des Plantes in Paris. I felt like a combination of
Julie Andrews as Sister Maria, and Bugs Bunny as Maestro
Toscanini. By the time we'd built the song up to its big cre-
scendo, we'd become a gleefully possessed chorus. Nothing
like a bit of singing to unify the masses! We'd also gathered a
little audience of confused tourists struggling to decipher the
performance. I would have been very pleased if at least one
tourist mistook us for busking musicians, but nobody threw
us a few centimes or anything.

When the song finished and we'd caught our breath, the
teacher thanked me and briskly checked off her list. Twenty
schoolgirls echoed her in chorus, *"Merci beaucoup mademoiselle!"* and off they scattered, vanishing with alarming swift-
ness behind the rows of linden trees. A few Germans hung
around, waiting to see what would happen next, so I shooed
them off in French, announcing, "That's all, folks!" Then
I gave them a big, toothy, American smile, gathered up my
things, and skipped down the path.

I didn't realize it at the time, but I was casting a spell on myself,
singing a song that set out my destiny, starting off with *Do, a
deer, a female deer* and ending with a triumphant *Do!*

Do what, exactly?

A deer, dummy.

The French schoolgirls knew all the words to the song but
not their meaning, and so we understood each other perfectly.
One of the perks of speaking a foreign language in a foreign
country is that nobody expects to understand you. To the
small pink ears of my fluffy new friends, Rogers & Hammer-
stein's definitions for the Sounds of Solfeggio were as good as
any in a city where wombats jirbled while lunting. (These are

actual words, by the way, taken from Jeffrey Kacirk's nonfiction book, *The Word Museum*. *Jirble*: "To pour a drink with an unsteady hand." *Lunting*: "Walking while smoking a pipe." *Wombats* are crepuscular marsupials with stubby legs. I have been accused of bearing a certain resemblance to them.) Like the schoolgirls, I thought I was on a scavenger hunt, scrounging for items that were terribly important at the time. If I'd been paying attention, I would have realized that the girls were doing the hunting, and the Do they'd found was Mi.

Now, there are millions of deer on the planet, but they're oddballs in the city. Do deer like shopping? Will they stay for lunch? No, they flee into the nearest woods, until they find something they can eat. That is how, by going around and around in circles and running a very long way, I ended up in a totally different place from where I started, because where things began, and where they ended, were both in Paris. One Paris was in France. The other was in Maine.

It would have been a more efficient use of my time on earth if I'd just figured it out right then, headed back to my home state, and started hunting for deer instead of singing show tunes about them to schoolgirls bestowing buttery kisses on my cheeks. But there is one thing that I'd learned from cooking my own meals: you can't rush the process or the dish will get burned. So I carried on in the archives, dutifully conducting research and feeding my curiosity, the only appetite I could indulge freely without worrying about emergency trips to the bathroom.

A famous nineteenth-century novel by Emile Zola, *Au Bonheur des Dames*, tells the story of a provincial girl who comes to Paris and gets a job at the Bonheur des Dames (Ladies' Paradise). Plain and penniless, Denise joins the flow of material goods imported from around the world. Caught up in the ritual of commercial exchange, she slowly loses her naïveté, her bad haircut, and cloddish shoes. It is not an improvement. The inspiration for the Bonheur des Dames was the Bon

Marché (Good Market) in the 7th *arrondissement*. The world's first purpose-built department store, the Bon Marché is still an impressive ode to commerce, but what sets it apart is its enormous gourmet food shop on the ground floor.

I couldn't afford to shop for groceries at the Bon Marché, but I'd visit every once in a while because it was always good for a laugh and cheaper than going to the movies. Once, I watched a portly woman in a hot pink dress going around the store with an empty shopping cart, and putting back every single item she'd picked off the shelves. Finally, after going round the store about six times, she picked out a square half-pint jar of honey, turned it round and round in her hand, and then she carefully placed the cube in the very center of her cart, creating a little island. Then she kept going.

She was clearly not Parisian. If she were, she would have known that the fastest way to a food decision was to make sure you had no way to carry it.

Here are ten more useful things to know about living in Paris that aren't in guide books:

One. Paris is not France.

Many French people think Parisians are snooty. Many Parisians would agree. What is the problem?

Two. Dogs are everywhere.

Dogs are to Paris what sheep are to Ireland: no matter where you go, there they are. And so are their cute piles of poop. Despite warnings, you will step in it. It will be your fault.

Three. The pharmacist will identify your wild mushrooms so you don't die from eating them, and will prescribe suppositories if you do.

Suppositories cure everything, including sore throats and freckles.

Four. Organ meats are omnipresent.

Livers, hearts, brains, tongues, and gizzards are featured on most respectable menus. If you get sick of cow and pig and ask nicely for a big plate of fresh vegetables, it is very likely that a duck will end up on your table. This actually happened to my sister. Vegetarians should consider themselves warned.

Five. Chic Parisiennes wear see-through blouses. Do not try this at home.

The "chic" part depends on the expression, which must be stern and flat chested. To complete the look, it is necessary to hold a man instead of a handbag.

Six. Apartments are very small, and closets are optional.

If they do have a closet, it is the water closet. It is rarely used for clothes. It often doubles as a library.

Seven. You get one outfit per season, and sometimes less.

In the Great Heat of 2003, for example, an unwritten rule emerged: you shall go totally naked in your apartment, all your naked neighbors will see you, and no one will ever speak of it. During the summer, the City of Light can intensify into an inferno, the air filled with a roiling, heavy heat as thick as puréed pumpkins. Very few buildings have air conditioning, yet there are also no fans. When I asked a French friend about this, she gave me a perplexed look. Then she replied politely, as if explaining Why The Sky is Blue: "I'd use it for two, maybe three days. Then what would I do with it for the rest of the year? Put it in the bathtub?" My fault for asking: I'd forgotten the Space Rule. This is . . .

Eight. There is room for only one of everything.

Over the years, I've stayed in various apartments in Paris, and none had space for a fan. Most barely had space for me. I suspect this is the reason why Parisians are so thin, as they live in studios that only have enough space for one glass, one fork, and one spoon. Who has time to wash the dirty dish in the sink? Wherefore Parisians, who really can't be bothered, zip around the city tearing off great hunks of baguette with their teeth.

Conclusion: Aerobic eating is a wonderful sport. As with most things, however, skill levels vary. It's harder to do than you think.

Nine. There is always a line, and the line is very long.

There are different reasons for this phenomenon. In checkout lines, for example, locals pay in cash, and give exact change. The cashier will take this change and count it back, often making a mistake and having to start over. This process can repeat itself two, three, even five times. Frustrated diners give up and head to McDonald's, thinking that "fast food" means "fast line." Disputes, haggling, and warm beer will ensue, leading to days of standing in long, defeated lines at the Préfecture de la Police.

Moral: In Paris, it's always better to go to a sit-down restaurant with waiters, because they carry machines that take Visa. Food will not arrive quickly, but eating will happen sooner.

Ten. The toilets do not flush. They concede.

When American toilets flush, they suck the refuse through a black hole that ejects the contents into outer space with the force of a thousand jet engines. French toilets sigh depressively at the bleakness of their job. "*Merde!*" they complain, and then they go on strike. When they do, the shit doesn't hit the fan, because there aren't any (see "Seven"). The shit hits your shoes. In Paris, there are delightful toilets called "Turkish" designed to send women straight to Chanel for an emergency pair of replacements.

At the Bon Marché, the bathrooms were upstairs. So were L. L. Bean camping clothes appropriate for "Le Week End," just in case tourists decided that fishing was the quickest way to sushi (see "Nine").

On this trip, because I was thinking about fast food, I made my way to the Great Wall of Canned Pâtés. Deer pâté, boar pâté, goose liver pâté, duck liver pâté, and random wild meat mashed with mushrooms, all in pretty glass containers small enough to go through airport security, and far better as gifts than nearby cans of *cassoulet* that were the size of small televisions. (No good: they required rolling suitcases to get home and would never make it past the bomb detectors.) Because I liked the label, I picked up a pâté jar with the rustic drawing of a rooting pig, and was busily inspecting the snout when the sound of a shrill voice screaming "Ajax!" broke my concentration.

"Ajax!" the voice screamed again.

If the accent had been American I would have assumed it was a brand-loyal woman desperate to find her favorite household cleanser. However, the accent was British, and it was coming from a fortyish woman with bright blue hair and black lipstick, a black tube top, an iridescent flowered miniskirt, no stockings, and combat boots, standing near the display of miniature vegetables. A small red-haired boy streaked past.

"Ajax!" she yelled. "Come here!"

The child did not comply, taking off instead in the direction of the domestic wines. This was much better than the honey lady. Blue Hair was definitely worth following.

Pig pâté in hand, I started tracking her.

She advanced with an aggressive, forward-hunched, lock-kneed step. "Ajax!" she shrieked, apparently uncaring that the entire store could hear her. "Bloody 'ell!" she muttered under her breath. "Leave him 'ere, I will. Let 'im find his own way back to the bleedin' hotel."

Ajax was nowhere in sight and not coming back on his own. She, however, had shifted her attention to a row of tomato pastes, which she studied with a disgruntled look on her face. "Bloody 'ell," she muttered again to herself.

As she spat and stomped and swore to herself, a small man at the fruit section started heading towards her. He had shorn gray hair, a prominent Adam's apple, ruddy jowls, and was bony except for a beer belly, giving him the look of a ferret whose biggest accomplishment in life was swallowing a whole watermelon. He wore a white oxford shirt and brown pants, both badly wrinkled, and clutched an empty picnic basket close to his body. As he sidled into view, Blue Hair's head jerked violently up. She glared at him.

His face turned ashen.

"Did you find the coffee?" she demanded angrily. "Well? Did you?"

He shook his head and blinked rapidly, a defeated look in his bleary eyes.

"Go on then, keep looking," she snapped, yanking up her tube top so high that her tummy popped out. He nodded his shorn head obediently and shuffled off in the wrong direction.

Still muttering and empty handed, she clumped off towards the region of the cheeses.

Ajax had still not returned. I thought it quite sensible of him.

Keeping one eye on Blue Hair, I wandered over to the barrel sacks of loose grains and started fishing through them, mostly to hear the pleasing sound they made as they tumbled. Suddenly, Ajax popped up on the other side of the barrel, throwing me a hopeful look. With the prescience of childhood, he recognized I'd been playing a game.

I nodded. He beamed. We began a curious round of hide and seek.

Ajax, running off to hide behind a kiosk of berries.

Me, fleeing over to the fresh fish.

Mr. Blue Hair, on a doomed quest for coffee.

"Ajax!" Blue Hair screamed.

I looked around and spotted Ajax skipping past the iced fish display. He'd grabbed one of the fresh octopuses out of a bucket and was mercilessly shaking its tentacles in the air.

"Do you know that boy?" an elderly French lady asked me in aggrieved tones.

"Which boy?"

"The one with the octopus." She gestured with her chin. She clearly thought I was his nanny.

"Nope!" I replied cheerfully.

She scowled at me. The *pain aux raisins* in her hands did not look convinced.

"He belongs to her!" I pointed nonchalantly towards the deli. As I did so, I realized that I'd been clutching a jar of pig pâté this whole time, and I brought it to my face, staring at it with a kind of wonder.

Blue Hair had trapped Ajax by a sack of couscous. She'd grabbed him by the back of his t-shirt and was dragging him forward with an air of dogged determination. His limbs were thrashing wildly but he wasn't screaming at all.

My new friend harrumphed in disgust, and turned away to resume feeding her bosom. She was breaking off small pieces of the raisin bread and dropping them down her cleavage. I could only assume that she'd squirreled a toy poodle under her blouse and buttoned it all under a jacket. But I wasn't sure, and there wasn't a good way to find out. I wasn't about to ask her to lift up her top and flash me, and staring at her chest until I'd resolved the matter seemed a very bad idea. No one else in the store seemed to take any notice, leading me to assume that letting pets ride around on your boobs was a perfectly Parisian thing to do.

Shrugging, I resumed my search for Blue Hair.

Blue Hair, Mr. Blue Hair, and Ajax had reunited and were headed towards the checkout counter. Ajax was still held firmly in Blue Hair's grip. Her black lips were set in a grim line, and the top of her tube was sagging to dangerously low levels. Ajax was struggling like a cat fallen into the bathtub. Mr. Blue Hair was slapping the boy's flailing fists away from his precious basket. Thrown off balance by the boy's jerking limbs, he got tangled in his own feet, and his basket tipped over. A single bottle of tomato juice smashed as it hit the floor. He regained his stance and stood clutching his traitorous basket, staring in anguish at the mess. Blue Hair flung an angry arm at him, letting go of Ajax's shirt in the process. The boy wasted no time: he broke loose and ran for the hinterlands.

The items that actually came home with me from the Bon Marché were a bag of basmati rice, a can of chickpeas, and a bottle of korma, an Indian sauce brought to France by way of Great Britain. When I'd turned away from Ajax's Great Escape and redirected my attention towards the shelves, this bottle of sauce was resting right in front of my face. Buddhists believe that our spiritual paths in life are dictated by our karma. I felt like mine was being led by korma, the same thing only off by one letter. Korma is karma that came out slightly imperfect at the soul manufactory, dooming those who receive it with terrible timing and a lousy sense of direction. I'd never sampled korma because I'd never run into it before, a classic case of kormic delay rather than karmic convergence.

By cooking, I could contemplate my korma and then eat it, too.

If you believe in karma, you have to accept what life brings you, since you brought it on yourself. Karma is not the same as Destiny, which predetermines every action, wherefore nothing can be changed. Karma is also not Comeuppance, which is a plot device in movies. Karma means that you inherit your own past from previous incarnations. This is why some people put nothing but pain into the world, yet they lead charmed lives of immense wealth and opulence. The punishment for their evil—if there is one—comes in the *next* lifetime, after they are dead and thus quite unable to care about being reborn as cockroaches.

Each lifetime has a lesson, but some people are very bad students.

If you struggle against your karma, that is your karma.

Until you learn to stop struggling, you will never understand karma. However, it is some people's karma that they will never learn.

Karma is very frustrating.

My jar of sauce stood off to one side, patiently waiting its turn. I picked it up and looked at it.

"KORMA," the label announced. "A delicious treat from India," it continued in English. A sticker on the back of the glass jar provided terse instructions in French:

Sauté meat.

Add sauce.

Cook for 40 minutes.

Serve with rice.

Under the rules of korma, life unfolds as a series of quirky accidents rather than important events. People who fulfilled their karma include world historical figures such as Elizabeth I and Marie Curie. People who fulfilled their korma include Alice B. Toklas and Pamela Anderson. Great kormic accidents in history include the apple falling on Newton's head, the invention of Post-its®, and the discovery that sildenafil didn't cure angina like it was supposed to. Instead, it gave men boners, and was remarketed as "Viagra." It still doesn't cure broken hearts, but men don't seem to care.

The kormic ideal is Inspector Clouseau, the greatest of French detectives, who always solves the crime but does it by accident. The kormic mascot is the bumblebee. It's an insect that can't fly but does anyway. The bumblebee thinks it's doing one thing when it goes questing for food, but as it dips here and there, happily humming to itself, it ends up accidentally pollinating flowers that couldn't survive without it.

It's quite possible that I'm doing something else when I think I'm doing another. Under my current formulation, that would be kormically correct.

Inside a universe governed by kormic principles, it makes perfect sense that I'm a terrible dancer. No matter how hard I try, the limbs won't coordinate. I cannot walk and chew gum at the same time. Talking makes my arms flap, in the manner of a light switch turning on a hair dryer. Because I am hopelessly bad at dancing, it's one of my favorite things to do. I have enrolled in jazz, salsa, and tango classes around the world, and am doubtless known in three continents as the worst dance student ever. In a dance class one summer spent going to school in Seoul, my sister put on a *hanbok*, the traditional dress of Korea, picked up a fan, snapped it open, and began wafting around like she'd been folk dancing forever. I managed to jerk forward and then promptly fell over, allowing my *hanbok*'s wraparound skirt to flap open at the same time that a visiting group of diplomats arrived to appreciate the beauty of Korean culture. A full moon was enjoyed by all. The teacher was horrified. I was unperturbed, because that sort of thing happens to me all the time. After she finished apologizing for my bad manners, I was trussed firmly into my *hanbok* and made to sit in a corner, where I was given a stick and a drum to bang slowly. This, too, was a task I failed miserably. All the other students began stumbling to my irregular beat, and my sister started glaring at me. This was not the proper flower-like expression for dancing, and it was my fault for putting a frown on her face. I was sent to another room to practice the Big Bow by myself. This involves prostrating yourself face down on the floor and staying there until you're told you can get up. I took advantage of this unexpected quiet time to take a nap, which merely confirmed that I had once again learned the wrong lesson from my punishment.

While all the other expats in Paris were doing yoga, I was belly dancing. Back in 2002, I'd watched the French television program, *Popstars*, a fifteen-minutes-of-fame series that managed to hook me despite the fact that I loathe game shows. Five girls were eventually chosen for a pop music quintet fabulous enough to overcome their dismal name, "L5." In English, this is medical shorthand for "Lumbar vertebrae no. 5." When pronounced in French, L5 ("elle cinq") sounds like "Hell sank." But the real star of *Popstars* was the woman with the thankless job of teaching the girls to dance. Mia Frye was a half French, half American expat who had an inimitable way of expressing herself in Franglish, barking orders like a drill sergeant and muttering curses under her breath. There was such pain on her beautiful face as she watched them floundering around the dance studio, their limbs jerking stiffly like defunct windmills. Their ineptitude was wounding her very reason for being, and she regularly told the five wannabes, in no uncertain terms, how severely disappointed she was with them. The Five glowered back at her in their baggy clothes, looking tired, sullen, and hungry. Madame Frye did not care. "I cannot *comprendre* the laziness!" she'd declare in astonishment. "You've only been practicing for five hours and you are behaving as if I am ordering you to go out and milk a herd of *vaches*."

In the U.S., Madame Frye would be labeled a bitch, and made to play nice in order to avoid lawsuits from their parents. In France, she was simply an *artiste*, and thanked for keeping up standards.

Despite my natural gifts at looking tired, sullen, and hungry, I was not interested in trying out for the next round of *Popstars*. Because I had watched the show many moons ago, however, I recognized a Hirschfeld-ish drawing of Madame Frye hanging in the passageway to the Café de la Gare, the Train Station Café, where it was posted along with dozens of other signs and notices for dance classes. Despite its name, the Café de la Gare is not in a train station. That is the Musée d'Orsay, which is a converted train station now full of naked nymphs, whose charming assets are such low hanging fruit that even my arms can reach them. The Café de la Gare is where people go to see warm bodies bending in mind-boggling ways, for it's in the courtyard of the Centre de Danse, which is probably the busiest spot in G-rated Paris. Ballet classes? Upstairs! Tango classes? Downstairs! Disco? In back! In the courtyard, the clashing soundtracks collected into a furious ball of sound chased by hundreds of stamping feet. With tapping toes and bouncing legs, I danced to the Main Office where new students could register for classes, because this was the only way to learn the secret location of the bathroom. "Too much coffee," I mumbled, as I pointed to Mia Frye's classes on the schedule.

Unfortunately, all the classes taught by Madame Frye were booked up until the next century and beyond. "Pardon?" I

blurted in surprise. Those classes will be taught by her cryo-
genically preserved head, the receptionist stated airily. Would
I care to try one of the Oriental dance classes? A new session
will be starting in ten minutes. And she blinked expectantly
at me.

I honestly had no idea how to respond.

She took my hesitation as a Yes. Briskly, she signed me up
for a trial lesson, took my money, and pushed me lightly off in
the direction of the restrooms. She'd set me on my path.

Bemused, I gratefully did my business and then wandered
in the halls, checking room numbers as I dodged returning students dashing to and from their classes. Newly released from
the *barre*, the ballerinas swept by me like so many varnished
broomsticks in leg warmers. As soon as I confirmed that I
was in the correct classroom and the other students started
filtering in, I realized why the receptionist had sent me here.
It was a belly dancing class, and all the women had genuine
bellies. I'd found my tribe! It was the highest concentration
of DD cups that I'd seen in this city of supermodels, and the
sight of them in costume—which is to say, in spangle bras—
was mesmerizing in the manner of salt-water aquarium fish
swimming around the tank in the gynecologist's office. I had
no idea what was going on, partly because the instructor, who
was perhaps Egyptian, had a very heavy accent, and partly
because who the hell knows the French words to directions
such as "PUSH the ribcage up and back, like riding a camel,
and shimmy!" In ballet, all the moves from *grand jeté* to *plié*
are already in French, so the English-speaking ballerinas taking classes upstairs had no new vocabulary to learn. My brain
was trying to translate orders to "*ondulez, ondulez*!" (undulate,
undulate—*arrrrrriba!* trilled the naughty Speedy Gonzalez
in my head), my body was struggling to emulate the moves,
and the result was belly dancing so remarkably bad it was . . .
remarkably bad.

But I digress.

I had a point, and the point was this: Korma doesn't care about your very good plans. One could say the same about karma. But some people's karma helps them win millions in the lottery, or rise to historical importance, or fall into the kind of love that has a soft-core landing. Korma leads the gullible to find meaning in a song from a musical, to belly dancing classes instead of to church, and to a cheap dinner alone in a tiny Paris studio, as happy as a clam can be. And who knows if clams are happy, really? They have no head, no eyes, and no brain. They do have a heart, a mouth, a cerebral pleural ganglion, and an anus. So, depending on how you look at it, they're the happiest creatures on earth.

Turns out I was only mildly allergic to my korma, which gave me the runs and a rash, like just about every other food on the planet. But, I survived to write this sentence, which is about the best I can generally hope for, my korma being what it is.

CHAPTER TWO

❧ ❧ ❧

Hustle

In good cookeries, all raisins should be stoned.
— *Amelia Simmons, American Cookery, 1796*

On my way back from the Bon Marché to my studio apartment, I'd often make a detour through the Luxembourg Gardens, where children would play with the toy sailboats in the central fountain. Each child would get a short stick and a boat with a numbered sail. They'd poke their boat with the stick, and off it would float across the rippled surface of the large circular pool. Eventually, their boat would drift back to the edge, coming close enough so they could poke it again. This activity involved a lot of waiting and chasing, because it was impossible to predict when or where your boat would return to the edge. The children were always trying to poke the wrong boat, just because it had drifted close to them.

This is how I feel about romantic relationships. "We begin by coveting what we see every day," Hannibal Lecter purred to FBI agent Clarice Starling, who'd been visiting him at a prison for the criminally insane. He was correct, but who takes romantic advice from a cannibal serial killer, even if he is a doctor with great teeth? Studies have shown that people tend to date inside a ten mile radius, because they'd rather pretend that proximity is destiny instead of fessing up to being lazy. What happens when the boys go after a girl who accidently drifted within poking range? They take a stab at her, and the girl floats away. The process repeats itself until the pokers get bored and leave.

No surprise, then, that Paris is a city of transients. A remarkable number of super-Parisians aren't even French. From Napoléon Bonaparte, who was born in Corsica, to Carla Bruni, the Italian-born former First Lady of France, a great chunk of those folks sitting decoratively in cafés are ex-pats who, by definition, came from someplace else. As a result, nearly 80 percent of Paris is unmarried but not necessarily single. Romance thrives in Paris because the city encourages the fine art of pitching woo, not the vulgar business of weddings. Lust has been around since the beginning of time, but it is only since the nineteenth century that it's been considered any basis to exchange vows, let alone remain legally bound until the hearse pulls up and starts honking for you. A Parisian's reaction to the news of an engagement is often perplexed confusion. "They're getting married? But why?" As far as people in this city are concerned, what kills a relationship isn't the fact that your lover snores like an asthmatic pig, but the contractual obligation to be by the pig's side 'til Death do you part.

One way or the other, marriage is fatal, and Paris is no place for the fainthearted in love. In this city, the pursuit of love demands a certain degree of flexibility and perseverance. Here is an example: When American porn magazine *Hustler* offered its first French edition a few years back, curiosity compelled me to buy a copy. Magazine kiosks typically place fashion, gossip, and health magazines on the customer's left, and hard news, international press, and hobby magazines on the right. The porn is always on the uppermost right shelves where pushy toddlers cannot grab it, and consequently it is too high for short and overly inquisitive women to reach. Wherefore the situation required that I ask for assistance.

"I would like to purchase a copy of *Hustler* (pronounced 'Oos-lair')," I said. "Could you please get it down for me?"

This is not a phrase often posed, by man or woman, in any language.

The kiosk vendor leered genially at me, and shook his head in refusal.

"How come?" I prodded.

"Because such things are not meant for young ladies."

I tried a few more kiosks, and each time, the vendor refused. When I related this experience to French friends with a request for an explanation, they chortled the French version of the clichéd line, "You ain't so young, lady." This unhelpful response did nothing to increase my respect for the French sense of humor. As a result, I have yet to resolve why the magazine kiosk vendors refused to take my money, but there's no use getting wound up about it. Proprietors reserve the right not to sell to patrons, for reasons they are not required to defend. A friend once visited me with her American boyfriend of the moment, a bossy fellow puffed up with wealth and convinced of his own importance. A few hours later, he returned from a solo shopping trip, huffing in outrage because a pricy boutique had refused to sell him a pair of loafers. He'd shouldered his way into the small store, bellowing orders. Wherefore he was simply ignored, as he had mispronounced the magic word. He thought it was pronounced, "Plat-ee-num Vee-sa." They were expecting to hear, "Please."

In the end, I convinced the humorless owner of a *tabac* to give me the small publicity poster plastered by the entrance to his establishment. Wordlessly, he peeled it down and handed it to me. Clutching my talisman, I marched back to my studio, unrolled it, and stuck it on my mini-refrigerator. Whenever I went for a snack, I had to look at a female mouth amusing itself with a stick candy striped in red, white, and blue, these being the colors of both the American and French flags. The poster wasn't much, but I liked it because it had required so much effort to get. The entire city seems to be constructed on this sadistic reward principle, with métro strikes, aloof waiters, and bad dates deliberately thrown into your path in order to make you deeply grateful for any crumbs of success.

Now, I wasn't hoping to buy French *Hustler* for the pictures. I wanted it for the *articles*. In order to improve my conversational French (which still isn't very good), I hoped to learn as many four letter words as I could, and I figured that an American porn mag translated into French would be a splendid way to learn. In English, my cussing tends to old-fashioned expletives such as "gosh!" "gadzooks!" and "golly!" In the larger scheme of things, it was far more embarrassing to wander around Paris, looking and sounding like Mister Peabody, the talking dog in the *Bullwinkle* cartoons, than to ask total strangers to sell me porn I was too short to purchase.

"But," you sputter, "porn isn't romantic!" Love + Lust = Lost without U . . . and a thousand candy hearts start to melt, for romance thrives in the spaces where hope meets confusion. And it is here that things start to get lost in translation, because in French, the word "fiancée" refers to your one-night stand.

Yes, I know. I'm a horrible, horrible person for bursting your bubble. But if you're reading this sentence, you should be older than twelve—and if you're not, please show this page to your mother so I can yell at her.

If I wasn't looking for love, then why was I was bootlegging signal at a café near the Centre Pompidou so I could search an internet dating site? I wasn't looking for myself. I was trying to help an ex-pat British scientist with a cat named Tara and a heart too soft for her own good. I was tired of hearing Cordula complain that there were no men in Boston where she lived, so I decided to send her a short list of bachelors worth meeting for a drink. That's when I stumbled across John's awkward profile. There was no photo, and everything about his information was wrong: almost-divorced dad, soccer coach for his son's team, corporate lawyer who lives in Wellesley, Massachusetts, a wealthy white Boston suburb favored by pedigreed dogs with weak bladders. My brain said no. A dismal fit for my bohemian friend. The back of my neck said yes. But yes for me, though everything he listed seemed a worse match for a girl who shops for groceries at flea markets.

I read his profile again, and the bizarre tingling sensation grew stronger.

Baffled, I sipped my coffee, and finally concluded an email to him wasn't poaching because my friend had no idea he existed. For that matter, neither did I. 'J-o-h-n' was merely a cluster of pixels on a screen. I sent him a message; within seconds, he replied. He later told me he'd been a member of the dating site for fifteen minutes and had received emails from three other women. As soon as my message came, he unsubscribed.

I wrote him that I read everything except for *Popular Mechanics* and gun magazines.

He didn't mention that *Soldier of Fortune* was in his bathroom.

I'm a political Independent with progressive leanings.

He's a conservative Republican who thinks that liberals are dimwits.

I refuse to marry or have children.

He's a family man.

Etc.

We were total opposites with nothing in common except the fact that we were both from Maine. I knew the towns where he grew up; he knew mine too. We disagreed about everything. Still, we kept corresponding, because lawyers aren't afraid of arguments, and that weird tingle up my spine wouldn't dissipate. My lizard brain knew something I didn't. What it knew, I had no clue. I was certain he wasn't a soul mate. I have met them before. The first words out of the man's mouth are always "Where have you been?" as if I'd popped out for a pizza and brought back beer by mistake. It's not me but the men who ask, plaintively, *"Now* what do we do?"* Perplexed words slipping out of unaccustomed mouths, for these are the sorts of men who don't read their horoscopes. Their eyes plead. Their bodies yearn. Wherefore I am unimpressed. So what? It's not romantic destiny to meet your soul mate. First of all, everybody has banana bunches of them, and if you've never met any, it may be time to leave your living room. Second, I find it pointless to pin romantic hopes on a companion who understands you deeply, listens to everything you say, bonds with you on an emotional level, and adores you beyond reason. Such perfection can only be found in a Golden Retriever. Or, says Cordula the Soft-Hearted Scientist, a horse. Not good options for me. (See "Allergies.") Third, I've never felt incomplete, as if I'd lost my other half in the dryer and needed to start taking long, romantic walks on the beach in hopes of finding it washed up and waiting for me. I'm fine by myself, thank you. Stop bothering me.

When I run into a soul mate, I shake his hand and I leave. It's keys-to-locks and perfect connection, blah blah blah, but so what? There's nothing new to learn from a relationship with your other half because it's already all about you. It's like expecting your left earlobe to teach your right earlobe a thing or two. Plus, if "soul mate" was a valid concept, I should have met one in the form of a hot babe slinging burgers, or a garbage man fresh from a dump. But no, it's always ridiculously dashing men with swollen bank accounts and a recidivist ability to recite poetry. I turn up my nose and run. This is also why I think reincarnation is 99 percent bupkis, because Larry, Algernon, and Ming all used to be Cleopatra. Just once, I want to meet a man who says that in a former life he used to be the daughter of Marie Antoinette's wigmaker. Then, maybe, I'd wait around to hear more. I'm still waiting—which is to say, I'm not.

I've been accused of being heartless, because only a bitch walks away from a man pinning his heart to her sleeve. I think, therefore I am unrepentant. To my critics, I say: please read more books, paying particular attention to the supporting characters. Remember the story of Odysseus and the enchantress Circe? He was on an odyssey, but for a year, Circe delayed his heroic journey by fulfilling his every need. *She* was deeply in love with the man of her dreams. *He* was having a fabulous island vacation with a real sex goddess! Inconveniently, she also turned all his men into swine. In one version of the story, she fed them to him every night. He dumped her, and resumed voyaging home to his wife.

Why is this a bad story? Oh, but it's not. Because he's the hero, Odysseus kept on running into gorgeous sirens who fell madly in love with him, and they unleashed all their feminine wiles trying to get him to stay home with them. They're soul mates! They belong together! Why else would a gorgeous, rich man with excellent table manners land in their laps, out of the blue, bringing shiploads of fresh food? The women are loamy of thigh with fertile wombs bearing many fruits, and the little bastards are never resentful when their father heroically abandons them. This is called Great Literature. My love story is terrible because I'm the one doing the running, and I look like a startled koala in spectacles. That's the part that confuses everyone. Given the men I've left behind, I should look like Lucy Liu trussed in thigh-high black leather boots. Instead, I'm Margaret Cho wearing thrift-shop sweatpants on a bad hair day. It simply does not compute. I'm too short to be fashionable, too fat to be chic, and too tarnished to be a trophy. Makeup artists cry when confronted by my face. My eyeballs eject contact lenses— it's something about "tight lids." I'm allergic to mascara, rouge, and hairspray. Common sense says I should be grateful that men want to marry me. Instead, I'm uncommonly aggravated. I mean what I say, and it isn't a ruse: *I don't want to.* The very fact that men ask for my hand in marriage—the hand being the wrong bit to try to persuade, by the way—means it would be a giant mistake. It's a perfect Catch-22.

To my secret glee, John won't fly to Paris for a weekend rendezvous with a perfect stranger, even if the perfect stranger is *moi*. "I have soccer practice on Sundays," he growled. Plus, he knew that I was moving to Boston for reasons settled long before our conversation began, and he didn't mind waiting for me to come to him. Was he seeing other women? I sincerely hoped so. To each other, we were big cumulus clouds drifting on wind. He did not inhabit my reality. I neither trusted nor distrusted him, for he was a character on an electronic page, more fiction than fact, writing himself into my consciousness but disappearing when I dreamed. A fickle proposition at best. It helped that he was painfully honest, answering every question I posed with a direct answer. He also drove a pickup truck, drank regular beer, and liked declarative sentences, all of which hinted that he was that elusive beast known as the Abominable Straight Man. I asked for a picture, and he sent me a photo of a blurry humanoid skulking in deep snow. He's the Sasquatch? My hypothesis was confirmed! Now I was really interested, because I'm allergic to everything else with fur.

"Sasquatches don't exist," Rose snipped, waggling her elegant finger in my face as we sat at an ordinary bistro near the Louvre. "Why don't you fall in love with a Frenchman and just stay here?" That's what she did, except her Frenchman was Dutch. An American stock broker who'd spent a few years working in the City (London's equivalent of Wall Street), Rose had had an exceedingly good year and decided to celebrate by divorcing her gay French husband. Gilles was one of her very best friends, and she'd agreed to marry him because he had ultra-conservative Catholic parents who strongly disapproved of 1) Hollywood movies, 2) margarine, and 3) gay men. He hoped they'd die deluded and happy, swept into their graves by old age and too much *confit de canard*. And they did! Is there a better time to end a fake marriage than after a real funeral? So she took the Eurostar train from London to Paris, and headed to town hall in order to file her divorce papers. As she stood in line, impatiently tapping her toes, she found herself being stared at by a gorgeous man in the next line. Pierre invited her to a party that same night. She agreed to go. They had sex in the coat closet. Once her divorce was final, Pierre proposed. They now have two absurdly beautiful children being raised as citizens of Paris.

This story makes Parisians jealous, because hardly any apartments in Paris have coat closets.

We sat down to green beans, giblet salad, and crème brulée, a classic lunch special available anywhere in the city. Years ago, I'd told myself I should do exactly as Rose suggested, since it was as obvious as the subliminal sequence of our meal. But I never did. Why not? There are lots of reasons, some of which even sound reasonable, but in the end, my not-so-good explanation is this: it's because I look grotesque when I eat. I'm not one of those women that can look all sultry when they swallow asparagus. It's beyond my powers to transform the licking of an ice cream cone into an erotic experience, as advised by *The Sensuous Woman* on tape. Published in 1969 and written by "J" (predictably, as "O" was already taken), it was a revolutionary sex manual at the time, teaching women how to please their men in bed. Today, it's pure comedy gold. Fast-forward a half-century later, the ice cream cone is now a raisin, and the focus is on women pleasing themselves. "I'd like you to start by examining your raisin," psychologist Lori Brotto advises her female clientele after passing around a bowl of Sunkist fruits. "Touch the raisin with a finger. Look into the valleys and peaks, the highlights and dark crevasses. Lift the raisin to your lips . . ." This sort of hilarity has become so mainstream that I read about Brotto's work in *The New York Times Magazine*. Nowadays, no scarlet letters are required; the analysis of orgasms has become a clinical exercise in head-shrinkage. Conclusion: It's not the woman's fault if penises make her laugh because female sexuality is "complex."

I dislike raisins. They're chewy and dried up. They happen to give me the runs, which is sort of beside the point, but what woman wants to think of her lady parts as shriveled black fruits? And lifting the raisin to your lips . . . well, if you extend the metaphor here, which is pretty much necessary for this exercise to work, it's teaching women how to become lesbians. Penises are funny/ Raisins are yummy/ Eat some today!

To which I say: sometimes a cigar is just a cigar, and a vagina isn't a raisin unless you're in therapy.

Clearly, I am no fun. When it comes to love, I'm literal. To me, all romance is fiction, too remote from real life to be anything but silly. Sweet nothings curdle my ears. I'm not interested in how things seem. I want to know what they are. The only way I can figure stuff out is by taking it apart and going back in time, all the way back to the Middle Ages when "romance" meant a story about pointy hats and disembowelments. When I chew on liver and giblets, my lips tell tales of blood and guts without me saying a word. Alas, chic women who carry tiny dogs in Hermès handbags don't want to know about the shit in the silver lining. This is why Rose and I are friends, because she's not ladylike in the least. Rose got married because she's American, but she lives in Paris because she's a flirt. "I'm a little in love with all my friends," she admits breathlessly. "Why shouldn't I seduce them?" And she bats her eyes at me.

She believes, profoundly, in love. Wherefore her version of what she shares with Pierre is terrifyingly X-rated.

"Let's go to the Louvre," Rose suggested as she sopped up the remains of her lunch.

"Why?" I asked in surprise, because we'd both been there hundreds of times.

"I need toilet paper."

Swathed in couture, she likes to go the W/C, apply a fresh coat of lipstick, smile dreamily at the face in the mirror and abscond with a giant roll of TP. Crabbily, I've told her that it's people like her that force people like me to carry their own stash in their pockets. She just laughs, and swipes the toilet paper anyway.

To this day, I don't know why she wanted it, but I suspect she was using the cardboard rings for an art project. The Louvre is very inspiring.

There is an old physics problem: If a train is traveling at 100 miles an hour and a fly is hovering above your soup, how fast is the fly flying? Why doesn't the fly hit the front of the car when the train suddenly stops? From the teacher's standpoint, the fly is doomed unless the student finds the formula to keep it hovering. In the real world, the fly does just fine, but I could never explain how. In physics land, the hypothetical fly falls dead, the hapless victim of my poor math skills. Grade: **F**. F for the Flattened Fly.

Just because I was moving to the Boston area didn't mean that my body was going to stay there. Call it an occupational hazard. Should one happen to be in a profession that starts with the letter "A,"—say, for example, "assassin," "arms dealer," anyone in the Army, "astrologer," "angel of Death," "acrobat," "anarchist," and, ho hum, "academic,"—moving around is part of the job. I once got the equivalent of a bill from a commission of interstellar planetary overlords who decided I'd used up too many minutes in outer space, therefore I owed them a Smoot of blood and turnips. Who am I to argue with Kang and Kodos, especially since I grew up listening to the original *Star Trek* on cassette tapes my brother had made? Long ago, I'd dispensed with my baggage in order to live out of a suitcase. Like one of the twelve called to be an apostle (yet another job starting with "A," I will note), I ditched my worldly possessions in order to follow an inner voice telling me to wander until the wandering was done.

No emotional safety nets. No trampolines to fall back on. My entire wardrobe filled an overnight bag, and the only shoes I kept were the ones on my feet.

For years, I lived out of a suitcase and then the suitcase was stolen, leaving me with nothing but the clothes on my back and the murmurs in my head. I should have been happy, or at least content. Instead, I found myself breakfasting in a nook, with a rescue cat warming my feet, and bouquet of resentments garnishing my table. As I stared into that crystal ball holding cut flowers withering in slow motion, I saw my future clearly: it was a bowlful of tap water that smelled like rotten spinach.

How to explain misery when life is great and God is good?

It would start with a gut feeling of wrongness that descended into dark wells. Was it hormones? Hysterics? A hissy fit? I tried on every explanation and concluded: it wasn't female trouble. Mine was the misery of the fly in the physics problem. A nameless, faceless entity had set me up for a head-on collision with modern life, and as long as I stayed obedient to the problem, indecisively hovering at 100 miles an hour, I would soon be drowning in a bowl of mass-produced chicken soup.

Mmmm, mmmm, not so good.

The trick to solving a problem is recognizing it in the first place. Flies have compound eyes made up of three thousand separate lenses. Their eyes are twice as large as their heads. Trouble is, their tiny fly brains can only process information from a few hundred lenses at a time. Their sight is blurred, because their brains are in their thorax, the part that moves their wings. Because of this, the fly pays no attention to the theatrics of history. It's too busy staying aloft so it can spit up in your food.

To get the answer you want, ask a better question. If you spend your time whining, "how come?" at random adults in the manner of a cranky two-year-old, you're likely to discover that all questions lead to a time-out and a cookie. If you search for answers in the wrong places, you will get the answers you deserve. It's all about the assumptions that get built in, the most famous example of which is: "Have you stopped beating your wife?" Do you see the trap? Many people don't, which is why Franz Kafka wrote a little fable called "A Little Fable," about the pathos of imminent doom. Real life isn't *Saw*, you see. It's not like there are clues.

> "Alas," said the mouse, "the world gets smaller every day. At first it was so wide that I ran along and was happy to see walls appearing to my right and left, but these high walls converged so quickly that I'm already in the last room, and there in the corner is the trap into which I must run."
>
> "But you've only got to run the other way," said the cat, and ate it.

Now, here is what's so frustrating about this fable. Kafka pointed the trap out, explained very clearly how to escape, and yet mouse after mouse will insist that no, the human's wrong, he's just an insurance adjuster whose biggest accomplishment in life was writing a bizarre story about a giant bug named Gregor. Clearly, Kafka was writing for cats, so why should mice care what he thinks?

Kafka wanted the mouse to live. The mouse just wanted to be a martyr.

Time and time again, I'd returned to Paris, mulling whether to turn left or stay gauche. I was trapped in a maze of my own making, lured in by the promise of stinky cheese and lamenting the path not taken. My fetal twin still wanted to be an artist, and it wasn't letting go of that ambition. Intransigent, it was the still, small voice in my belly that was my version of an addiction, an unreasonable craving that wouldn't relent no matter how many times I tried quitting.

There was no way out of the trap, at least not as far as I could see. The fly did not agree, because it had 2,998 more eyes than me. All I had to do was to follow its lead . . . for at the end of the day, when the train has stopped and all the chatty mammals have departed, comes the Hour of the Fly. Released from the physics problem it didn't understand in the first place, it's free to flirt with other flies, and they will make baby flies called maggots. They will take over the world, because they have quick reproductive cycles and no birth control on their side.

One of the most famous cafés in Paris is *Les Deux Magots* (and no, it's not a typo, though it would be funnier if it was). The café became famous because literary lovers such as Simone de Beauvoir and Jean-Paul Sartre used to argue over his infidelities there. The word *magot*, which is the same in French and English, comes from *Magog*, as in the Book of Revelations:

> When the thousand years are over, Satan will be released from his prison and will go out to deceive the nations in the four corners of the earth—Gog and Magog—and to gather them for battle. In number they are like the sand on the seashore.

Though the prophecy is grim, kids love the story of Gog and Magog because it's almost a palindrome, "Gog am Gog," which is pretty much how a bored child in Sunday school would expect a Gog to identify himself. Theologians haven't decided what the prophecy actually means, but in kid-brain it's the hellfire n' damnation version of the joke: "Pete and Repeat were on a boat. Pete fell off. Who was left? (Repeat!)" In Bible-ese, the joke comes out: God and Gog were on a boat. God kicks Gog out. Who's left? (Magog)! Over time, *magog* came to refer generically to people from heathen lands, thus the "two Magots" in the café are a pair of lifelike sculptures representing Chinese men. They are mounted near the ceiling. For a hundred years, the two Magots have hovered over countless tourists slurping bowls of soup, and there they will stay until the day when the trains stop for good.

Then what? It depends.

Satan and his minions get thrown into a lake of fire. Everyone else, including the dead, gets to stand before God, who reads about them in a Book of Life. People who aren't in the Book of Life get tossed into the lake of fire, where they get to die for a second time, sort of like what happens when sunlight hits vampires. The only way I'd get into that book is if I wrote it myself. Now there's a thought! If I wrote my own Book of Life and pulled off a switcheroo, could God tell? It's not like He'd already read it. For sure He didn't write it—that would be the Fickle Finger of Fate doing the writing. All I'd have to do is figure out where God stashes his triple-F bedtime reading. I'd already been to the Library of Hell, which is, naturally, in Paris. Where's the library of Heaven? (Wrong answer: the Vatican.)

The world is wide, the mouse had insisted, right up to the moment when the walls converged and it was too late to form a better opinion. In a perfect world, the mouse would have whipped out a saw and hacked her way out of the trap. Not possible for me, because my hacksaw had been confiscated. It was one of two items missing from my bag when I'd rummaged around for that song in the Jardin des Plantes. ("Surely, my dear Watson," said Sherlock Holmes, "you noticed that a hacksaw was curiously not among the items she'd had with her?") The other missing item was my Swiss army knife. I used to carry both everywhere, until the airport people started objecting to them, asking me: "Exactly what, young lady, did you intend to do with these things?" I'd give them a dirty look. "Well, gee, isn't it obvious? How else am I going to fix my supper?" The uniformed men would scowl

at me, and then swipe my cooking tools. No wonder my fetal
twin was howling for blood. She was hungry, and needed to
be fed.

So what should I do, now that I had come to another fork
in the road?

It was time to pick it up, find a new knife, and hack my
own trail through the woods.

It was a busy morning, so it was noon in September before
I made it to the cavernous lobby of the Boston tower where
John had asked me to fetch him. Hovering behind a dais,
humorless security guards pointed me to the express elevator
to the 15th–20th floors. The lawyers were all wearing the same
dark suit, but only one was pacing the perimeter with his head
down like the bears in the Paris zoo. That was John.

In greeting, he gave me a jar of jelly his mother had made
from wild blackberries picked from the back of the house in
Maine. I gave him a glass Christmas ornament shaped like
an alligator. We were opposites right down to the kinds of
gifts we'd exchanged. He'd given me a jar of sentiment. I'd
given him box of symbolism. The ornament didn't survive the
final leg of its journey; the tail had snapped off en route. I was
mortified. He just chucked the broken shards in the bin and
whisked me to a French bistro around the corner.

There was so much chemistry between us that even total
strangers commented (to me, in the Ladies' Room, giving me
"thumbs up!" under the stalls): "Are you guys on a date? He's
really cute!" Uh, thank you? This date was a beacon of hope
for pudgy women everywhere. But I wasn't besotted, infatu-
ated, or convinced I'd met my destiny. He happened to be six
feet tall with thick hair and broad shoulders. So what? I don't
eat with my eyes. I smell with my tongue. Why should I care
what he looks like? All that matters is that his skin whiffs of

honey. To another woman, he might stink like an elephant after a hard run. He was, after all, a Republican in a liberal town, exuding white male privilege from his well-scrubbed pores. Didn't smoke, drink, or do drugs. Loved this great country, and liked to shoot guns.

"Err," I started, casting around for a conversational-type response. Finally, I squeaked: "I don't shave my armpits!"

"Good," he replied, and polished off the last bite of his steak.

Man-like, he ate everything placed in front of him without comment or complaint. The only problem with his food was that there wasn't enough of it. Hungrily, he eyed the other half of my lunch. "Would you like to finish it?" I asked politely, thinking that he really should. He waited two beats and polished off the rest of my meal.

Beep! Time's up!

He'd warned me that he had a business meeting at one, and so lunch ended with a swift peck on the cheek and a bellowed, "Bye!" as he hurried down the street.

What?

John wasn't the kind of man who'd say, "I'll call you," just to have something to say. I'm not the kind of woman who sits around waiting for a man to call, because I hate the phone. Even for me, though, the end to this meeting was abrupt and strange. The more I thought about it, the more perplexed I became. Jumping on the T, I took the Red Line to Harvard, where I sat and fumed at Widener Library, working myself into a furious lather until I finally reached the point where I folded my arms across my chest, crossed my legs, scrunched up my face, and told myself: "If he doesn't call me in ten seconds, I will never speak to him again." Then I started a silent countdown. "ten … nine … eight … seven … six … five … four … three … two …"

My cell phone rang.

This is why I hate the phone. Having a phone gives callers the strange idea that you'll answer it.

The horrible device kept ringing. Students were giving me dirty looks, so I grabbed my bag, dashed into the vestibule, flipped the phone open and hissed, "What?"

"Hello?" John said in a slightly perplexed tone. "You called. So I'm calling you back."

"I didn't call," I said sulkily. "I've been in the library. *You* called *me*."

There was a silence. "But I *heard* you . . ."

Let's not start up with that, shall we? "How was the meeting?" I cut him off.

"Fine." There was another silence. "Do you want to have dinner?"

"No," I replied peevishly. "I'm not hungry. We just ate, remember?"

"I didn't mean right away," he sighed in exasperation. "Tomorrow. That's Friday night. Okay?"

"Okay."

"Come meet me in my office, and we'll go from there."

"Fine," I grumbled.

"Fine," he grumbled back. "I gotta get back to work," he said abruptly, and hung up the phone.

No wonder chit-chat over lunch was a disaster. To communicate, we had to bicker.

To my great relief, we never made it to dinner. We argued all the way to Wellesley, and I ended up staying all weekend. He took the opportunity to explain to me that when a woman puts off meeting a man for months, and then makes a date for lunch and shows up wearing *pants*, the man will assume that she's not very interested in him. As a rebuttal, I pointed out that a) I'd been in France, 2) the pants were Parisian, and iii) I'd warned him from the outset that I was fussy, and it was

unlikely that I'd be attracted to him. I didn't want to give him
ideas. My argument was just as convincing as you'd expect,
given that I'd spent the past three days in his bed.

My sister was not amused. "What if he's an axe murderer?"
she objected, because she thinks all corporate lawyers are axe
murderers.

"He's not an axe murderer," I said firmly.

"But how do you know?" she fretted.

I knew because of the third law of Newtonian mechanics. We were equal actions and opposite reactions, agreeing on
nothing, alike only in our stubbornness. He was bullheaded
and impatient. I loathe being rushed. We fought. Real sparks
flew, the kind that singed my skin and vanished in a tiny puff.
John could make me so angry that I refused to talk to him for
days, imposing utter silence that was worse that ignoring him.
It turned him into a thought bubble yet to be filled. He had to
come find me if he wanted to have words.

And where was I? I'd gone to Arizona for a semester. Surprise! We fought about the fact that I was in Arizona. Then,
bellowing loudly, he came to visit. We went on hikes through
red rocks in the desert. I returned to New England. Pretty
soon, I was back in Paris for the summer. Howling furiously,
he came to visit me. We had a hilarious time chasing cows
in Normandy. I returned to the U.S. Before long, I landed
in London. We fought about the fact that I was in London.
Then, complaining bitterly, he came to visit me. We laughed
our heads off riding the double-decker buses to the Tower.
This back-and-forth went on until I got so tired of him calling
me all the time that I moved in with him in Wellesley. The
only thing that changed was that I started doing more of his
laundry.

Little things for me started appearing around the house as
if clever mice were making them. A baking dish. A purple
hairbrush. A pair of fuzzy slippers. A list bearing a strange

similarity to the "pan, a comb, and maybe a cat" that Scientologist grooms promise their brides. In what unfathomable place in the male psyche are these things located? Thankfully, there was nothing sentimental about any of these items. They were even less personal than the nylon stockings my *halmoni* would send every Christmas, the thigh-high kind with tourniquet elastic tops sized for legs the size of chopsticks. By the time I'd become a decrepit spinster of twenty-two—"Too old! Why you not marry?"—she'd given up the stockings and switched to bath sheets, which is a Korean grandmother's way of saying "Too fat! Regular bath towels too small!" John knew perfectly well that the fact that I was living with him did not make us a couple. There was him, there was me, and there was lizard brain. The reptile kept me coming back, because it really liked honey. But I will leave, as I always do, because the world is wide and it is my nature.

Then, one day, he surprised me with a gift. It was a plastic grocery bag coated in crumbs from the forest. I opened it. Inside was the heart of a deer he'd shot himself.

Perplexed, my mouth opened. Then it closed. I didn't know what to do with it.

To place it in perspective: my sister's cat Buster was a legendary urban hunter. His fame was such that he earned a place in Clea Simon's book, *The Feline Mystique* (see index, "Cat, loud shorthair.") He'd been a mewling larva, blind eyes tightly shut, and he grew into an enormous black-and-white tomcat that showered with her and left whisker stubble in the sink. At night, Buster ("Holstein") the Cat slept next to her on his back, his head on a pillow, tucked in with his paws over the covers and held straight by his sides. They both snored loudly. Sleeping was their favorite activity. At daybreak, he'd shiver himself awake, lick back his hair, give a good stretch, and head out to work. By the end of the day, he'd drag home a mangled bird and meow loudly, demanding to be admired.

Messy though it may be, it melts your heart when they do this. Cats bring you presents when they love you, "love" being in cat-brain the desire to ensure the continuation of the human most willing to provide Pounce® treats. A bleeding hunk of protein was the most sincere form of affection that Buster could give her. "You have to respect that," my sister sighed, stroking his contented, blood-spattered face. "It's disgusting, but *he* doesn't think that." She looked at the half-eaten pigeon on the floor. Pretty soon, Buster would start to vomit. She sighed again. "It's the thought that counts."

Standing at the threshold in his muddy rubber boots, John held his heart in his hands and offered it to me. His whole body glowed with pride. So I thanked him with a kiss, took the gift, and made him strip down and hose off on the porch so he wouldn't track mud through the house.

He was pretty happy about the naked part. I was pretty happy with the meat.

But a deer heart isn't a present so much as it's a loud chest-thumping demand, a request to know where, in this relationship, did he stand? He'd given me a gift that money cannot buy. A precious thing beyond price, and a deeply romantic gesture. For when I went away, leaving him alone for months at a time, he wasn't out chasing other women, even though he was free to do so if he wished. I'd said that he could. And it was true. I just wasn't sure what I would do if he did. He didn't sit around waiting for me to return. Instead, he started going to Maine every weekend, tracking whitetail deer in the forgetful forests behind the house where his parents live. John's heart was proof of those sustained years of effort without promise of the prize. Uncertainty didn't stop him, though sometimes he felt discouraged, sitting solitary in the cold sunlight, listening to the muttering pines.

Is the heart seized by a coronary the same organ pierced by Cupid's arrow? To horny males, all prey looks the same. To the hunter, nothing could be further from the truth. A hunter's quarry is singular, different from all the others because it knows how to get the better of him. The origins of the word "quarry" can be found in the Latin, "cor," which means heart. Wherefore *cordial*, that which warms the cockles of the heart. To succeed in his task, the hunter must combine good luck with careful timing and unwavering commitment, forging a unity of mind, soul, and body yearning to catch the heart that flees not out of fear but because it will not wait for you.

John could not heave his heart into his mouth, so he took the matter into his hands. He hoped I'd understand. And I did.

He loves me like fresh meat loves salt. So I cried.

Here is my recipe for deer heart (serves four-six):

---

1 fresh deer heart, soaked overnight in clean, very cold water, changed frequently

1 cup port

½ lb bacon, minced

1 yellow onion, minced

2–3 medium carrots, minced

2 garlic cloves, crushed

1 bay leaf

1 cup red wine

Salt and pepper, to taste

Wash and clean the heart, removing all membranes, arteries and veins. Pat dry, and slice as thinly as possible. Place slices in a medium bowl, cover with port, add salt and pepper, and marinate overnight in the refrigerator. Using a large sauté pan, cook bacon at medium heat until fat renders but the bits are not crisp. Add onion, carrots, and garlic to the fat, cooking over medium heat until onion is translucent but not browned. Turn heat to high. Lift heart slices out of port marinade, and sauté quickly until just browned. Add bay leaf, port marinade, and enough red wine to cover. Bring to a boil, then lower heat to simmer. Allow liquids to reduce. Do not overcook. Remove pan from heat and allow to rest. Remove bay leaf; add salt and pepper to taste. Serve with creamy polenta, roasted red peppers, and asparagus.

Take away the hide, the color of the skin, the firm flesh and bones bowing as they age. Discard the irrelevant, the conventional, and the romantic fantasies that inherit failure, as they must. In your mouth, as you savor and chew, you hold the oldest story ever told of being in love, a story for which you alone can produce the ending.

The irreducible self is not pretty. It is mortality incarnate.

The deer's heart is still safe to eat. In the modern world, the brains are too dangerous, being prone to conveying madness.

CHAPTER THREE

ॐ ॐ ॐ

A Liver with Onions

Lord, confound this surly sister
Blight her brow with blotch and blister,
Cramp her larynx, lung and liver
In her guts a galling give her.
— *J.M. Synge*

t this point in a proper romance, the heroine should find herself facing a large obstacle challenging her bliss, such as a rival in stilettos, or an inconvenient war. Since the nineteenth century, the conventions of the genre have been consistent: the heroine runs away from marriage, a clever suitor figures out how to win her, the heroine finally relents, they tie the knot and live happily ever after. From Jane Austen to that Mormon lady who wrote *Twilight*, authors always make the heroine marry Mr. Right in the end. If he wasn't Mr. Right, the heroine would not have married him.

When the woman ends up with Mr. Wrong, she isn't the heroine but the sidekick. She is there to make the heroine look thin. I didn't want to be heroine or sidekick. I wanted to be Tolstoy, so I started writing about John and turned him into the heroine. Turnabout is fair play. Besides which, he was the one who always wanted to talk about The Relationship, asking me awful things like, "How do you feel about us? Where do you see this relationship going?" "What relationship?" I'd reply in astonishment. "We're living together!" he'd bellow in disbelief. "So?" I'd retort, and refuse to speak to him until he apologized for being so mean to me.

Exasperated, my friends told me I was being unrealistic. That social conventions would indicate that living with a man means that I am in a relationship with him. From my perspective, I was in a monogamous heterosexual cohabitation experiment and doing my best not to bias the scientific outcome. Expecting it to turn out a certain way undermined the entire process, and so I was just living it day to day, and seeing what happened. Talking about "the relationship" just created unreasonable demands based on the bizarre belief that I would stay with him.

Consequently, I did not get worked up when John asked me to accompany him to his parents' house in Maine for the weekend. For generations, John's people have been from Bethel, a ski-resort town in a southwestern part of the state that I ended up not knowing very well on account of my dad being the way he is. As it happened, my dad had been assigned a church in one of the nearby towns, and we were all set to move there. Then the minister who'd been appointed to the Houlton church refused to go, because it's so far north that the local television stations are Canadian. To keep the peace, my dad agreed to switch churches with him.

It's fun to wonder if John and I would have been summer sweethearts if my family had moved to the Bethel area as originally planned, but I wasn't much interested in boys back then. My mother was convinced that the bad influence of boarding school had tipped me over the edge and turned me into a hairy-legged lesbian. (Somewhere on a Venn diagram, the brain spheres of minister's wives and frat boys are intersecting. This is why I love Venn diagrams. They illuminate our shared humanity.) In her mind, being a lesbian was still no excuse for not getting married and giving her grandchildren.

Just as, in my mind, going to Maine with John did not mean we were getting serious. It was not to meet the parents, though such a meeting was a corollary effect of staying at their house for the weekend. It meant that my cohabitation experiment was shifting to a trial application phase.

After I agreed to go, the conversations began to change, so I started taking notes in an effort to extract relevant data from subject B (John), with myself as subject A. He didn't notice, because I was writing an academic book about zoos at the time, and he was used to me staring at him with an odd expression on my face, frowning suddenly, and then typing furiously on my laptop. Up to this point, everything that had passed between us was prep work: the mundane but necessary task of setting parameters, clarifying objectives, and controlling for variables. Now that I've agreed to travel with him, the parameters shift. From now on, everything unfolds in the imminent present, because this is still a monogamous cohabitation experiment and not foretold by fate. I don't know the outcome, and neither does he. Which is why he asks this awful question:

"Do you want to enter the wife-carrying contest at Sunday River?" John asks sweetly over breakfast.

"What for?" I ask suspiciously. Sunday River is the resort where John grew up skiing. Along with other warm-weather activities, it hosts a wife-carrying contest when the snow melts.

"Obvious, isn't it?" He gives me a big, sunny smile.

Now, some women might think this is a man's roundabout way of proposing. However, John is nothing if not direct, and he also knows better than to ask me. Because we are opposites in all things, he is the marrying kind. I'm the kind that flees. We live together successfully because he's good at running after me. "We're not married," I point out, and calmly eat my eggs.

"True!" he grins, peeking at me from behind his newspaper. "But the man doesn't have to be carrying his *own* wife. She just has to be married."

"A weirdly literal sort of race," I squint at him. "And it still doesn't apply to me!"

"I'm just making that up!" he laughs. "The race people changed the rules! No more 'wife,' so I can carry you!"

"That *is* interesting," I muse aloud. "Do you think there'll be straight men carrying lesbians? Or gay men carrying straight men? Or . . ."

"I don't care about that," he cuts me off in aggravation. "I want to know if you'll enter the race with me. The prize is the 'wife's' weight in beer!"

"You still have to carry me," I remind him.

"So?"

". . . in a *race*."

". . . weight in *beer*," he repeats, setting down his newspaper and getting up from his chair. Then he leans over, scoops me up, tosses me over his shoulder, and starts jouncing me experimentally.

"What if" (jounce jounce) ". . . it's a brand . . ." (jounce jounce) ". . . of beer . . ." (jounce) ". . . you don't like?"

"Completely missing the point." He puts me down and soothes me back in place. "Can we practice anyway?" He smiles winningly at me. "Please?"

Eventually, I give in and say yes because I'm curious to find out what will happen. I suspect this is the same reason many women agree to marriage, thinking that it's going to be a romantic lifetime of being swept off their feet, only to find themselves in goofily compromising positions never mentioned in ladies' magazines. I'm thinking he'll put me in a fireman hold and sling me across his shoulders, or maybe toss me over his head and let me ride piggyback. The image in my head is vaguely like ice dancing, sparkly and graceful, featuring me wearing a flippy skirt and a tiara as adoring crowds cheer, huzzah! Instead, he's going to use the "Estonian hold," which means that my legs will be wrapped around his head and my nose buried between his butt cheeks.

"No, no," John interrupts me before I get too lost in random thoughts. "Not 'butt cheeks.' Sand pits!"

"Excuse me?"

"We're going to practice in the sand pits out back," he declares. The Wellesley house is not only walking distance to his son's school and next to a fishable pond, it's also a few steps from a dirt sidewalk the town grandly calls the "hiking trail" because it cuts through the woods. The sand pits used to have something to do with men cutting ice from Morse's pond and shipping it to Boston in freight cars, so a defunct railroad line runs by them. This spot is great fun for kids practicing tricks on their dirt bikes. It also works pretty well for men running off with women slung over their heads.

So that evening after supper, we pull on ratty clothes and head to the sand pits. It's light outside for a few more hours, and the early fall temperatures are pleasant.

"You ready?" he asks, as we teeter at the rim of the main pit.

"Yah."

"Good!" All of a sudden I am once again upside down on his back, my nose planted between his butt cheeks and legs wrapped around his head. With a bellow, he plunges downhill through soft sliding sand. "Comfy, baby?" he hollers thoughtfully as he tightens his grip on my thighs.

"Mmmmf mmmf!" I reply.

"Hang on, baby!" he cheers. Once he reaches the bottom of the sand pit, he charges full speed ahead.

It is harder than it looks, being carried upside down by a large man running full tilt with a few Friday-night beers in him. You can't just hang there like a sack of potatoes, not if you want to enjoy yourself, and certainly not if you expect your team to win. I had to tighten my arms around his waist and press my head into his ass, fusing my belly along his spine. Hold too tightly, he can't breathe. But if he forgets you're back there, you can squeeze out his brains with your thighs. It's all about finding a yin-yang sort of balance between cooperation and homicide. I make sure he likes it by humming the tune to *Rocky* as he runs. It's amazing what making happy noises down there will do for his ego.

He huffs and puffs around the sand pit, then flips me back over his head and sets me down on the ground. "D'you know what Patrick said when I told him I wanted to enter the wife-carrying contest next year?" Patrick is John's youngest brother, a confirmed bachelor who lives full time in Maine. Patrick said, "You need to get one of them skinny wives!" And John busts out laughing as if it's the funniest thing he's ever heard.

So John has been telling his family about me *and* showing them pictures. I am not sure how to interpret this, but I believe it means—to him, at least—that we are now a couple. "Har, har," I grouch. "Besides which, don't you want me to gain weight? Ten more pounds on me means ten more pounds of beer you might win!"

He scratches his head and gawps at me as if I'd just asked him to invent time travel.

"You need to eat, honey bear," I tell him soothingly. "Your brain doesn't work."

"Hur," he agrees and, because he's too tired to talk any more, he picks me up and carries me back home, piggyback style.

In 1793, shortly after the Revolutionaries of Paris, France, decided to behead their king, the good citizens of Township Number Four, Maine, renamed the town. They picked "Paris." Nobody knows why. Township Number Four didn't have a king. They didn't even have any queens. What they did have was churches and dentists, which explains why John's people who live around here brush their teeth religiously: twice a day, with waxed floss and mint toothpaste. In this neck of the woods, everyone is related to everyone else, either through bleeding gums or through Christian community.

The first church in Paris, Maine, was founded by the Calvinist-Baptists in 1795. Then the Free-Baptists established their own church. Soon enough, pronounced the *Maine Gazetteer* in 1886, there were also societies for Baptists (who are not, I should add, to be confused with General Baptists, Regular Baptists, Separate Baptists, Universal Baptists, Primitive Baptists, Old Regular Baptists, Two-Seed-in-the-Spirit Predestinarian Baptists, or, Lord help us, Anabaptists, better known in this country as the Amish.) The nineteenth-century town of Paris also had one society for Congregationalists, two societies for Universalists, and three for Methodists. With a population of about two thousand eight hundred, Paris wasn't especially churchy. It also had five post offices.

Improbably, I find myself standing in the driveway of John's parents' house, which is outside of the town of Paris and about ten miles from Bethel. Bethel is often praised in travel magazines as one of the prettiest small towns in the U.S. But in Hebrew, the word "Beth-el" means "House of God," and this house is halfway between Paris and Bethel in more ways than one. The house backs right up to a mountain, and there's a cleared sixteen-acre field doubling as the front lawn. More mountains rise up in the distance, the kind of natural monuments that aren't looming and dark, like Mount Doom, but nice, friendly mountains that can be climbed by chattering Boy Scouts. The house itself is scaled large, because John's father is nearly twice my height and the rooms were built around him. It's a big house. It seems perfectly obvious to call it the Big House.

"'Big House' is slang for prison," John growls.

"I'm still calling it the Big House," I insist. Because that's what it is.

For lack of a better way of putting it, this weekend is a trial by meat. Our back-and-forth relationship has been going on for years, but this is the first time I've met John's parents because his father doesn't like to travel. Don and Ruth are aware that I exist, and they're relieved John's found a . . . a . . . a *something*, let's say, uh, "friend," which is better than them calling me "the shameless hussy what's leading our son down the path of iniquity." They're trying to be supportive. They want him to be happy. They're just not sure if I make him happy or just drive him crazy. Factually speaking, I'm a never-married woman corrupting their firstborn with her fancy feefle-farfle. ("What is she?" I can hear them complaining inside my head. "A Pentacostal?") It was bad enough that John became a lawyer instead of signing up for the military. The Maine plates on the back of Don's Ford truck say VETERAN, same as Patrick's truck, whereas Ruth's truck is a lady-like two-seater with an old Bush bumper sticker. John's pickup is a Nissan with out-of-state plates, and me in the passenger seat. I'm just another symptom that he's been living in Massachusetts too long and heading straight to Blue Dog Democrat hell.

The spacious house is spick and span, warm with pine and handmade braided rugs. Inside, there's no evidence that the men hunt. No rifles, taxidermied heads, or mounted trophy racks on the wall. Outside, however, there's a deer in a flatbed truck.

It has been gutted and tagged. Both warm dark eyes are open. Deer die with their eyes open. Soldiers die that way too. The buck doesn't look like it's staring, and it doesn't seem asleep. It doesn't look alive, but it also doesn't look dead. Lying on its side, its limbs are loose, its pelt soft and clean. There is no visible wound except the slit up its belly, but the fur masks the gap. To find it, you have to go looking. It has a perfect set of antlers, gracefully curved, no points broken and no chips marring its smoothness. The buck weighed in at 195 lbs. of hide, muscle, and hooves. The same as John standing naked in a snowdrift wearing nothing but boots.

"Been tracking this fellow for three days," Patrick states with pride, pointing at the buck. He's tall, affable, and rangy, with a loping gait and large hands. "Early this morning," he narrates in a strong Maine accent, "I saw a group of does, about ten of them, down low on the mountain. I could tell they were heading up, so I just followed. I listened to him crashing about for a least an hour before he came into range. He was standing in a cope, hidden behind some trees. As soon as he poked his head out, I took a shot. Hit him right in the liver. There's nothing left of it." He looks at me appraisingly, and adds, "Sorry."

Nice to meet you too! Carefully, I lift up the deer's side as if it were a toupee worn by a giant. The inner cavity is empty and perfectly clean.

"Get the tenderloins out before the butcher steals them," John's father reminds Patrick, gesturing behind my back and over my head. Don is more than a little bit scary. He is not a smiley fellow. He's a man of few words because he lost part of his hearing in Vietnam and it never returned, like so many things taken for granted and lost in the war. He doesn't approve of existential navel gazing. That's okay. I can do it for him since his navel is pretty much right at my eye level.

"Already got them," Patrick affirms without elaborating, but his hands are empty, and the truck bed is glaringly clean. All it holds is the deer. I have no idea where he put these choice lumps of meat. The obvious place is one I can't check and, unlike my sister, Patrick doesn't expand while he eats.

The deer looks out with warm soft eyes free of judgment. It doesn't seem to have a belly button.

John's mother Ruth wanders out of the house to see what the fuss is about. She has no official opinion of me. As far as Ruth is concerned, my main virtue is that I am not John's ex-wife, a nightstand Buddhist whose preferred meal is bean sprouts served on a yoga mat. The ex-wife wanted the divorce because she thought John was too boring, but her favorite form of entertainment still seems to be yelling at him for being a rightwing conservative who watches the Military Channel and expects to eat a hot breakfast, lunch, *and* supper. I think this very funny, because I yell at him for the same things. Otherwise, I don't think about her at all.

So far, the only part about this visit that surprises me is how young his parents are. John is a year older than me, but his dad is at least fifteen years younger than mine, and his mother is still quite heartily alive.

"Hey, Ruthie," Patrick's hunting buddy Keith calls out, his face lighting up in greeting. He's sitting behind the wheel of a muddy ATV. Like Ruth, Keith is a ruddy-cheeked type with short white hair and water on the knee. "You want a liver?"

". . . a liver?" I echo, my ears perking up.

"Folks down the street took a buck yesterday," Keith explains. "They don't want it so they gave it to me," Keith natters. "It's just sitting outside 'cause they butchered the buck themselves. I don't care for it. Why don't you take it?"

"Sure," Ruth replies easily.

"I took a shot at a buck yesterday," Keith says conversationally, "but one of the points was dropped. So I know it wasn't the same deer as this one. This one is bigger, too," he adds, making Patrick beam with pride. "Can't keep up any more," Keith shrugs, a rueful expression on his wrinkled face. "That's how it is when you get old." He shakes his head, chuckling, but he knows, the way all terminally ill people know, that laughter will not cure what ails you.

He's dying. But so are we all.

"This one here dropped right away," Patrick elaborates, "but I couldn't find him at first, 'cause he'd tumbled down into a ravine. First I had to find him, and then I called Keith on the radio so he could come up with the ATV."

"I wasn't much good out," Keith apologizes. "That's the trouble, only having one lung. Can't breathe in cold weather." He smiles wanly.

"It was a lot of work getting him out," Patrick says reproachfully to his large empty buck, which doesn't say anything back. "We had to make a sled out of sticks, you know, an Indian hammock, and drag it out that way. Then we tried tying the sled to the back of the ATV but that didn't work. The deer kept on flopping over and the ATV was just popping wheelies. So we ended up tying it to the front." He's wearing a full set of hunting woolens coated with tree smutch, and his face is grimy from the forest. He's tired and hungry but none of that matters. Every once in a while, a silly grin slips out, ruining his practiced air of nonchalance. "It was a lot of work," he repeats.

On nights when clouds hide the moon, the forest is very dark. Hunters in Maine have eighteen hours to get the deer out and tagged, and they have to take the entire animal. If you must leave the carcass overnight in the woods, the best thing to do is to string it up to keep the coyotes from getting it. In deep winter, the carcass will simply freeze. In the warmer months, however, the venison may spoil. So you bring it out, even if it's so dark you can't see your own feet.

This, too, is hunting, and it's not about killing animals. It's about caretaking their graves.

As the men stand around and chatter in the driveway, breathing in the cold and basking in the sunlight, Ruth heads off somewhere down the road. A while later, she comes walking back with a plastic grocery bag swinging from one hand. Wordlessly, she hands it to me. I untwist it and look inside. It's a liver.

"There's a leaf on it," I tell Ruth.

"That's because the deer was gutted outside," she explains, as if it's perfectly obvious why it came decorated with plant life.

Holding the bag, I march into the house so I can clean the contents for dinner. Ruth is an excellent cook but she's happy to let me deal with the liver. She knows I grew up cooking for church suppers, thus I know how to portion for large quantities. This is important, because the men in this family have serious appetites. So far this weekend, she's watched me pare apples and chunk up the squash without slicing off my thumb. It remains to be seen if I can handle the forest's version of a slippery wiggle pudding.

The liver is large, dark red, heavy, and flexible. The texture is perfectly smooth, with just a few surface pimples clustered in a small area. There are two large lobes, flat and thick like giant lima beans. But a liver looks like nothing else, not even other livers.

In France, I'd once stumbled into an outdoor market with a stall that specialized in variety meats. The butcher had set out a showcase of fresh livers from cow, calf, pig, sheep, goat, rabbit, goose, duck, turkey, and chicken, just one of each, lined up like specimens in a natural history museum. They were pretty pink purses filled with everything a girl needs, thicker than butter and softer than ripe peaches. Groaning with strong cheese, woven baskets bounced merrily around me as I stared and stared, unable to wrap my head around these livers of good lives, fragrant with lemon wedges and fresh sprigs of thyme, so I tore myself away and pottered under the big tent, tasting wild honeys, sampling olive oils dipped in good bread, and poked and prodded and nosed and ogled until I was back at the meat booth again, staring at the goodies under glass. Somehow they'd rearranged themselves while I wasn't looking, like mischievous toys coming out to play while the grownups were asleep. It was so exhausting trying to choose between goat liver and pig liver that I gave up without buying anything.

In French, the word for liver, *foie*, sounds the same as the word that means time, *fois*, which is hardly different from the word for faith, *foi*. I sometimes wish I had more time and some faith, but I do not. Perhaps this is why I crave liver, since it's the only one of the three that can be bought with money. My father is a man of faith. He trusts in God and he is content.

His life is good and he is blessed, regardless of all the tragedies that have happened to him. He knows it is God's plan at
work, and he puts himself in God's hands. He's living proof
that God works in mysterious ways, and in order to accept my
father I have to concede that his beliefs are true for him, even
when they don't make sense to me. He has refused worldly
success, turning down promotions that would put him in
positions of prestige and power, choosing instead to stay poor,
not a bishop but a pawn to be mocked and used by others, as
the poor always are. He doesn't feel that way, you know. He
has no money but his faith gives him joy and he gets health
insurance from the Church. So when you consider the larger
picture, he's doing pretty well.

He doesn't judge others, because only God can. Officially,
however, he disapproves of the fact that I'm living in sin. He
knows perfectly well that I'm temperamentally unsuited to
marriage but he must protest against my trolloping ways
since that is his job. He also suspects that what binds John
and me together is not a meeting of minds but a collision of
flesh. Because he is nearly eighty, my father worries that bodies wither, that strength dwindles, and warmth fades. I run
cold. John runs hot. Like a lizard, I bask in his body heat until
a strange equilibrium is reached.

"What if he's not hot anymore?" my sister clucks disapprov-
ingly, because disapproving of me is everyone's favorite activity. She also knows, even though she'd really rather not, that
John and I have already been together for two years and we still
entertain each other extravagantly in bed. By now, the ladies
magazines say, he should be bored silly of me, especially since
my unmentionables come in packets of three. My bourgeois
baby sister waggles her married finger in my nearsightedness,
tsk-tsking me for being so shallow, then we burst out laughing because she sounds just like Mom. "Aigu!" she shrieks,
and topples over laughing again. But John isn't my friend. He's

my man. That pretty much sums up what I expect from him. John knows that his hotness is terribly important to me. He also knows that when he stops being overheated, he'll be a corpse in the ground. So I really don't worry about some kind of cooling effect over time, whether in terms of his core temperature or his inexplicable ardor for me. I may not have faith but I do trust him. He has a good heart. It will not conk out on me.

My liver is weak, said the Chinese doctor who diagnoses Chi, but I hold a good one in my hands. *Ma foi, il y a une fois, un foie.* . . Welling richly with blood, this portion of the deer can't be bought, and it can't be gotten just by asking. Thus it is like true love, decent neighbors, and world peace. The wellness of the liver shows this is a good spot, here at his parents' house in Maine, where well water burbles in the backyard and wild strawberries grow freely.

Carefully, I rinse the slices and soak them in milk. It makes good visual poetry—the milk, the blood, the stuff of vampire lust—but it doesn't do much in terms of improving the taste of something already lavished with health. Either you like liver or you don't. Sexing it up doesn't change the sound of swallowing inside your head.

Because there is plenty of good daylight left, all the men go out hunting again except for Keith, who goes home to rest. A few hours later, after dark, they come back empty handed. They are tired, dirty, and hungry, but they don't look disappointed. Hands washed and faces wiped, they come to the table still wearing their hunter's woolens. Dinner is deer liver with onions, served with potatoes, squash, green beans, and bread, followed by apple pie and ice cream for dessert. The only food items that come from the store are the wine and the butter. From well water to firewood, John's parents' house is an almost self-enclosed food system.

Almost, because they don't have a cow to milk, though there are plenty of dandelions for wine.

Almost, because I'm here. A food system includes the eaters.

Crusted golden brown, the liver looks and smells delicious. But "the proof of a pudding is in the eating," cautions the British expression, because the "pudding" was a sheep's stomach stuffed with meat and oatmeal. Around this table, the men take dainty forkfuls, hesitantly smacking their lips. A verdict has been reached: the liver is good. Under the table, John squeezes my hand.

The men begin eating in earnest, pausing between bites to recount the details of the hunt. As the humans chat and eat, Basel clicks around the table, looking for scraps of attention. Mostly German shepherd, Basel sleeps inside the house, just like indoor cats that eat tuna from a can. He belongs to Patrick's latest girlfriend, who is from New York. Christy's family is Italian-Polish—"big hair people," she says wryly—and her entire clan views the Great Outdoors as a mistake to be avoided. She doesn't know how she ended up a plain talker who can handle a rifle and a chainsaw, but she had the good sense to move to Maine when it became clear that it wasn't a phase.

During the summer months, Christy works as a park ranger. In the winter months, she works odd jobs that pay the bills. Unfussy with long dark hair and chapped lips, she's blessed with the kind of long-limbed looks that mean she'll still be attractive when she's sixty. It doesn't bother her that Patrick's beagles go hunting every day, taking Patrick along with them. But she usually tries to make herself scarce when the field dressing begins. She doesn't have the stomach for it.

"So . . . what happens to the hide?" Christy finally asks.

"It gets thrown away," Patrick shrugs.

"What!" she exclaims. "Can't you give it to someone?"

"Who?" Patrick replies. "Right now cow leather is so cheap, dealers can't make a profit from deerskin. It costs them more money to scrape and tan the hides than they'd make from selling them. They can't even break even. If I drove the skins to the tanner in Norway that'd cost me at least ten dollars in gas, and I'd get nothing for it. So I'd be losing money by trying to give it away."

"But it's disrespectful of the deer," she complains. "There are some things more important than money. That deer *died* because of you. It deserves to be treated with consideration."

Patrick gives her a look. "Well, if it wasn't for people like you, who won't wear leather or fur, then maybe there'd be some use for the hides. As it is, there's no market for them."

"Can't we tan it ourselves?" she asks plaintively.

"Sure," Patrick snorts, "if you want to scrape off the hair and then sit around chewing the skin for a few weeks, the way the Indians did it. Otherwise, you have to buy a whole bunch o' chemicals, and they're nasty and expensive. And then what would you do with the hide? It would be too small for just about anything, and you'd only have one."

Christy glares at him, but she's stumped. States have different bag limits on deer, but in Maine, the annual limit is one. It would take years to get enough hides for a shirt. Plus, the "nasty" stuff he's talking about is lime and battery acid.

How did the Indians cure hides? According to Theodore R. Davis writing in *Harper's Magazine*, 1878, the entire process is both difficult and time-consuming. The pelt (of a buffalo, in his example) is stretched out on the ground, flesh side up, and secured at the edges with little wooden pegs poked through small cuts made in the skin. Using sharp stones or shaped buffalo bones, two or three women scrape the hide free of all fat and flesh, reducing the thickness of the hide in the process. The scraped hide is then moistened with water in which buffalo brains have been steeped, producing "brain water," and for ten days the stretched hide is kept damp with this fluid. Once a day, the women unpin and rub the hide using only their bare hands, a task that nearly takes their own skins off, Davis tells us, because the hides are so rough. This process continues until the buffalo skin is soft enough to be used as a robe. The tender, yielding results are white as snow. According to Davis, the hides were often traded for sugar, coffee, and other coveted items.

I do not know what was in the brains, but apparently it was powerful stuff.

The "brain water" method was all-natural, non-toxic, and utterly dependent on the gendered division of labor. Scraping hides was women's work. Men literally never touched them, not until it became clear that money could be made by processing them in giant batches. According to the *Hunter's and Trapper's Practical Guide* of 1878, it began by giving the hide a good soaking in warm water, after which point the flesh and fat could be scraped off. The cleaned hide should be hung in a warm room "until the hide begins to give off a slight smell of hartshorn." Take the skin down, scrape off the side with hair, and then soak the skin for two to three weeks in weak lyme water. Rinse the skins clean, scrape them again, and then soak them in wheat bran and water for another two or three weeks. Throw the skins into a "pickle of alum, salt, and water," stir well, and then throw them back in the bran water for two or three more days. Take them out, and then partially dry them in a warm room. The partially dried skins should then be thrown into a trough filled with a paste made of 3 ½ pounds of salt, eight pounds of alum, twenty-one pounds of wheat flour, and nine dozen egg yolks. Dissolve the alum and salt into water, mix in the rest of the ingredients, add enough water to cover the skins, and beat the mixture into a froth. Remove, dry, stretch, and smooth with a warm iron. Then sell, sell, sell!

Quasi scientific, with fancy chemicals and precise measurements, this method for tanning deer hide is a lot like modern cookery. It requires a list of added ingredients as long as my arm and enough eggs and flour to make twenty-two pound cakes. It only sounds quaint and charming. It *smells* like rotten eggs. Unlike the American Indian system, the whiteman's version requires an extensive network of specialized supplies that paves the way to NAFTA. You don't want to buy foreign supplies? Try making your own alum. It happens to be the essential ingredient in baking powder, which transforms cakes into light and fluffy confections. Without it, your biscuits will be harder than hockey pucks. The 1875 edition of the *Encyclopedia Britannica* provides several helpful recipes for alum, including a method used in Paris, France, where this trace element is not naturally found in the soil. It instructs: Mix together 100 parts of clay, fifty parts of niter, and fifty parts of sulfuric acid of the specific gravity 1-367. Put it into a "retort" and distill it. If the ingredients are mixed correctly, "aquafortis comes over, and the residue in the retort being lixiviated with water, yields an abundance of excellent alum." Easy-peasy! I lixiviate and retort daily. But where do you get niter and sulfuric acid? How do you make those? And down the rabbit hole you go . . .

Here is the ingredient list for the Indian way: buffalo, sunlight, water. Hides can be tanned without leaving the woods as long as there's a stream nearby. Still, before the romantic haze sets in, turning the world before the White Man into a banquet for bunnies, I will repeat two words: brain water. A dish best poached, not fried. Those who wore these snow-white buffalo hides wore the skins of Indian women too. With every silent scrape of short fingernails they bound themselves to the hides, marrying body to body and skin to skin. The human touch made the finished hides soft and beautiful but the cost to make them was very high, because they extracted beauty from women in return. Naturally, in today's market, these hides are worthless. As Patrick says bluntly, no one will take them. Not even Christy, who can't afford them because she's a young woman with good looks. She does not want to sit outside, under the beating sun, scraping and rubbing for days and weeks and months until her skin crisps in the heat and her back begins to crack, turning her into a hunched and leathery crone nobody wants.

Beauty for beauty. Skin for skin. A pound of flesh. Fresh, the hide weighs much more than that. Care to donate an organ? Lend a hand or two?

Who pays? As always, the animals do.

"Pass the potatoes," Don growls to Ruth, who is sitting at the other end of the table, blasé in the company of two of her three grown sons. All the slices of liver are gone.

Nature gets hungry too. So the deer skins get thrown to the wolves, the potato skins go to the insects, the apple peels feed the worms, the eggshells go to the garden. And the earth is fed.

Basel clicks around the table, hoping for treats. He doesn't like liver, so I pet him instead. Under the table, John keeps holding my other hand. It's been a good day for both of them.

CHAPTER FOUR

Bite Me

Biologically speaking, if something bites you,
it is more likely to be female.
– biologist Desmond Morris

John's father is shooting gray squirrels from the kitchen window, trying his best to scare me away. Now that John has started bringing me to Maine every weekend, the Big House isn't big enough for the both of us. It isn't personal. It's political. I'll always be a liberal, and it's best if John realizes this sooner rather than later and moves along to a nice conservative girl who isn't so noisy when she eats. The three-month hunting season on squirrels lasts through the end of December, and there's no bag limit because they're a pest species. Specifically, the little criminals have been nesting under the hood of his truck and stealing from the bird feeder. The gray squirrels are also bullying the red squirrels out of the neighborhood, even though grays and reds don't eat the same food or chase the same girls. The red squirrel is small and sleek, resembling a chipmunk without stripes. But he can't eat acorns. Instead, he mostly eats pine nuts. As a result, he tastes like pine tar, the stuff in turpentine.

Fat and heavy, gray squirrels eat everything humans eat. They taste like duck.

As it happens, gray squirrels are gray, and red squirrels are red, so it's easy to tell them apart without tasting them. It's not always so simple: some red foxes are black, some black bears are brown, and weasels turn white in snowy winters. With squirrels, fortunately, a color-coding system works unless you make the bad decision to leave the country instead of staying home and reveling in the glory that is American plumbing. Annoyingly, the North American red squirrel has a cousin, Squirrel Nutkin, who lives in Britain with his brother, Twinkleberry. A hundred years ago, they posed for a picture book by Miss Beatrix Potter, who also made Peter Rabbit sit for her, and now the three of them are more famous than Ziggy Stardust. No such good publicity for the small tribes of American reds quivering in the woods. Indeed, your average zit-faced teenager thinks that gray squirrels are the only squirrels that got a right to be here and all the black and red squirrels snuck in illegally, getting it exactly backwards. Don't matter. If might makes right, gray squirrels win. They're everywhere.

As a toddler, I was bored by *The Tale of Peter Rabbit*, a British story of rabbit pie that my sister and millions of other sunshiny preschoolers adored. Instead, I loved Potter's *Tale of Squirrel Nutkin*, 1903, which is the kind of book that kids today never read because the story is very weird. Frankly, I'm amazed it hasn't been banned. There's no way this "tale of a tail" would be published today, not even with the gorgeous watercolors confusing parents into thinking it's a cute story about resourceful rodents. It's the story of an owl called Old Brown who rules Owl Island, a bountiful Eden loaded with delicious nuts. The red squirrels have to get Old Brown's permission to take the nuts from his land, so they bring him gifts in exchange for the rights to harvest. But instead of asking nicely like all the other squirrels, Nutkin runs around teasing Old Brown with terrible riddles:

Hitty Pitty within the wall,

Hitty Pitty without the wall;

If you touch Hitty Pitty,

Hitty Pitty will bite you!

I would laugh and laugh at this line, my favorite. It was a mantra for my two-foot self, because adults were always trying to pick me up and pet me as if I was a tame baby panda. Then they would scream and drop me when I started to talk. Pandas aren't supposed to know words like "hypocrite" and "alcoholic."

If you touch Hitty Pitty,

Hitty Pitty will bite you!

Hahaha! It worked with kids in school too. I hardly ever had to bite anyone, because I also knew how to land a punch. I got lots of practice at home fighting with my older brother. It was practically an aerobic exercise after dinner.

Eventually, Old Brown gets fed up with the bad riddles and decides to eat Squirrel Nutkin. The owl is getting ready to skin the squirrel, holding Nutkin's tail in his claws (using proper human techniques for squirrel-skinning, I note). Suddenly, the tail breaks, and the squirrel escapes. A happy ending, and Nutkin lives to see another day. Old Brown doesn't seek revenge, and the squirrels never return to Owl Island. The story seems sweet until you stop to examine it, for the "gifts" the squirrels brought the owl are animals they killed as tribute: "three fat mice," a "fine fat mole," "seven fat minnows," etc., the emphasis being on *fat* (and therefore scrumptious), confirming that bribery, animal sacrifice, and random violence are perfectly acceptable inside a feudal order. Old Brown can kill Nutkin and his mates don't protest, for such is the Way Things Work. Owls require fresh meat to survive.

In a land of milk and honey, owls would starve to death. So would red squirrels.

Still, the menu isn't the real trouble in this story. The death of mice, moles, and minnows don't get most folks riled up about animal cruelty, especially since cute fluffy squirrels are doing the killing. So what if they're offering up lesser animals as sacrifices? It's the only way that the owl won't eat them, for the powerful are blessed by God, and they keep their wealth by doing His will. Only a nut rejects a perfectly profitable system that forces the poor to beg for food and pay a hideous price for the privilege. Hey ho . . . hello, Nutkin! He's a red-headed rebel, a leader of the autonomous collective, a socialist-communist-Nazi-anarchist-terrorist-tree-hugger out to sow chaos in Eden. Wherefore he's the Devil's handmaiden. To shut him up, the Owl decides to devour him, this being the best way to get rid of uppity poorlings who refuse to respect customs. Lawbreakers should be punished, should they not? But the squirrel escapes his executioner—not due to cleverness, but because his tail breaks. The maiming strips him of his power of speech. For the rest of his days all he speaks is gibberish—"Cuck-cuck-cuck-cur-r-r-cuck-k-k!"—instead of the King's English. His disenfranchisement is complete.

A political parable? Nope!

Squirrel Nutkin, you see, is suffering from Tourette's Syndrome. In a 1995 article, "Excessive Impertinence or Missed Diagnosis?" published in the esteemed *British Medical Journal*, Gareth Williams argues that Nutkin's socially inappropriate behavior and strange verbal outbursts revealed a pathology, not an ideology. Nutkin is a flawed hero with a misunderstood disease named after Georges Albert Edouard Brutus Gilles de la Tourette, a nineteenth-century French neurologist who studied mental illness. One day, a paranoid patient shot Monsieur Tourette in the head. Tourette survived the injury, but he went insane and died in an asylum.

And so, Nutkin tics, squirms, and blurts obscenities because he cannot help it. Tourette's Syndrome is making him do it.

The imperfections of Miss Potter's anti-hero make him strangely human: a mini Mr. Monk who commits crimes rather than solving them. You can't criticize the disabled. That would be mean.

But *I* still have teeth. And I like to chew on things.

In England, the gray squirrel is an invasive species. Eating these fat foreigners has become a nifty way to solve an ecological problem while feeding national pride. The slogan for the national campaign is: "Save a red. Eat a gray!" The gray squirrels taking over England are native to the U.S. of A. They've become very popular on trendy London menus.

I'm forbidden to cook the gray squirrels foraging by the Big House, because they eat garbage—perhaps the most human of human creations, for we produce it without thinking about it, and accuse the other guy of making it. Gray squirrels are the rodent equivalent of pigeons, which are basically feral chickens. Every city of men has its share of these loathsome birds, but they're not wild. They're descendants of domesticated pigeons who fled life in the coops, going from the unique hell of the utopian collective to the strange joys of the hardscrabble streets. It's a choice some humans would make, if they could. The cubicle life isn't for everyone.

Many chefs consider Squab the Pigeon the finest bird to eat. Many hunters think that Gray the Squirrel is a gourmet treat. Blue State America learned about squirrel cuisine during the 2008 campaign for President of the United States, when Southern Baptist minister and Republican candidate Mike Huckabee revealed that he used a popcorn popper to cook squirrels in his dorm room at Ouachita Baptist University. I don't know what bothered foodies more: the fact that he sullied the popcorn popper by using it as a skillet, or that he didn't provide his recipe. Ah, but where did he get those squirrels to cook in the first place? Did his mom send them in a care package? It isn't as if you can pick up a few pounds of squirrels at the grocery store, because squirrels aren't farmed in factories or mass produced in vats. So I waited for reporters to ask him where he got them. None did. So I waited for one to ask: was he frying up red squirrel, black squirrel, red fox squirrel, gray squirrel, or . . . ? Reporters didn't ask that question either. The job of asking questions now seems to be left to Oprah and The Comedians, but they're obsessed with fat jokes. I was left to assume that Mike Huckabee, man of the cloth and aspiring POTUS, knew how to shoot a .22 well enough to hit a small cute target and not feel the least bit guilty about it.

It is a forgotten fact that the most pious of hunters were priests. He was "a manly man, to be an abbot able," wrote Geoffrey Chaucer of his Monk in the *Canterbury Tales*. An eater of wild meat and lover of wanton women, this Monk kept a stable of greyhounds and wore robes lined with fur. It didn't change the fact that he called himself a holy man and enjoyed all the privileges of the Church, including the right to hunt the forests where the tasty deer lived. The rules meant that all peasants were poachers. If caught taking deer in the King's Forest, à la Robin Hood and his Merry Men, the poacher's arm would be chopped off, unless the king was in a bad mood. Then it was "Off with his head!" and too bad for the peasant's starving family, but those are the rules. So what if the monks helped themselves instead of helping the poor? They believed unquestioningly in the existence of God and they knew that Hell was real, just as they knew that the earth was the center of the universe and so do you. Why else would the deer be sacrificing themselves to the priest's arrows, unless there was a Divine Plan at work? How else were these men of God to continue their Holy work, unless they were well fed?

"Cuck-cuck-cuck-cur-r-r-cuck-k-k!" said the hungry peasants. But nobody listens to one-armed bandits, not even other bandits.

Squirrels weren't on the priest's dinner menu, because they were vermin. To eat them was to define yourself as a meek, not a monk. As meek, you were one of those people who will inherit the earth eventually, someday, not now, but for sure after you're extremely dead. Ergo, the peasants could eat as many squirrels as they could catch, using nets and baskets and their bare hands, just as long as they thanked the earth for giving them an advance on their inheritance.

"My old hairdresser ate squirrels," my sister said primly. For a long time, during her indie rock-star years, my sister got her Korean hair dyed white-blond at a black salon in Somerville. As a bleached blonde in a swamp rock band, my sister played a full-size accordion wearing high heels and a neon pink mini-dress. Onstage, she looked like a live version of those animated dancing popcorn boxes chirping, "Let's all go to the lobby!" before the regular movie starts. As soon as she strapped on the accordion, she turned into a giant bellows dancing on two legs, with just a thatch of bleached blond hair frizzing over the top. The Giant Dancing Accordion had groupies. My sister retired from the music business years ago, but every once in a while on the Boston subway, an old fan will spot her biceps, do a double-take, and blurt out excitedly, "Hey, I know you! You're that accordion player!" My sister will pretend that she has no idea what he's talking about, and he'll moo in adoration, " I love you!" unaware that the other Redline T-riders are staring worriedly at him, because "Asian chick" and "polka player" are not thoughts that usually go together in the brains of Harvard students. For me, the funny part is trying to imagine how a conversation between my sister and a Somerville hairdresser whose own sister enjoyed the lovely name of Pajama Female ("PAH-jah-mah Fee-MALL-ee") would lead up to ". . . well, my uncle used to trap squirrels," because my sister favors sugar, spice, and everything nice, preferably prepackaged as a cookie. Her exotic food brain, such as it is, tends to wander in the direction of rice milk, kefir, and the health benefits of raw garlic. Until she got married, she used her oven to store books. Somewhat obviously, she does not cook. She especially does not cook squirrel.

During my travels, I have learned that squirrels make poor barbecue and excellent conversation. It's amazing how many people eat them, at least in the disreputable circles in which I travel. They're the deep-fried Twinkies of the back woods, and a guilty pleasure among citified Southerners trying to hide their roots. Unless you grew up skinning them, they're a lot of work to prepare, and yes, they make pretty good stew. But I don't usually think of gray squirrels as dinner. Mostly, I see them as competition. When we were little kids, our mother would tug on a floppy straw hat, leather gloves, and a pair of old sneakers, and go out into the woods. Hours later, she would come back with baskets full of stuff, none of which looked very tasty: green stalky things, short bristly leaves, dandelions, and acorns. Lots and lots of acorns.

"I'm not eating that," my sister would declare.

"Why?" I'd ask in surprise.

"How do I know it's not poisonous?"

"It's not," I pooh-poohed, but what the heck did I know, except the animals thought they were good?

As we got older, we started harvesting acorns too. There we'd be, bent over by the side of back roads of Maine, asses waggling in the air as we picked up nut after rubbery nut off the ground. They would become *dotori muk* (pronounced "mook"), an acorn jelly cake that looks like a brick of translucent tofu. *Muk* tastes the way fresh acorns smell. It is slightly bitter with a distinctly nutty taste. It is only as good as the nuts, this being the case with any wild food, with a taste ranging

from awful to good. It is a giant pain to make. Reducing a
bushel of acorns to that quivering brick gives you a whole
new respect for the work that deer and squirrels put in just to
extract the tasty bits.

Muk-making starts with the nut gathering. Luckily we
were used to going to church, because this part also involved
funny hats and a sustained bout of worshipful prostration on
our knees. Once the basket was full, we took the acorns home,
picked out the munched ones and the greenies, and peeled
them. There were two methods to remove the husk: 1) close
your eyes, smash the acorn with a mallet, then pick the tiny bits
of nutmeat out of your hair, or 2) jab a very sharp knife into a
slippery surface the size and hardness of a marble shooter, and
pare it carefully while trying very hard not to bleed. In other
words, it's the kind of work that's *perfect* for pissed off little
kids with small hands and limited manual dexterity.

Smash! Stab!

Smash! Stab!

"Eeek!" my baby sister shrieked, and fled into the living
room, never to return to the dread horrors of the kitchen.

The next step consists of grinding the nut meats into flour
and steeping it in cool, fresh water. This step is essential,
because acorns have tannins, which are plant compounds so
acidic that they're used to "tan" pelts into leather. Once the
brown water runs clear, the remaining stuff is essence of muk.
Boiled and poured into molds, it hardens up to the consistency
of Jell-O®.

Dotori muk is the food of war, not of childhood. It's something Koreans of my mother's generation knew how to make,
just in case war broke out again. There's nothing "peaceful"
or "non-violent" about making muk from scratch, never mind
what the skinny blond lady on TV says. John ran across her
on a cable show called something like *Take a Nature Break!
with Moonbeam Goody*, and he thought she was so funny he

made me watch her. A Martha Stewart clone with organically whitened teeth, Miss Goody No-Shoes was trying earnestly to make muk, but she got so frustrated by the husks that the show abruptly cut away to a commercial in order to let the fairy helpers smash them off camera. Then she popped back, holding the magically smashed nuts in her hands with a crazy smile plastered on her face and singing something about rainbows. By the end of it, facing imminent muk failure, her grin was so demented I thought her eyes were going to bug out of her head, in the manner of a Martian Popping Thing. I was very disappointed when a giant hand didn't reach out and give her a good squeeze. It would have relieved some of that tension in her face.

Nowadays, if you have cash money, you can buy muk powder at just about any H-Mart grocery store. You can also buy muk ready-made in little plastic tubs. This is a great timesaver for home cooks, but no fun at all for the deer and the squirrels working the assembly line, squirting munched acorns out of their butts. The next thing you know, the moochers will be demanding three meals a day, same as the house pets, and then they'll want all the same rights as Fluffy and Spot, including free health care and birth control paid for by the taxpayers.

Don takes aim, poking the rifle through the ruffled curtains, and nudges the barrel through the open window over the kitchen sink. Slowly . . . slowly . . .

BLAM!

Still clutching the rifle, Don peers intently out the window with a deep scowl splitting his face.

"Stop that," Ruth complains loudly, as she walks into the kitchen in a nightgown and fuzzy slippers, because it's six o'clock in the morning, and loud noises seem louder when the sun is hovering on the horizon.

Glowering, Don mutters, "If you don't scare off the squirrels, they'll start coming into the house."

"Well, I can't make coffee with you standing over the sink," she says, making shooing motions with her hands.

"Bah," he scowls and keeps standing by the open window.

John shuffles into the kitchen and yawns sleepily. "Is there any coffee?" he asks hopefully. Like his father, he is fully dressed in work clothes and ready to tend to the forest out back. I'm in my female pajamas and doing my best to avoid everybody's line of fire by hiding behind the couch.

"No coffee," Ruth says in an annoyed tone of voice. "*Somebody's* got to move out of the way so I can get the pot started!" Her Maine accent thickens on account of her irritation.

"There's too many people in here," Don mutters darkly under his breath, and stalks outside with great strides, taking his rifle with him. I believe he has realized there's a socialist Nutkin doing her best to be very small in the living room.

Ruth grabs the coffee pot and fills it with water. "He should have been outside in the first place," she declares loudly.

"Blam!" the rifle agrees.

Emerging from my hiding spot, I walk over to the kitchen, stand on tiptoe and peek out the kitchen window. It's a Disney tableau of squirrels scampering around the bird feeder, none of which seem deterred by the efforts of a large human to blast them to bits. "Gosh," I say. "Those squirrels are persistent!"

"Golly," John teases me, giving me quick butt-squeeze and smooch. Thoughtfully, he does this behind his mother's back so she doesn't see, as this will give her the vapors and it's too early for fainting.

"Wrrrrrr," the coffee grinder announces, as it pulverizes the beans. Efficiently, Ruth whips up a hearty breakfast, and the three of us sit at the kitchen island, working our way through eggs, bacon, pancakes, and toast.

"Get your clothes on," John prods me as he gulps down the last of his coffee. "We're going to take care of trees."

A short time later, we hike a little way up the mountain
out back and spend the morning pruning pines. "Don't bother
with that one," he says as he stops me from taking branches
off a cute little tree. He looks around. "Focus on the dominant trees. We take off the lower branches, keep them healthy,
they'll grow true." There are also co-dominant trees, sister
trees, and suppressed trees, he explains. No sense pruning the
suppressed trees. They'll die anyway. Most of the trees seem
to fall into this category, including the one I'd started pruning.
The worst trees are thin and weak, with reedy branches and
brittle needles, their trunks as frail as fashion models.

"But aren't the little ones just younger than the big trees?"
I object. In the back of my head, I'm thinking it's mean to
ignore weak trees. The strong ones are doing fine without our
help. Shouldn't we nurture the ones that aren't doing so well?

Carrying a chainsaw, Don strides up to join us, shaking his
head in wonder at my foolishness. Scowling, he points up.

Surprised by his sudden appearance, I obey without arguing. As I tilt back my head my mouth opens like the lid on
a jack-in-the-box. I'm ready to swallow the sky. The highest
trees are at least thirty-five feet tall with bushy green tops. It's
a foliage quilt wrought by butterflies.

"Now follow the trunks down," he orders brusquely.

The forest shifts.

Suddenly, it becomes apparent why the big trees are big,
and the small trees are small. The forest has made its selection.
It is not kind. It does not negotiate. All around me, in the glade
and the quiet, a mighty war is being fought between fierce
shoots and ferocious seedlings, the weak dying by the tens of
thousands as a handful emerge above the rest. The squirrels
have munched abundantly on seeds, denying thousands the
opportunity to grow. The moose have trampled on shoots,
crippling more. Through luck, a few saplings survived. The
trees that are greenest at the top have the biggest trunks at

the bottom. But they are not only bigger than the rest, they are straighter, their bark smoother, their limbs symmetrical and pleasing. The large trees get that way because they get the sunlight to grow. That sheltering spread of branches above keeps light from reaching the weaker trees below. The rivals die slowly of starvation.

John nods to his father, who nods wordlessly back, and the two of them walk off, leaving me to ponder this new knowledge while I wield my little pruning saw on the lowest branches. In the distance, I can hear two sets of chainsaws starting up.

> The meek eat the muk,
> The monk shoots the meat,
> The owl skins the squirrels,
> Cuck-cuck-cuck-cur-r-r-cuck-k-k!

CHAPTER FIVE

❦ ❦ ❦

Sex Ed Chicks

Leave the gun. Take the cannoli.
— *Peter Clemenza, in* The Godfather, *1972*

flock of baby chickens has arrived at the house in
Maine. They started out as sixteen "unsexed" chicks,
meaning the males and females weren't sorted before going
into the box. Odds are that the ratio of male to female will
be 50/50, but the actual contents are a surprise, kind of like
one of those Jumbo Mystery Boxes sold by the novelty shop
Archie McPhee, America's foremost purveyor of "fighting
nun" windup toys and the classic rubber chicken. How to sex
a chick? I pick one up and eyeball its X-rated parts. No dangling bits. It's a hairy eyeball with little whirling legs. Peep!
Peep! But, alas, no show. It's such a tricky task telling the
boys from the girls that "chicken sexer" is an actual job, and
even the professionals get it wrong. I do an internet search of
"sexed chick," and get dozens of strange hits. The top entry?
Sex Ed Chicks.

The omniscience of math prevails: precisely eight of the
baby chicks turn out to be males. Seven are dispatched right
away. Translation: they are killed. They expire whether or not
you approve; blissful ignorance does not change the way of the
world. To placate their children, parents buy pastel-colored
chicks at Easter to celebrate the resurrection of Christ. These

baby birds come dyed. No surprise, then, that they don't live very long—drowned in dog slobber, smothered in chocolate kisses, set free so they can be promptly run over by an SUV. Pet owners absolve themselves of these deaths, because it wasn't their fault. The cat did it.

In the blink of an eye the chicks turn into pullets, meaning they still have pinfeathers and are neither fluffy nor cute. They are the chicken equivalent of skinny teenagers who distrust grownups and huddle in sullen groups. One pullet has a broken toe. She occasionally tries to eat it, mistaking it for a worm.

Barred Rocks have round bodies and small heads. Each bird sports a bright red coxcomb, including the hens. They spend their days scratching for bugs and pecking each other the way kids slap each other upside the head. Exuding skittish energy, they eye me sideways with mechanical tilts. At first glance, they are just eight birds running around, posing exactly like the propaganda chickens promoting free-range organic eggs in the commercials. As soon as they decide you're not a fox, a chicken, or a member of the paparazzi, they turn into thugs. They spend their free time attacking each other, going after bellies, butts, whatever body part is close to the beak. The strong bully the weak. A dominant hen rules the flock, and the pecking order goes all the way down the seven that remain. The Queen is not visibly bigger or stronger than the others. I suppose it's a matter of a stronger inclination to violence, as is the case with all bullies.

The young rooster, known as a cockerel, is supposed to help limit the girl fights. Chicken folk swear that hens behave better when there's a rooster running around. The ancient Roman historian Columella recommended one male for every five hens: a Sultana rooster and his happy harem. In flocks without roosters, a hen will sometimes step in and assume his authority. She becomes the man of the hen house. This interesting behavior doesn't change the fact that chicken society is sexist.

I like the rooster. He's funny. But he's not very useful. At the crack of dawn, aged four months, the handsome boy starts to crow.

In Korean: 꼬끼요 (Kkokkiyo)!

In French: Cocorico!

In English: Cock-a-doodle-doo!

In Oz: Kut-kut-kut, ka-daw-kut!

Only English and American ears hear "doodle-doo" when a rooster starts shrieking his head off—an expression that, soon enough, you start wishing were literally true. The first time the rooster goes off at 5 A.M., it's charming. An hour later, city people are ready to wag their finger vigorously at him and lecture him strongly. In case you're wondering, "cock-a-doodle-do!" is what the Master hears when he "fiddles with his fiddlingstick/ And knows not what to do." Bored, the Master says to himself, "Forsooth! Methinks I shall doodle-a-cock!" Today, however, the line has been updated to conform to modern language. It is now called "watching internet porn while hiding in the loo."

In theory, roosters crow as a warning. The sound marks their territory and scares off predators. Some roosters will crow all day long. These roosters are especially good at getting eaten by hawks. Sure, the farmer can cover a cock's eyes so he thinks that the sun never rises, but what's the point of having a rooster that sleeps all the time? Instead of resorting to this extreme, some chicken farmers cut off the bird's balls, turning him into a capon. Unfortunately for the farmer, castration is not guaranteed to keep the rooster quiet. As a bonus, though, capons are delicious.

True capons aren't widely available in the U.S. because they take twice as long to reach market maturity as a broiler, and the end product is three times more expensive because they can't sing like Farinelli the Castrato. In French, this bird is a *chapon,* and its creation is part of the nation's gastronomic heritage. I learned these things during my first attempt to buy a fresh chicken in France after I quit being vegetarian. This decision required an extended discussion with the poultry man as to which type of bird would best suit my cooking needs. "Mademoiselle," he gargled sternly, "a 'chicken' is not a chicken. This bird comes in many forms." Behind me, a long line of shoppers murmured in agreement. "Are you feeding yourself, mademoiselle?" the butcher asked solicitously. He inspected my roundness and raised a calculating eyebrow. "Perhaps you need a bird for a group of friends? Is it a special occasion or . . . ?"—he eyeballed me again and tut-tutted. To my consternation, the whole line leaned forward to hear my reply. Eh, a good butcher can size you up and cut you down at the same time. This is very Parisian. The questions match the bird to the cook, as both sides have their own flavors and quirks. There is the *chapon* (a castrated male), a *coq* (an adult rooster), a *poule* (an adult hen), a *poulet* (a virgin hen), or a *poulard* (a teenage chicken of either sex). In the end, I wasn't entirely sure but I think he gave me a farm-raised, organically fed, non-breeding young hen. He definitely didn't give me a tough old rooster. If he had, my girlish self wouldn't have known what to do with it.

That was years ago. Now, I have a killer recipe for *coq-au-vin*—i.e. old rooster stewed in red wine. It works on young roosters too. And I know exactly what to do with a cock in three languages.

Cock-a-doodle-doo! the cock crows.

I grin toothsomely.

Cock-a-doodle-doo!

Cock-a-doodle-doo!

Cock-a-doo . . .

And then there was silence.

"Where'd he go?" I ask Ruth.

"Away," she shrugs. "That's all I know."

It's a mystery what's happened to him. Nobody is talking, not even the hens. And if there was roast chicken for dinner? Why, that was pure coincidence.

The chickens live in a windowless hutch made out of a converted tool shed. The front section of the shed holds sacks of feed and wood shavings for chicken litter. The back section of the shed is walled off with a door for humans. A narrow ramp—a "chicken way"—leads to an outdoor pen. When they get the urge to lay an egg, the hens hop up to a roosting plank and scooch into a laying box. The boxes protrude outside the henhouse, and they have lids that can be lifted from the top, so it's easy to reach down and grab eggs without bothering the birds. Since it's already getting cold at night, a light bulb throws off enough heat to keep the chickens warm. I think of Easy-Bake ovens.

Sometimes I wonder what it feels like to a hen when they have to lay an egg. Does it feel like having to go number one or number two, or something altogether different? Once I lifted the lid on the laying box looking for eggs, and caught a hen in the middle of doing her thing. I thought she'd jump down in a huff or starting pecking my hands, but she didn't move. She just looked up at me with a slightly reproachful glance, as if to say, "Privacy please!" The laying process can take a half hour or longer, and they don't get magazines to read. Afterward, some hens like to cover their eggs and start the hatching process. This requires forcible booting off the egg, prompting some hens to brood, darkly, as they mull over the egg that might have been. To break their obsessive ruminations, housewives used to grab their hens and dunk them in water. Hence the phrase, "mad as a wet hen." Funny how only some of them brood. Funnier still that a dunking makes them forget. It's a reminder that chickens will never become good Baptists.

The hens roam freely outside during the day but stay close to the house. At nightfall, without any reminding, they head back to their coop. This is because the chickens know that predators come out at night: foxes, coyotes, bobtails, falcons, and owls. Raccoons steal eggs. Weasels will too. And, of course, humans do. We're the biggest thieves of all.

Unrepentant, I go to check for eggs. An early snowstorm has arrived, dropping great piles of snush: snow and slush combined into heavy wet stuff that behaves like bleached quicksand. By tomorrow, because this is Maine, it will be warm again. "I hate the wind too," I tell the chickens soothingly, doing my best to look like a very large mother hen. But it doesn't seem to help; my ruse is not meeting with success. They coo-cluck and ignore me like always. It seems perfectly normal. Ergo, something is definitely wrong. Perplexed, I go back outside and head around to look at their pen, expecting to find a tear large enough to admit sharp paws. Then I spot it through the wire. A sodden bundle of feathers. A dead heap of bird. It must have died in the night, because it's frozen to the ground.

Empty handed, I plod back in the house, and announce the sad news. "Why did she die?" I ask plaintively, saying aloud the question that, sooner or later, everyone must ask and thus end childhood.

"They just do," Ruth said blandly.

"Aren't you worried that it had a disease?"

"One was a little red around its butt," Don says grimly to the room, pulling on his coat and heading out to the henhouse to deal with the carcass. I am glad that no-one expects me to dispose of the body, but it's mostly out of fear that I'll turn it into a terrifying food experiment and serve it for dinner.

"It's probably the same chicken what started laying tiny eggs," Ruth muses. She makes an O with her finger and thumb. "No yolks." She tilts her head toward the refrigerator. "One's in the egg crate."

I get up from my chair, open the refrigerator door, and rummage about for the specimen. There it is, lying at the bottom of one of the egg crate cups. A wee little egg that looks like it came from a hummingbird.

"That's how they started out when they first begin laying," Ruth remarks. "The eggs were small like that."

From the outside, the egg is perfect. It's just too small for respectability. It's a bead of roe, a dried jellybean, a nipple on a male supermodel. I picture snake eggs, spider eggs, and ant eggs. I think about humans who lay eggs. Me, to be specific. I think about Willy Wonka's Eggdicator machine, and Oompa-Loompas rolling eggs down the chutes, and Veruca Salt being a bad egg and falling down, down, down, and coming out the other end of the world as baby Evita.

I don't know how I lay eggs. I just know that I do. Small ones without yolks that don't obey a schedule.

I stare at the too-small egg, and wonder about mine chugging down the fallopian tube until it falls down the chute. Bad egg! Bad, bad egg! What made it come out wrong? "So was there something messed up with it?" I blurt. "What happened to the chicken?"

On cue, Don stalks back in the house, throws another log into the woodstove, then sits down in the living room and settles into his lounger. "It's hanging out back," he announces to the room. "Tomorrow it goes on a tree out front and we'll see if the coyote comes. More likely crows will get it first."

John comes stomping up the basement stairs. "It's been a bad year for deer," he adds randomly. "The coyotes are getting them." For reasons that escape me, he is wearing a Wellesley soccer t-shirt that clashes spectacularly with the shotgun he's carrying.

Closing up the egg crate, I put it back into the refrigerator while pondering the possibility of painting the little one in pretty pastel colors. "If the coyotes are getting them," I say, "then why haven't I seen carcasses? How come I haven't seen any tracks?"

"Coyotes don't hang around posing, you know," John reminds me. "I've seen a couple."

"I haven't seen any," I say, as if my failure to notice them means they don't exist.

"That's because you don't spend enough time in the woods," he says bluntly.

This is true.

He adds: "There's a coyote making a trail right near the house."

"Really?" I say interestedly. I'm not afraid of coyotes. I just worry it might have gone crazy. Why else would it hang out near humans? Except for lap dogs and the occasional rabid raccoon, all sane mammals shun our company. Even house-cats aren't interested in us. They just like the smell of fungus that grows between our toes.

"Yes," Don interjects unexpectedly, and goes back to ignoring us. He doesn't seem to notice that John's parked himself on the big sofa in the living room, and he's pulling the trigger on his shotgun.

Click, pause. Click, pause. Click, pause.

"Why are you doing that?" I ask crossly.

"Doing what?" he asks innocently.

I waggle my finger at him. "Pulling the trigger on your shotgun."

"It's not a shotgun, it's a rifle," he replies calmly.

"Shotgun, rifle . . . it's a *gun*. In the living room! I mean . . . geez . . . you can't . . . there's . . . there's *bread dough*!" Indignantly, I point at the kitchen counter where a ceramic bowl is covered with a damp towel. "It's *rising*!"

Behind me, Ruth stifles a snort and goes out to fuss with some pies cooling on the porch.

"It's a Ruger," John explains unhelpfully. "I'm going to fit it out with a scope."

I park myself in front of him with my hands on my hips, doing my best to give him crabby looks without making him laugh. "So why are you sitting there, pulling the trigger?"

"Because it sticks," he answers succinctly. He's squeezing the trigger again and again so the action will smooth out.

Click, pause. Click, pause. Click, pause.

Glare, pause. Glare, pause. Glare, pause.

"Here," he pats the beige couch cushion next to him and smiles winningly up at me. "Come sit next to me," he asks nicely, and pats the cushion again, repeating the annoying gesture until I am forced to sit on his hand, which is of course his plan. "Watch me first," he orders happily. "Then you try." He squeezes one more time, a soulful expression on his face, and then he retrieves his hand and starts taking the gun apart so he can show me how it works. There is a safety, and a widget, and the rifle won't go off unless you know which part to turn first. It may seem obvious but it isn't. It's not like the movies. As I watch, he reassembles it. "Now pick it up," he says, handing it to me.

The Ruger is a lot heavier than it looks, and the butt feels pleasantly firm. I start to laugh, because it reminds me of him.

"Focus," John growls. He does not have a sense of humor about guns.

Dutifully, I stifle the giggles and return my attention to the rifle. "It's not loaded?" I ask dubiously, seeking assurance that I'm not going to shoot the television by accident.

"Of course not," he says dryly. "Here, look," he says, handing me a thing that looks like a bullet to me. But it's a dummy, not a blank. There's no powder in it. "This is what's in there," John explains. "If I was loading live rounds, the last place I'd be sitting is the living room." He means it. When I was seven, my family went to the Sussmans' house on Christmas. Santa brought my friend Stevie a toy gun. We ran around the outside, rolling around in the snow, hiding in snowdrifts and burrowing under the porch, and then Stevie ran into the house and pointed the toy gun at the grownups. He got in Big Trouble for that. Stevie's dad was mad. He spanked Stevie right there in front of everyone and took the toy gun away. Stevie knew better than to complain. You don't aim a gun unless you're prepared to shoot it, and you never, ever point a gun at your dad. Especially when the unarmed minister and his wife are visiting. It's very rude.

Cautiously, I jounce the rifle on my leg. The barrel is aimed at the ceiling, where a spider is catching flies for lunch.

"Go ahead," John urges. "Squeeze."

I squeeze. Nothing happens.

"Squeeze, but gently," he instructs. "Don't tug. Just keep squeezing until it clicks."

I try again.

Squeeze.

Squeeze.

Squeeze.

CLICK!

I scream and drop it. It lands with a loud thud on the floor.

"You can't do that," he scowls, reaching down and picking the rifle up. "Stay calm!"

"But it startled me!" I protest.

"It's not loaded, it didn't make a loud noise, and there was no kick. What's to be startled?"

"It just did. There wasn't any advance warning and then it just kind of jerked."

"Well," he sighs, "that's part of the problem with this one. You want the action to be perfectly smooth." He checks the rifle quickly and hands it back to me. "Try again. You need to learn how to handle it."

Gingerly, I pull the trigger again. The barrel is pointed at the ceiling. The spider is gone. The gun is still unloaded.

Squeeze.

Squeeze.

Squeeze.

CLICK!

I jump again, but this time I don't drop it. I just flail and feel like an idiot.

My twitchy reaction is "commonly called 'flinching'," intones *The Hunter's and Trapper's Practical Guide* of 1878. "This is fatal to good shooting, *and must be overcome*." Failure to do so is tantamount to death or starvation, neither of which I feel like trying today. The *Practical Guide* recommends balancing a quarter on the end of the barrel of an unloaded rifle, taking aim at a target, and pulling the trigger until the quarter doesn't fall off. Rain or shine, day and night, you must practice, practice, and practice until you can perform on command.

"Huh," I say out loud, and stare banefully at the gun, which suddenly looks a lot like my violin.

Rolling his eyes, John reaches over to take the weapon away from me. I'm happy to give it up. Bouncing that thing on my lap has worn me out. It's more exhausting than playing with someone else's baby. A gun does not seem natural in my hands. I'm too Korean-aunty to pout sexily and stay upright while shooting a machine gun in stilettos, like the Asian actress playing French super-spy Nikita on TV. However, it's very easy to picture me squatting in a doorway, yelling in 한글 at the cable guy as I hurl raw squid at him.

"You gotta practice," John intones, and starts pulling the trigger again.

Click, pause, Click, pause. Click, pause.

Sulkily, I slide back into the couch and start kicking the sides aimlessly with bare feet. I can do this because my feet don't touch the floor when I sit back on the seat.

He stops squeezing and gives me a thoughtful look. "There's a kid's rifle downstairs. You can use that."

I'm so surprised that I stop kicking the couch.

"Sure," he says blandly, as I resume bouncing on the cushions. "It will be a better fit."

Click.

The only firearm I've ever shot was a BB gun to scare away raccoons that hung around the parsonage. I used a broom to kill the bats that flew into my bedroom. Worn down to a nub, the broom was useless for sweeping up the floor, but when swung like a bat, it whacked bats good. Was I exposed to rabies? Why, yes! Raccoons and bats are carriers. Did I ask for a pistol? No interest. When loud noises became necessary, as they often are for kids, my brother just blew stuff up with his Mr. Science chemistry set.

In everyday life, I'm a goofball, but when a real crisis hits, I get calm. When I was a graduate student in Chicago, I was mugged at gunpoint. It didn't occur to me to buy a gun. When my Hyde Park apartment was burglarized, I was traumatized, but still, no thought to buy a gun. When I was robbed on the no. 6 Jeffrey bus by a man who sliced open the side of my leather satchel with a box cutter, all he got was my lunch, because I still wasn't carrying a gun. When I tote up the number of times I've had to file police reports around the world, it's really quite depressing. But none of these experiences prompted me to stop traveling alone or buy a firearm to protect myself. However, I did learn something useful. I'd thought that criminals targeted me because I'm an excitable Asian chick. The Chicago police just laughed at my naïveté, and waved a hand around the station. A good chunk of the other mugging victims were burly men, and they came in many shoe sizes and a satisfying assortment of colors. It was just the omniscience of math again, otherwise known as "the odds," which I am. So get over yourself, lady. You're not special.

One way or another, I am constantly running into guns, so it seems a good idea to learn how to handle them. Frankly, it's simpler to haul John around for protection, because he's much better at being armed. He's also better at opening jars, taking out the garbage, and shaving without nicking himself. But, that attitude is terribly sexist. And so, *poule* that I am, I'm going to learn how to shoot for myself.

❧ ❧ ❧

CHAPTER SIX

Bard the Joint

Let the meat cake.
— "Mary Antwinet," "leader of the French revelation,"
from blog, shitmystudentswrite.tumblr.com, 2012

The recipe begins: "Skin the coot. (Do not pick). Wash in salt and water and let stand overnight in a solution of 1/4 cup salt and water to cover." According to the editors of *Yankee Magazine*, who decide such things, "Stewed Coot" is a Maine specialty. The problem is that I have never seen a coot, let alone eaten one. I don't know if it's animal, vegetable, or mineral. I've heard that they are both crazy and bald, as in "Crazy as a coot" and "Bald as a coot." This information is not very helpful, because I could say the same about Britney Spears.

I decide to check out Cootworld.com, because "if you want to know about Coot's [sic] this is the place." To my surprise, a coot is neither a relative of raccoons nor a cucumber pickle. It's an All-Terrain Vehicle (ATV) that twists 45 degrees in the middle, exactly like a Dancing Barbie. The coot is both funny looking and tough. It lives in tricky water environments such as whitewater rapids and shallow lakes with rocks. I have never seen anything quite like it in the wild, but it went extinct in 1985.

By contrast, standard American coots are still flying around Maine. They are not ducks but waterfowl, a group that includes other curious mouthfuls such as teal, widgeon, and snipe. Sometimes called a mud hen, the coot resembles a black rubber ducky with a white shield on its forehead. "Coots are good shooting; good eating," the U.S. Fish and Game Office hastened to assure dubious hunters in 1944. Mostly, the U.S. Fish and Game Office noted, there were a lot of them, especially when tasty ducks and geese were "mysteriously" nowhere to be found.

Elsewhere, there are recipes, most of which go like this:

Clean the coot. Place a brick in the cavity, and roast in uncovered baking dish for twelve hours. Add one bottle of red wine, and roast for another twelve hours. Continue adding wine and roast until the brick is soft. Then discard the coot and eat the brick.

Like many waterfowl and wild turkeys, the bird is not to be plucked but skinned. This is because its feathers stick to your eyeballs, and its skin is tough as shoe leather. I remain unconvinced of deliciousness.

"Can you bring me a coot?" I ask John, who has just stomped into his mother's kitchen, where I am rolling biscuits.

"A what?"

"A coot. It looks like Daffy Duck."

"Nope," he says, and tosses back a cookie from the jar. "That's upland hunting. I need a dog for that. But you can have a partridge," he declares, plopping himself on the couch. He starts riffling through the newspaper. "I got one this morning."

"Where?" I prod skeptically.

"Out back," he says absently, putting down his paper and picking up *Uncle Henry's Swap It Or Sell It*.

"Is it really a partridge, or was it a grouse?"

"Both. Either," he grumbles. "What does it matter?"

"They're distinct species, like moles and voles."

John snorts, hunches over and buries his face in his small reading, which means: I don't care as long as it tastes good.

"Well," I snip, "you *will* care if the cooking methods for partridge and grouse turn out to be really different. You can't cook a duck like a chicken, for example. If you try, your duck will be awful." I walk over to the couch and poke him in the arm with a floured finger just to make sure he's listening.

As usual, he doesn't seem to notice, so I poke him again. This time, his head pops up. "Here's a good one!" he says, grinning widely as he flaps *Uncle Henry's* in my face.

"Don't change the subject."

Ignoring me, he begins reading aloud. "'I have a Yamaha Blaster that the motor blew back in 2001'—"

"What's a blaster?"

"It's an ATV," he answers impatiently. "Now shush and let me read this to you!" He takes a deep breath and resumes: "'I had got in a wrestling accident in 2001 so never rebuilt it until late 2003 and never finished it. It has new crank shaft and piston, needs a starter and clutch cable, other than that everything is in good condition.'"

"Why are you looking for ATVs?"

"I'm not!" he replies gleefully and holds out the publication for me to see. "I'm looking for guns!"

I stick my face in the pages. It's listed under "Firearms." "So this person has an ATV that doesn't work and wants to trade it . . . ?"

". . . for guns!" he grins.

"What would really be funny is if this ad was run by a little old lady named Millicent."

"Could be," he acknowledges. "This is Maine! The little old ladies can be tough."

"It would even be funnier if the ATV was edible. Like the coot that someone,"—I give him a meaningful look—"is going to bring me for supper."

"Get me a new 16-gauge shotgun," he shrugs. "Then we'll talk." He sinks back into the couch and resumes studying his options.

Annoyed, I walk back to the kitchen, pop more biscuits in the oven, and then do a bit of research. Not only can Millicent turn a coot into a shotgun, her ancestors could turn a grouse into a partridge. Recounts British author J. Turner-Turner in *Three Year's Hunting and Trapping in America and the Great North-west*, 1888:

> I managed to knock over what the Virginians call a pheasant, the correct name of which is ruffed grouse; but in America, and especially Virginia, it appears to me they rarely lose an opportunity of calling everything by its wrong name, and I often think they must have searched the dictionary through to hunt up the most inconvenient words wherewith to express themselves.

The Hunter's and Trapper's Practical Guide of 1878 offers a fabulously cranky variation of the same complaint, and then it keeps on going.

> Often a name is applied to some game-birds which is not only senseless, but a name belonging to another variety than the one improperly given it, as is the case with our Ruffed Grouse and Quail, both of which a re known indiscriminately as 'Partridge,' which is not to be found in America, but is the true name of an English game-bird.

I am utterly charmed by the guidebook's final jab, which seeks to clarify this muddle by turning to *Herbert's Nomenclature for Hunting*, which is to hunters what the *Oxford*

English Dictionary is to Scrabble enthusiasts. Snippily, *Herbert's* explains (with asterisks included):

> Grouse, before they can fly, is a brood.
> Grouse, after they can fly, is a pack
> *Pheasants, a single hatching of, is a nide,
> *Partridges, a single hatching of, is a covey.

Unfazed, *Herbert's Nomenclature for Hunting* is as snide as a Frenchman mocking British cuisine and as impatient as a frontier schoolmarm teaching teenagers in kindergarten. The pearls of wisdom are many. Who knew that hunters were so wise about human nature? For example, the experienced hunter knows that two grouse are called a "brace." Three grouse are a "leash." This makes perfect sense if you think about it, because that's how they look as they strut single file through the forest. It goes on:

> Two rabbits are a couple. Three are a couple and a half.
> Two hounds are a couple. Three are a hurdle.

True, and true.

I am thinking to myself, the world would be a better place if we all read *Herbert's*. We would know better than to confuse a whiteness of swans with a gaggle of geese, and there would be no more fuss over plural wives, boy toys, mistresses, or ménages-à-trois. All that matters is that humans ask themselves before they couple up: am I a bunny, or a hound? Bunnies make bunnies happy. Hounds make hounds happy. Add a bunny to a bunny couple, and all the bunnies snuggle. Bring

---

* Observe here, that neither Partridge nor Pheasant existing in America, the words *nide* and *covey* are useless. What is generally called, therefore, a *covey* of Partridges is a *pack* of Ruffed Grouse. [To which I would add: Observe here, that the first sentence above being grammatically incorrect.]

another hound into a hound pair, and it's a whole mess of trouble. Specifically, according to *Herbert's*: a multiplying of husbands, an incredibility of cuckolds, a nonpatience of wives, and a herd of harlots.

In other words: a hound plus two bitches = a team of divorce lawyers.

John happens be born in the Year of the Rabbit, which makes him a bunny, romantically speaking. His bunny-ness may explain his stubborn fascination with threesomes. I'm born in the Year of the Dragon. I eat bunnies for breakfast.

Bing! the oven complains. The biscuits are done. I open the oven door, take out my biscuits, and set them on a cooling rack. As they cool, I clean up the dishes, and then I butter a few biscuits for John.

"Did you hang the grouse?" I ask him nicely, setting down the plate of snacks on the coffee table in front of him.

"Nope," he replies from behind the *National Review*.

"Where is it?"

He waves a hand towards the fridge, and then the hand snatches up the biscuits, which he tosses back and gulps down like a trained seal.

Soon enough I am staring at the plucked and skinned bird, wondering how best to prepare it. Here and there, black feathers stick out like fake eyelashes off a drunken showgirl. Unlike a factory-farmed chicken, there are no clumps of yellow fat tucked under the thighs and frilling the front of the breast. Pleasingly white and translucent, the flesh smells like fresh water, scented of air and sunlight. As I hold the bird in my hand, I imagine it in the bush, staring sideways at John with its blank beady eye. Blink. Blink. Hop. Blink.

BLAM!

John was using a shotgun, and he got it with one pellet to the neck. The bird is whole and unblemished. The breasts are plump and robust. The thighs are wee and shapely. It's a shame to cut it up. I am going to stuff the grouse with cara-melized sweet onions and roast it whole in the oven.

But the ideal way to cook it, according to William Hamil-ton Gibson's *Camp Life in the Woods and the Tricks of Trapping and Trap Making*, 1901, is to build a good fire and let it burn down to embers. Take the bird, gut it, wash it thoroughly, soak it in water so the feathers are saturated, and then place the whole thing directly on the hot coals and ashes, and bury it. "When done, the skin and feathers will easily peel off," Gibson says, "and the flesh will be found to be wonderfully sweet, tender, and juicy." The bird will be improved, he adds, by a stuffing of smashed crackers and "minced meat of any kind," or by using "Indian meal" if you can get it. "A fowl thus roasted is a rare delicacy," he declares with enthusiasm.

I'm trying Gibson's recipe the next time a grouse saunters into gunshot range. The tasty grouse don't usually do this, by the way. Only crazy coots do.

I didn't bard the bird, mostly because I didn't have any caul, or what the French call *crépine*, "lace fat." To obtain *crépine* in the U.S. requires a whole pig and serious butchering skills, and I had just two hours to find, buy, and unwrap one. I have been called many things, but "fast shopper" is not one of them. I also wasn't going to ruin my lovely bird by larding it up with store-bought fatback. Wrapping meat in slabs of uncured streaky bacon is a crude version of barding, but the cook risks imparting unwanted tastes, namely "smoke," "salt," and "nitrite." So I ended up massaging it with butter and roasting it under a tin foil hat, to be removed for the last ten minutes to give it a crisp golden finish.

By the time I'm done carmelizing the onions and prepping the bird, everyone else has disappeared. Pleased to be alone, I sit in the sunny living room, riffling through Ruth's collection of old cookbooks while I wait for my nose to tell me when the bird is done. With game meat, there's really no other way. Use your eyes, and you'll be wrong.

Very little summarizes the conflicted state of game cuisine better than the banishment of the opossum from the American cookbook. Its exile has been so complete that most serious chefs have forgotten they're edible. A good example of this is *L.L. Bean's Game and Fish Cookbook*. Adopting the lofty tone of a museum curator, this gorgeous book tells you how to prepare photogenic creatures such as moose, elk, deer, woodcock, quail, and grouse, along with all kinds of freshwater fish. Because it is a game cookbook, its back section illustrates the basic procedures for field dressing, though it uses bloodless drawings and skips the really gruesome bits. The editors figure you don't want to know about things such as the "Amazing Butt-Out!" tool, which lets the hunter extract a deer's intestines using the most direct means possible. This cookbook also omits recipes for classic American varmints such as raccoon and opossum. To learn how to prepare them for the family, the intrepid cook has to turn to the monumental oddity that is the *Joy of Cooking*, first written and self-published by homemaker Irma Rombauer in 1931.

In the dry tones of a train schedule announcer, the widow Rombauer orders her unblinking readers to skin the raccoon, then scrape the fat off the carcass, blanche the flesh for forty-five minutes, add baking soda, boil it a bit more, drain it, rinse it, add more cold water and boil it again, take it out, stuff it with bread, stick it in the oven and bake it covered for forty-five minutes, uncover it . . . and then, yes, bake it some more until doneness is achieved. By comparison, the recipe for opossum is a haiku of gothic horror: "Trap 'possum and feed it on milk and cereals for ten days before killing," she instructs crisply. "Clean but do not skin. Treat as pig . . . roast as for pork." Rejoice, serve, and eat!

Nowadays, few home cooks have dealt with a pig up close and personal, let alone a possum. It doesn't seem as if pigs and possums would have much in common, especially in the flavor department. True, both are pale snouted omnivores that breed without birth control, helping them colonize the planet almost as successfully as humans. Unlike pigs, however, possums have thumbs on all four of their creepy doll hands and they always seem to be smiling with too many teeth. When confronted with danger, possums secrete an enzyme that makes them appear to be dead. It is a strange defense mechanism, made even stranger by the fact that it's useless against clever hunters called Mom. All housewives had to do was scare the possum into falling over into a dead faint, then pick it up, stuff it in a sack, and there's your dinner. It was still smiling as Mrs. Cleaver shoved it into the oven.

I've never tried possum, because I find their appearance to be deeply disturbing. This is completely irrational, I know, but there you have it. Then there is the cultural divide. New Englanders don't go possum hunting, which is generally cast as a Southern thing. And even if Maine is sometimes called the "South of the North," possum casserole never once showed up at any potluck dinners at my dad's church. But in the South, possums are still hunted as game, and they were once staples of slave cuisine. For that, they deserve respect as good meat. It's over a century since the Civil War, and today, the economic outlook is as bleak as the Great Depression when Rombauer wrote her book. Now is not the time for squeamishness, especially since possums are everywhere, just waiting to be run over by cars driven by homicidal old people named Granny.

Because humans have been eating meat ever since being kicked out of Eden, I've run across recipes for swans, dormice, rats, elephants, and just about every mammal or bird on the planet. But if possum has disappeared from the American cookbook, recipes for skunk and porcupine never appeared in the first place. This is when you have to talk to people who battle cute creatures armed with annoying defense mechanisms. By "people," I mean Patrick. After much prodding for info, he eventually burps out: "Me and my hunting buddies, we eat them all the time. They're good." This is all I can get him to say on the matter, because he's just lost all the hair on his head to a bonfire.

Here is what happened: over the weeks, the pile of debris from his small lumberyard had grown too large. The plan was to set it on fire, because the best way to make sure that a brush pile doesn't catch on fire by accident is to burn it all down first. Hours later, the bonfire was steadily burning but the huge mass was still intact, and his day permit was running out. To speed things up, he threw one arm over his nose, climbed up the smoking pile, and dumped kerosene on the wood. The fire flared, singeing the hair off his head and giving him bonfire sunburn, making his face as red and grainy as a raw beet. It looked bad, but no big deal. The hair would grow back. It always did.

Then his arm got hot. There was the sweet smell of roasting cotton, followed by the aroma of grilled meat. Kerosene had splashed on his sleeve, and it was burning hot and fast.

No need to panic. Just stop, drop, and roll.

Down he tumbled. On the way to the bottom, he started to bleed. Then the cut started to gush. He'd rolled over a jagged edge of wood, slicing open his elbow but missing the tendon. The clinic stitched him up, wrapped his burned hands in thick gauze bandages that turned them into giant Q-tips, and sent him home with painkillers.

Which explains why he's here, recuperating on the couch.

"Don't bother with them hunting magazines," he tells me impatiently as he pushes awkwardly through the door of the Big House and settles into the living room. "It's all rock climbing stuff written by guys who live in New York City. Those guys *want* to be me," he declares staunchly. This from a man whose bald head is not only bright red and peeling but whose face has no eyebrows, making him look like an enormous naked mole rat that fell into a vat of cherry Coke. By tomorrow, maybe the day after, he figures all will be back to normal except for the hunting, which he can't do on account of the Q-tips. "I don't need some guy sitting in a padded chair in a city office telling me how to hunt," he adds indignantly. "I want practical information, like ratings for ammo." He works himself into such a state that he flops, exhausted, into the couch. The skin on his eyelids is white.

Experimentally, I sniff. The roasting releases a tantalizing aroma that is curiously unlike chicken. I am a teensy bit relieved that it doesn't smell like kerosene. The oven timer hasn't gone off yet, but the grouse smells as if it's ready for finishing. Bouncing with anticipation, I shuffle over to the kitchen, pull open the oven door, and lean over to inspect my roasted bird.

BLAM! BLAM! BLAM!

That's not the usual chiming noise the oven timer makes. I close the oven door, straighten up, give the oven an appraising stare, check the timer, and tilt forward again.

BLAM! BLAM! BLAM!

The racket is coming from outside. Quickly, I straighten up, letting the oven door spring shut, and rush over to look out the picture window. In the distance, John and Don are shooting clay pigeons in a far corner of the front lawn. On the couch, Patrick is sound asleep. The sound of gunfire doesn't wake him from his nap.

I dash back to the oven, take the grouse out, pull on work jeans, work boots, and a fuzzy jacket, and wander down to watch. As I approach, I wave both arms energetically to make sure that John and Don see me. They are both wearing protective ear muffs for shooting, and I am coming up from behind. They'll spot me when they reload.

"Pull!" Don calls out.

Poof! the clay pigeon shatters.

"Pull!"

Poof!

Then they switch off, so Don is shooting and John is pulling the spring arm that launches the clay pigeons high into the air. It looks easy when they do it. Both of them hit the spinning disks every time. The clay pigeons sail into the air, whizzing like small Frisbees, and poof! they shatter into a thousand little pieces, raining orange from the sky. They now come in biodegradable nontoxic versions that still break easily. The exact word for their crumbliness is "friable." Not to be confused with fry-able.

The clay pigeons come neatly stacked in boxes and look like the drain plates that come attached to cheap flowerpots. AS FRAGILE AS EGGS, the packing box warns. They are no longer called clay pigeons because it's too confusing. People who skeet shoot tend to be literalists, as in "birdshot" is for shooting birds, "buckshot" is for shooting bucks and no, you cannot switch them. There's nothing birdlike about a flat orange disk. So "clay pigeon" is out. It is now "clay target," as in "round thing to be shot at," and all is right in the world.

But I insist on the old term, because it's important to remember that magicians and newly-marrieds used to destroy passenger pigeons (charmingly called "doves") by the thousands, just for the satisfaction of getting revenge on them. We can scarcely remember that the arrival of a pigeon flock used to be an epic natural disaster. Flocks numbered in the millions, and when they passed overhead, they "stretched as far as a person could see," wrote a horrified New Yorker in 1854. "There would be days and days when the air was alive with them, hardly a break occurring in the flocks for half a day at a time." They ate everything in their path, raining shit from the sky, and Lord help you if they picked your woods to roost in for the night. In the popular imagination, they've been replaced by flying saucers hurling down burning wrath from the sky. The effect is the same: crowds stampeding, babies crying, preachers intoning, "Judgment Day hath come!" as the monstrous flying mass blocks the sun from the sky, promising to wipe out the human race. Defiant and armed, Americans grab their shotguns and start shooting until they obliterate the enemy in the sky. The last remaining alien is shot by a brave little boy, who thus saves mankind.

"You wanna try?" John asks nicely, as he reloads the machine that flings the clay pigeons into the air. Because it used to hold live pigeons, the flinging machine is called a "trap."

"Sure!" I reply.

John reaches into the back of the Kubota and hands me a kid's .410 shotgun that he'd tossed in the back. I take it, pleased by his thoughtfulness and annoyed by the fact that I'm so predictable.

John takes the shotgun out of my hands and starts rifling around the Kubota, searching for the correct ammo. He finds it, takes the shotgun from my hands, and starts loading it for me. "I won a competition once," he says conversationally.

"Where?" I demand.

"In Scotland."

"Why were you in Scotland?" I exclaim.

"For the lesbian wedding."

I give him a look.

"It was long before I met you," he laughs. "It was very fancy. They kept moving the launch site around so it was harder to hit the pigeons. But I hit them anyways."

I thwack him on the leg because we are in the middle of an open field, surrounded by forest, shooting clay pigeons on a sunny day in Maine and yet, somehow, he manages to fit lesbians into the conversation.

"Here," he says nicely, handing me the live shotgun and a pair of pink ears. The kid's version isn't weaker than a regular shotgun, it's just smaller. "For little people!" John teases. Because, yah, I have stubby limbs: the regular shotguns are too long for me to handle. It's the same problem I had as a teenager trying to play my dad's trombone. My arms weren't long enough to extend the slide very far, so my tunes were limited to three notes.

I move into position a few yards away from the trap. Experimentally, I point the shotgun up at an unsuspecting, defenseless cloud.

"Do I put the bead on the target or should it be below?" I ask.

"On the target," John replies.

"First sight the target," Don instructs patiently as I get into position. "Never put your finger on the trigger until you're ready to shoot. Lean forward on your left leg. Put the butt of the shotgun nice and tight on your shoulder. It will kick a little, but not very much."

I nod, raising the shotgun to my shoulder, and trying to gain a solid stance. Then I stop, pause, put my ears on, and raise the shotgun again. "READY!" I shout, and point the shotgun up at the empty sky. "PULL!" I command, feeling very English gentry ("Care for a spot of tea, Mum?") even though the friable pigeon and I have a wee too much in common.

Zwing! The trap launches the clay pigeon and up it twirls through the air. Peering down the barrel of my shotgun, I follow it . . . follow it . . . follow it . . .

. . . and then it lands.

"IT WAS TOO FAST!" I exclaim indignantly, still wearing my ears. I turn around. John is leaning on the trap, trying to keep a straight face. Don just looks happy that I didn't shoot one of the crows by accident.

"Try again," John says encouragingly.

"Okay," I agree, and carefully resume position. "PULL!"

Zwing! The trap launches, and the clay pigeon flies through the air. I follow it . . . follow it . . . and take a shot.

BANG!

The clay pigeon sails by, landing soft and perfectly intact on the laughing lawn.

"That was terrible," I acknowledge sadly, pulling off my protective earmuffs in defeat.

"Let's try shooting at a stationary pigeon," John says soothingly. "That way you can practice hitting it while it's not flying away."

The two of them set up a clay pigeon at fifty yards, and then gesture for me to shoot.

I inhale, take careful aim, and shoot.

I miss.

Sighing, the men set up again at thirty-five yards, propping up the clay pigeon with a soda can so it's easier to hit.

I miss so badly that the crows around it don't move.

Twenty-five yards? No.

Fifteen yards? No.

Ten yards? Ahem. No.

With the two of them telling me where to point the barrel (which is to say, Don stands behind me and moves the shotgun around until it's pointing in the right place), I finally hit the clay pigeon. Poof! It shatters into a tired heap instead of bursting redly in the air. Even the clay pigeon is embarrassed to surrender to the likes of me. It's so close I could hit it if I spit with conviction. It's a round disk made of baked earth, for goodness's sake. It's not sticking out its tongue at me or trying to run away.

"Next time you're trying to shoot rabbits," John teases, "just tell it to come in closer and sit still!"

"This is hard," I say dejectedly, and hand the shotgun back to him.

"Your head's too big. That's why you can't properly sight."

"Do you mean that for real or are you just being mean?"

"Actually," he replies with a serious expression, "your head's too big. You're an Asian-chick Neil Cavuto."

I don't know if I should be insulted or flattered.

"A gas-powered gun with a speed sight will work for you," he declares blithely, as he checks the chamber and reloads.

"But you'll have to be custom fit if you're ever going to hit anything."

"You need to shoot more," Don says with dour finality. With that, he's done wasting time with me and puts his ears back on, blocking out the chitchat and the yammer. Cocooned in silence, he grabs his shotgun, nods at John, and the two of them resume their fun, hitting the clay pigeons with the greatest of ease. Just to annoy me, John switches to the kid's shotgun. In his hands, it looks like a toy.

"Yes I know," I grumble to myself as I sit on the grass and watch. "I am a terrible shot. You don't need to rub it in."

A few rounds later, the men adjust the spring in the trap, turning it into a crafty baseball pitcher playing the minor leagues. First it sends out fastballs. Next it throws a couple of curve balls. Once it even does a lob. The easiest clay pigeons to hit are the ones that fly sideways, streaking orange across the sky. The most challenging are the ones that go directly away from the shooter, which is how I'd expect a bird in real life to behave.

Fly, fly away home, fake little bird!

Fly! Be free!

BLAM.

And joyfully it shatters and falls to earth. Ashes to ashes, and dust to dust. Because, after all, the clay pigeon is made of dirt. The earth is where it longs to be.

After they run out of ammo and fall turns into winter, we walk around the field, collecting the clay pigeons that I'd missed and stacking them back in the box, then smashing the broken shards into the sharp grass. They crumble apart, as delicate as Necco wafers. The three of us stomp the ground in a Charlie Brown dance to silent music, crushing the last remnants of clay creatures already broken.

Compliant, they vanish beneath the weight of my boot and, like magic, they're gone.

CHAPTER SEVEN

❦ ❦ ❦

Vampires Suck

If the [zodiac] stars are animals, what food do they eat?
— *nephew of Adelard of Bath, 12th century*

"The neighbors had been losing chickens," Ruth remarks over dishes in the sink. "Kept finding them with their heads gone."

"—and . . . ?" I prod. She's washing. I'm wiping. With one eye, I look through the kitchen window, scanning the hen-house, but it's the middle of the day. Outside, nothing moves. No birds. No insects. Just flakes of snow, swirling on invisible breezes, falling in the gray light. It's utterly silent until the winds start to whip. Then the whole house sets to rumbling. These snowflakes sting if they hit you in the face. The edges are like little razor blades, but they are very pretty.

"They set out traps," she continues, her arthritic hands bus-ily scrubbing a casserole dish. "Finally caught a white wea-sel. He'd been decapitating them." She shakes her head and scrubs some more, marveling at the peculiar thirst of animals.

Weasels want the blood. Rats attack the flanks. Foxes deci-mate the bird, leaving nothing behind but cracked bones and feathers. Americans want the breasts, putting the rest into fancy feasts for cats. The hunger reveals the beast.

In winter, brown weasels turn white. When sold, weasels turn into minks. The weasel is beautiful, its body lithe and head small and despite all the blood, it sleeks away with fur and soul unstained. It is practically miraculous how a mammal can sever an artery and drink life's blood dry, lick its lips and trot away, spotless, ready to sleep the untroubled sleep of babes.

Up, down, and around, the Great Outdoors has become a blank page. Gone are the mountains, the sky, and road. It's just snow and more snow. When it gets like this, I wonder where the wildlife goes. Add a few toy deer and we're the teeny tiny paper people inside a panoramic sugar egg. The snow's proof that global warming is a myth, the TV news people announce, because it's December and there's a big storm heading up the East Coast. How could snow in winter be possible, the commentator sarcastically remarks, if the world was warming up?

Because the moon is bigger than your thumbnail, Princess Leonore, even though you can't see it when you stick your thumb in front of your eyes.

I want to see the world from the weasel's point of view. I don't think I'm alone in this. What else accounts for the vampire mania out there? We obsess over these drinkers of blood, beautiful monsters who are slender of frame, nocturnal of habit, fanged of teeth, and utterly indifferent to laws made up by hairless monkeys. We call them ermines when they've become expensive coats. Why not call them vampires too?

Because that would be a mistake. Vampires are weasels but weasels aren't vampires. They don't live a romantic haze of idiotic dribble. They kill to survive, and we only complain when we paid for their meals. The rest of the time, we don't care what they do.

> All around the chicken coop,
>
> The possum chased the weasel
>
> The monkey thought t'was all in fun,
>
> Pop! goes the weasel!

Nobody knows what the lyrics to the song mean, but everybody is certain that it has nothing to do with shooting weasels.

Because Patrick's dogs are bored, we're heading over to his house and taking the dogs out for a rabbit hunt. Basically, this is winter hiking with beagles and guns, except Patrick is the only one who's armed.

"For rabbits, I usually start pretty late in the day," Patrick says. "Maybe seven or eight in the morning. I can be out here all day, and the dogs will run the same rabbit until sundown."

"Don't they get hungry?" I ask.

"You mean the dogs?" he asks in surprise, as if the thought never occurred to him. "Nah," he shakes his head. "If you feed them before a hunt, they'll just puke." He shrugs. "Sometimes beagles will puke anyways, to lighten themselves before a hard run."

Beagles are bundles of energy bursting from every pore. They can run and run and run. They can stand some cold but not too much. They can lose a lot of weight in one outing. Beagles don't have the thick fur and tufts between their toes that keep Huskies comfortable in the cold. They have to move in order to stay warm. As soon as the dogs spot Patrick heading to his gun safe, they're off the couch and at his heels, tails wagging furiously.

"Where's Homer?" I ask, looking around for the fourth dog, a male who replaced Scratch and Big Red after they turned on each other.

"Dunno," Patrick replies. "He disappeared."

"Meaning . . . ?" I prod.

"Mebbe the coyotes got him," he muses, as we walk downstairs to the sawmill portion of his house. "But the most likely explanation is that hunters stole him."

"But it's *Homer*," I point out. "He's a lousy hunting dog. Who'd kidnap him?"

"The kidnappers are stoopider than Homer!" Christy chimes in sadly. She's put on warm clothes and joined us downstairs. Despite his lack of brains, Homer was her favorite beagle.

Ironically, Patrick had gone all the way to a breeder in New Hampshire looking for a beagle that didn't have the smarts bred out of him. He'd planned to name the new dog Homer. He'd come back with a puppy named Homer. "It was already his name," he'd mumbled contentedly. One look at those big eyes, rolling in ecstasy over donuts, and your heart melted faster than butter in the microwave.

Alas, it quickly became obvious that this dog's namesake wasn't Homer the Bard but Homer the Simpson. Like that yellow paragon of misguided persistence, he was loud, stupid, and prone to falling into absurd situations involving angry skunks and mayonnaise. On a good day, he'd wake up in the morning, yawn, stretch, and lovingly lick your face. Then he'd lift up his stumpy leg and pee delightedly on the bed. It quickly became obvious that Homer the Beagle had the attention span of a goldfish and the brains of a daisy. Turned out the dome-headed look of "lovable lunkhead" was a symptom of line breeding. "You're getting him fixed, right?" the veterinarian asked, giving Christy a stern look over wire-rimmed glasses.

It wasn't a question. Christy understood. His ding-a-lings were snipped.

Contemplatively, Patrick tugs at one ear. "Guys come up here from Massachusetts; they see a beagle all alone out in the woods, so they grab him." He shrugs. "They're counting on no one on their end asking questions, and the dog being too far from home to figure out how to get back." Patrick shakes his head and chuckles. "I figure that one of these days, the guy who stole him will bring him back!"

Patrick's three remaining beagles all wear I.D. tags and collars, but Beebee and Daisy get homing devices when they go hunting. Maggie, the "fat one," doesn't need one because she's too fond of home. Their bodies wiggling in ecstasy, the dogs trot up to Patrick so he can attach the homing devices to their collars. He checks the radio signal, and then off we go into the winter: four humans, three beagles on short leashes, and one mutt dog named Basel.

Out in back of Patrick's house, there's an old logging trail cutting through the woods. For simplicity's sake, we're sticking with it. Everything is covered in snow, but the old path is still visible. As soon as we reach the main trail, Patrick leans over, unhooks the beagles from their leashes, and off they go into the woods, sniffing eagerly for rabbits. Basel strains to join the beagles, but Christy holds him back by his collar. "He can't follow the girls," she explains. "Every time he tries, he runs into a tree or pokes himself in the eye." Basel's impulse to run doesn't last very long. As soon as the pack is out of sight, he settles down and resumes his usual lope.

Four humans and one dog walk, quietly, searching for sign. An hour into the hunt, John is far in front, keeping a steady uphill pace. Every once in a while, Patrick stops to scrutinize the ground. He points at small indentations in the snow. "Rabbit tracks," he says.

"Fresh?" I ask hopefully.

"Not sure," he replies, crouching down. He plops two bare fingers into the snow, raises them to his nose, and sniffs them. He shrugs. "Nope."

He straightens up and continues up the trail. Christy and Basel follow on his heels. I am still hovering by the tracks, wondering how he can smell anything off snow. Irrationally, I peer into the brush, searching in the direction of the tracks, hoping to catch a glimpse of the rabbit that was there many moons ago. Abruptly, there is flash of fur in the spot where I'm staring, followed by Maggie. She starts baying. "Aroo! Yip yip!"

"It's Maggie!" I holler up the path. The worst hunter of the three is on the scent, not far from the tracks that Patrick smelled. I stand and wait . . . one potato . . . two potato . . . three potato . . . and here come the other two beagles zeroing in to the spot.

"Aroo! Aroo!" the beagles announce.

Patrick backtracks to find me. "Did you see it?" he asks.

"Yep," I affirm. "Saw it run right into that group of trees"—I point through the puckerbrush at a nice stand of pines—"and Maggie was right behind."

"Aroo! Aroo!" comes through faintly in the distance, but a good gust of wind buries the sound. The baying is now alarmingly far off.

"It's a big one," Patrick comments.

"How do you know?" I ask.

"The size of the circle," he shrugs, and draws a big O with his arm.

Rabbits don't run in a straight line. They run in circles. This technique confuses predators because the scent tracks back on itself. The bigger the rabbit, the bigger the circle. Or, as Sir Peter Beckford claimed in 1781: "A hare, generally, describes a circle as she runs; larger or less, according to her strength." Notably, Sir Beckford added, this O-making does not apply when the woods are very dense. Instead, the rabbit's circles will be meandering, random, and tight, posing "a constant puzzle to the hounds."

I don't know what "dense" means to a rabbit. To a hunter, however, I suspect it means "machete."

Sir Beckford's *Thoughts Upon Hunting* caused a minor uproar at the time, signaling the first stirrings of a repressive morality that would reach its fullest expression during the Victorian Age, a hysterical period so prudish that piano legs were covered lest the sight of them incite lust in hapless young men. Huffily, Sir Beckford pointed out that the same people doing all the protesting about the "cruel" sport of rabbit hunting were happily eating mutton for dinner, completely oblivious to the fact that an adorable little lambikins died quite gruesomely for them. Lambikin sang,

> To Granny's house I go,
>
> Where I shall fatter grow,
>
> Then you can eat me so.

And so he was gobbled up.

Lambs are marinated in the symbolism of self-sacrifice: Christ is the lamb of God that taketh away the sins of the world. He's not the rabbit of God. Abraham slits the throat of a lamb in place of his son, Isaac. Again, not a rabbit. If anything, rabbits are associated with paganism and witchcraft, given all that unmarried promiscuous sex they're having. That's why bunnies live at the Playboy mansion. They like it there, because bunnies enjoy salads and rainbows. So what's my point? Well, vegetarians would have nothing for dinner if a single pair of fertile rabbits was allowed to bunny at will, because the British countryside has no wolves or coyotes and very few foxes remaining, leaving sickness and a few predatory birds to eradicate garden pests. You'd think that rabbit hunting would be fully backed by horrified Christians pleased to rid the countryside of these hungry little heathens. But the anonymous attacks against rabbit hunting were actually targeting a privileged system of landownership. Peter Beckford could rabbit hunt because he was a Sir, just like Chaucer's Monk could hunt because he was an ass. The United States is one of the few countries in the Western World where hunting is not the sport of popes and kings, but pioneers and playboys.

"I'll be right back," John announces abruptly, as he backtracks down the hill and suddenly leaves the trail.

"Where are you going?" I ask in surprise.

"To get a rabbit hunting license and my shotgun." And off he disappears into the woods.

"Uh," I start to say, but he's already well out of earshot, his footsteps swallowed by the wind and the trees.

Christy laughs. "He'll find us. Don't worry."

"Uh . . ."

She laughs again. "No, Patrick won't mistake him for a rabbit."

"Oh good," I exhale, relieved. It's too cold for cell phones and no one brought walkie-talkies, so even perfectly good Maine directions such as "I'm by the old refrigerator at the dried-up brook" won't do. The only way he'll know where we are is by listening, I guess. It's amazing how much his hearing improves in the woods.

Now that the beagles are on the scent, the hike turns into a hunt. We walk and listen, walk and look. The dogs are so far off that none of us can hear them. Basel is in the deep snow, turning and turning, chasing his tail in slow motion.

"He's making a nest," Christy says fondly.

"Why?" I ask curiously.

"He's old. He needs a nap."

"Out here? While we're hunting? In the cold?"

"He doesn't care," Christy shrugs. "He's got fur."

Basel is now settling into his snow bed, intermittently looking up at Christy and closing his bleary brown eyes to rest. Gray hairs tuft the top of his head and salt the end of his nose. Since he's a rescue mutt, Christy doesn't know how old he is, but he's at least seven since that's how long they've been together. It's the longest relationship she's had.

"Go on," she says to me, as her old dog falls asleep in the snow. "I'll catch up."

Nodding, I resume marching up the trail. The hunting expedition is now down to two humans. Patrick is still the only one who's armed.

Human tracks are easy to follow. They leave a heavy impression wherever they go. A few minutes later I find him, because he is still stopping intermittently to study the snow.

Patrick stands up from his crouch and resumes walking up the trail, going deeper into the woods.

"Do the beagles know where you are?" I ask him eventually.

"Nope. You have to figure out where to wait."

This is where the radio collars come in handy, but they don't work with pinpoint accuracy. It's not like in *Aliens*, where the grunts had tracking devices that showed exactly where the space monsters were hiding. There's no beep . . . beep . . . beep noise to alert you when the dogs are close, because that defeats the entire purpose of walking as quietly as you can. Still, given the amount of noise the dogs make as they chase their prey, I can't figure out why we're supposed to be quiet.

The dogs are very far away. The sound of baying is barely audible to my ears. Carried forward by the winds, it is close enough to be heard, but I can't determine the direction. As minutes pass, the baying gets louder, but I still can't tell if it's in front, behind, or to one side.

Suddenly the rabbit goes zipping by right in front of us, a gleeful blur streaking across the trail, followed by all three beagles in quick succession.

"Aroo!"

"Aroo!"

"Arooooooo!"

And just like that, they all disappear into the woods. The trees swallow the sounds of beagles barking.

"Well," I say, blinking in surprise. "That was . . . uh . . ." I pause. "Well. Huh."

It all happened so quickly that Patrick didn't even get his gun at the ready.

He shrugs, unbothered, and keeps walking.

The rabbit is running in large circles. Here is the fascinating thing: it's not worried about the pack chasing behind it. It's worried about the dog hiding in wait on the side. And by "dog," the rabbit means us. So Patrick says. I am skeptical. Surely no animal enjoys being chased? A pack of beagles, barking furiously as the rabbit runs for its life . . . this does not induce fear?

"Naw," Patrick says dryly, amused by my questions.

A rabbit doesn't panic when it's being chased. It fears being trapped.

The hunger of dogs. This, the wild beast understands. Not so animal lovers who try to pick it up, cooing, "Look at the furry widdle wabbit! Wooky wooky woo!" This makes no sense from the rabbit's point of view. It will run away as fast as it can from humans who believe that small woodland creatures are their friends. The rabbit that lives in the forest is a wild animal. It's prey, not a pet. Such is the rabbit's life, to be chased. Every carnivore on the face of the earth calls it food. Snakes, owls, hawks, foxes, stoats, weasels, raccoons, opossums, bobcats, housecats, and wily coyotes indistinguishable from Lassie the Good: its enemies are above, behind, and beneath; nocturnal, diurnal; reptile, mammal, avian, and everything in between. Given how many predators find rabbits delicious, it's amazing that any rabbits survive. Yet they do, and they survive by being smart, fast, and lucky. And by reproducing as quickly as donuts at a drive-thru.

According to the *Young Sportman's Miscellany* of 1828, a single pair of rabbits, left alone for four years, will end up as 1,274,840 rabbits. That's a lot of rabbits. They are also famously clever. Rabbits are known for their ability to outwit hunters such as Elmer Fudd, the lisping weekend hunter who wears color-coordinated outfits as he minces through the forest. In the normal course of hunting, however, rabbits routinely escape the manliest of woodsmen. Through the eighteenth century, they were reputed to be witches in disguise, what with their strange habit of disappearing into thin air before astonished eyes. This sounds silly until you actually see one vanish right in front of you, and you aren't quite sure how to explain it to your friends.

All of a sudden, John is right behind me. He is now holding a shotgun and, presumably, he has a rabbit hunting license in his pocket.

Conversationally, by way of greeting, he says, "You know you can't take a shit in the woods, not if you've got the dogs."

"Huh?"

"If you take a shit in the woods, the dogs will roll around in it."

"So what do you do?"

"You've seen those trailer-hitch toilets. They work!" John teases me, because we've been hunting rabbits all afternoon and it's winter, which means that I am experiencing deeply conflicting impulses. *Must pee. . . but it's so cold! No good tree to hide behind. . . my butt will freeze! Why didn't I bring snacks? I'm so hungry. . . what if the rabbit decides to jump into my lap while I'm doing my thing?. . . maybe there's a candy in my pocket. . . gotta peegottapeegotta pee!. . .*

"You got your rabbit license?" I ask John, since he wasn't gone very long and I'm trying to distract my bladder by talking.

"Yep," John answers cheerfully. "Went to Dougie's and got it."

"Where did the shotgun come from?"

"The truck," he says.

"How did you know where to find us?"

He laughs. "You're really loud."

I glare at him. "Okay, fine. I'm loud." My perfectly normal down jacket makes noises when I walk. The zwick-zwick of waterproof exteriors. The crinkle of plasticized protection. These are not sounds found in nature. They are the sounds made by credit cards when they're swiped.

"You swing your arms when you walk," John points out, cocooned in his morally superior woolens.

"Zwick zwick," my arms lisp in annoyance.

"Aroo!" the beagles call, the sound once again very faint and far away.

I cannot hear the rabbit when it runs. Its silence is the sound of rabbit joy.

Hours later, we end up chasing the dogs, because it's nearly dark and time to go home.

"Maggie! Beebee! Daisy!" Patrick hollers to all four corners of the world. But the dogs are not tired; they do not want to come in. Fifteen minutes of trekking later: "Maggie! Beebee! Daisy!" Patrick repeats.

This time around, Maggie comes skidding out of the forest, wagging her tail in happy greeting when she sees Patrick. She bounces along next to him, looking remarkably peppy for a dog that has been running in mad circles for five hours.

The rabbit has outrun the sun. We are returning empty handed. The hunt began too late in the day. As dark descends and the moon comes out, the air turns frigid in our wake. Squeaking, the snow announces our exit as the forest exhales in relief.

"What about Beebee and Daisy?" I ask, as we trudge along the path.

Patrick shrugs. He'll go out tomorrow and find them. Or the beagles will figure it out and come back. He's not worried about them.

"But it's cold out here!" I protest.

"They're dogs," Patrick points out dryly. "They have fur."

So does the rabbit. Nobody expects the bunny to come inside because it's winter. But, there's the Homer Incident to consider. So Patrick hands Maggie's leash over to John and pulls out the tracking device from his pocket. He flicks up the radio antennae, and starts waving the plastic control around, turning 360 degrees as he follows the rabbit's invisible orbit, watching the little lights flicker up and down the control panel.

"Daisy!" he hollers decisively as the little lights begin to dance in excitement. Still staring fixedly at the controls, he walks headlong into the brush. Soon enough, he returns to the path, a beagle tucked under an armpit. "Here," he orders, plopping the squirming bundle of joy into my arms. She is belly up and blinking placidly, and off he goes into the brush again.

"Hullo, Daisy," I say to the beagle, who looks utterly bored by me, and then I set her four paws back on the snow and clip her into her leash.

"Aroo!" she howls in protest, but she seems resigned to her fate even as her ears twitch and her tail stands at attention. She knows where Beebee and the rabbit are hiding. A few minutes later, Patrick emerges from the brush in the direction she's staring. He's carrying Beebee, who looks exactly like a little kid throwing a fit.

We resume walking, each of us handling a pissed-off dog straining at her leash. "Where's Christy?" I ask Patrick after we pass Basel's empty snow nest.

He shrugs, and keeps walking.

After a while, in the distance, the house glimmers into view. Inside, the lights are on and the chimney is smoking. The sight of that warm haven makes me feel how very cold it is out here.

We walk faster, and blame it on the dogs wanting to get fed.

Back inside, we're greeted by the sight of Basel with a big patch over one eye. He'd ended up bleeding from a big gash, because he tried to give chase and walked right into some branches, just as Christy had predicted. So they came home, had a snack, and Basel read *Skating to Antarctica* while Christy had a nap.

Patrick busies himself watering the beagles, and I busy myself feeding everybody else. As a concession, Patrick offers me a rabbit that he's thrown in the back of his truck.

"Won't a fox steal the rabbit if you just let it sit there?"

"It's frozen already," Patrick points out. "It wouldn't have any luck."

"Me neither," I say sadly.

Their faces wet with water, the beagles commandeer the couch and collapse into exhausted doggy heaps. Patrick sits down next to the woodstove, unwinds the duct tape wrapped around the top of his rubberized boots, throws the boots into a corner, and lumbers over to join the beagles on the couch. One-eyed, Basel is following Christy around, hoping for attention, and John is sitting in an armchair, waiting to be fed. Today, nobody took a shot so the guns don't need to be cleaned, but there's melting snow to be mopped up and wet clothes strewn in front of the woodstove. It is hissing in annoyance.

Dinner is dry dog food for the beagles, wet dog food for Basel, and store-bought spaghetti and hamburger meatballs for the humans. I imagine the rabbit is eating Mr. McGregor's French beans and lettuce. Poor Mr. Fox gets nothing.

CHAPTER EIGHT

🐾 🐾 🐾

The O in the No

The cat that cannot reach the meat says it stinks.
— *Persian proverb.*

Seven A.M. Sunday. There is no hunting today, so John is sitting morosely at his breakfast, eating French toast made with warm eggs just laid by the hens. I swear the chickens looked proud of themselves when I went to the henhouse this morning. Some days, they are too busy bickering to notice me hovering by the door in my pajamas and boots. Other times, they press forward, expecting me to give them nice tasty worms. Today, they practically stuck a name tag on each shell so I'd know which hen laid which egg. By the time I trundled back to the human house, John was sitting at table, waiting for his breakfast, and reading *Uncle Henry's* because I hide *Guns & Ammo* on church day. *Uncle Henry's* has a "Firearms" section that he checks religiously. He also looks for snowmobiles, ATVs, and tractors.

His mother wanders in the kitchen, looking for coffee.

"Hey Mum," he calls without preamble. "You want a peacock?"

"No," she says flatly.

"But peacocks are useful," I interject. "They're guard birds!"

"So are geese," she points out, unimpressed.

"Patrick should get geese," John says, as if he's stating a matter oft-discussed and definitively settled, though I have no idea why Patrick needs guarding. He flaps *Uncle Henry's* in his mother's general direction. "Someone's offering peacocks for free. Also free Nubians, free chickens, free horses, free cows, and hmm,"—he flips the page—"some alpacas for over a thousand each. That's deluded," he snorts. "Who's going to pay that kind of money for alpacas around here?"

"Any llamas?" I ask hopefully.

John checks the pages. "No llamas," he reports gravely.

"Llamas guard sheep," I say, in my backwards way. "I want sheep."

"We used to have sheep," Ruth says absently, as she pours orange juice for herself and settles into her chair in the living room.

"I thought you were getting a flock?" I ask, because they've been talking about getting sheep since I met them last fall at the end of deer hunting season. But it is always "not now; in the spring," for this is when the new lambs arrive. No one tries to start a new flock in the middle of a Maine winter. Now that spring is here, there's no real excuse not to get some.

"Well," she demurs, "it's hard."

I don't know if this is a yes or a no.

She adds: "Sheep don't cooperate when you go to shear them."

"I can do it," I volunteer, ". . . as long as John helps." I look over at him. He's studying the gun section in *Uncle Henry's* again, and not paying the least attention to the conversation.

I've sheared sheep before, having been taught by a parishioner in my dad's church after he retired from the ministry and kept on preaching anyway. It's easy to do badly, and difficult to do well. Shearing, that is, though I suppose it's also true of preaching. The only way to improve is to practice on a live, bleating flock. It is not a skill that can be learned from books. I'm not afraid of the shears or worried about hurting the animal. They struggle, but not because shearing is painful. They struggle the way a little kid struggles when he has to sit buckled in the back seat on a long car ride to grandma's house, and he's jacked up on Skittles and has to pee really badly. Are we there yet are we there yet are we there yet? Baaaa! Can we stop now can we stop now can we stop now? Baaaa! The sheep sound like they've been tossed into a bag full of cats, but it's just because they're cranky. It really is as simple as that.

I like the "Miscellaneous" section of *Uncle Henry's*, because it's always interesting to see what doesn't fit in a category when we're already talking about the kind of flotsam and jetsam that shows up at swap meets. For example:

Three religious statues, about four feet tall and in excellent shape. Great decorations for home or gazebo!

These are Jesus-y versions of lawn gnomes, which sometimes land in *Uncle Henry's* under the category, "Sporting Goods." Or:

Three burial plots, each one can be used for burial plus three cremations.

If anything belongs under "Miscellaneous," it's a family plot the whole family can share!

Katahdin sheep, no need to shear, 5 ewe lambs, 4 2-yr-old ewes, 1 gorgeous ram, and 3 meat lambs.

This is a good one. Originally bred in Maine, the Katahdin sheep is named after the tallest mountain in the state. It likes the cold, loves the snow, and the ewes don't need help giving birth. But the sheep's most unusual feature is that it doesn't grow wool. It has hair like a dog, but it only sheds once a year. So it's a sheep-dog, not to be confused with a sheepdog.

Then there's the business of the "meat lamb," which puts things rather too bluntly for city folks who buy their apples at the store. "Amateurs," I mutter to myself. In these parts, it's:

Pigs ripe for eating. One dollar a pound live weight.

The ads in *Uncle Henry's* offer miniature portraits of rural life, offering life and death in one stroke.

Free piglets. Get started on your Christmas sausages now!

Rabbits, pet or meat.

Roosters for sale, $3 dollars each. If not sold, will be in the stew pot.

This is a pragmatist's poetry, unsentimental and spare. These lines conjure up images of bucolic pastures where the flowers always bloom, and then they rip off the curtain to reveal the brutal machinery making dead roses smell good. Make-believe isn't well tolerated in a world where good manure comes composted, aged, and screened. I sip my black coffee, flip through more ads, and marvel at the tiny tempests erupting when hopes collide with reality:

I have a pair of Woman's Steel Toe boots for sale size 8. I bought them thinking 1. They'd fit and 2. I was suppose [sic] to be moving in with my friend and working on the horse farm she was gonna buy, I take size 7 ½ so they're a little too big and make my feet go numb. ONLY worn a couple times, I'm selling because I'm not moving in with my friend and no longer have a use for them. I will not ship sorry.

Woman's Plus Size 24 White Wedding Dress. Comes w/ train/ veil/ storage bag/ puff slip.

It has long sleeves. It has never been worn.

Wanted: Older gentleman. Do you have one you're not using?

Then there are the little mysteries:

I have an unknown sexed bearded dragon.

Arthritic salmon with flies in box.

3 year old running walker female trained on coyote cold nose will run non stop parents were cat dogs.

Gaggle of running gravelys. Too old to pull the straps. Two gravely walk behinds.

Twin nannies, does usually triplets.

There is an entire world of fantasy tucked inside these pages, should you care to find it. It all depends on where you look, and your point of view on the small business of being alive.

Abruptly, Patrick's head pops through the garage-side door of his mother's house, followed by the rest of him. He wanders into the kitchen and stamps his feet, his cold nose sniffing coffee. "What you got there?" Patrick asks me without preamble, a vague note of accusation in his voice.

In reply, I wave *Uncle Henry's* at him.

"Been looking for that," he announces loudly, as he reaches over and takes it from me. "Every Thursday, I take *Uncle Henry's* and read it on the crapper."

"But it's Sunday," I say.

"Yup," he glowers, and stalks off to the bathroom.

As usual, Fox News is blaring in the background. Predictably, the guests are complaining about health care and mocking Dems who are whining about death threats. On her Facebook page, Sarah Palin has posted the names of pro-health care reform Democrats and labeled them with crosshairs. So what's the big deal? This is all in good fun, the talking TV people explain. Obama, Oprah, Olbermann: only lily-livered liberals would get upset about being in the crosshairs because the crosshairs are *fake*. No actual guns being pointed and no triggers being pulled. Stop complaining, ya sissies! On and on they gabble, the Fox TV people mocking the alphabet channels and I wonder if they know that a fox is considered vermin by people who read Aesop. Nowadays, however, that's pretty much no one, because these fables come with morals, and morals are bad for business.

For folks who tweet, here is the limerick version of the "Fox and the Grapes," from *Baby's Own Aesop*, 1887:

> This Fox has a longing for grapes:
>
> He jumps, but the bunch still escapes.
>
> So he goes away sour;
>
> And, 'tis said, to this hour
>
> Declares that he's no taste for grapes.

The fable is the origin of the phrase, "He's got sour grapes," which is a way of poking fun at bitter folks badmouthing fine things out of their reach. But Aesop was a Greek slave and a pagan to boot, so who gives a flying fig what he thinks? We're indivisible Americans, pledging allegiance to one nation under God, dammit, not to one fox under grapes!

As it happens, these same greedy foxes also appear in the Bible, and it's pretty much SOS for poor Reynard: Shoot On Sight. "Catch for us the foxes, the little foxes, that ruin the vineyards, our vines," sings Solomon the Wise in his Song of Songs, because foxes really do eat grapes, though they'd rather eat mice. Without grapes, there's no wine. Without wine, there's no women. Without women, there's no song. No bottles of plonk, no gallons of Gallo, no champagne wishes and caviar dreams. Just plain water at royal weddings, and Christ isn't on the guest list to perform handy miracles. The faithful panicked. Obligingly, eighteenth-century Baptist preacher John Gill unleashed a righteous rant damning the fox to extermination. Thundering mightily from the pulpit, Gill warned his flock that foxes practice wily ruses. Such tricks confuse good Christians, for foxes are very appealing. Yet by their nature, foxes are deceitful,

> they put on sheep's clothing, transform themselves into angels of light, mimic the voice of Gospel ministers, use their phrases and expressions, that they may not be easily discovered; and are abominable in their principles and practices, and to be shunned by all good men.

Try defending foxes after that sermon full of holy hellfire and brimstone. My father never preached like that. He preferred heartwarming parables that made everybody feel better about their place in the world. He told stories of honoring God through good deeds, and reminded the congregation to love thy neighbor as thyself. His sermons were the polar opposite of the kind of stuff Gill wrote in his remarkable and very long *Exposition of the Entire Bible*. Published in the 1740s, it identified Solomon's fox as a false teacher hiding God's truths. Such a creature hides in plain sight, like the serial killer who tells Miss Prim his date, "I'm a bad, bad boy," with a crooked smile and a twinkle in his eye, and she feels lucky instead of running away at full speed.

"He will beat you all at piety," Samuel Johnson had commented of the wicked winners in this world. It's one of the first things I think whenever bibles start getting thumped at me by women cloaked in humility but wearing expensive boobs. I'm good, thank you. Go thump yourself.

"Stop watching TV," John interrupts me.

"But . . ." I protest, wiggling my hands at the screen. "A puppy is going to be on Fox News!"

"They'll show the dog again," he says drily, tugging me towards the back door. "I need you to be my spotter. I've got to sight in my rifle."

"Why?"

"So you'll have venison for supper this fall."

"I thought your hunting rifle has a scope on it," I say.

"Yep," he replies briskly.

"So what's there to do?"

In reply, he pulls me to my feet and starts prodding me outside. "Targets are already set up out back," he tells me as he tugs me through the sunroom and onto the deck. Then he adds, as an afterthought. "They're political signs."

"We're shooting at political signs?" I repeat, as visions of sour grapes dance in my head.

"We're aiming for the O," John instructs, as he hands me a spotting scope and parks me next to the railing on the deck. "Stay up here," he orders, as he walks down the steps and starts setting up a shooting table on a patch of ground to my left. If he reaches up with his right hand, he'd be able to grab my left foot. "Don't ever get in front of a man with a gun," he reminds me. "And confirm where I am *before* you start moving, if, say, you decide you have to pee. I'll always tell you before I'm going to shoot. I won't take a shot until you give me a verbal response."

He natters on with the usual safety instructions, but my brain is still stuck on ". . . we're aiming for the O." Oh no! my head shrieks. The political signs are pretty far away from the house but one is black with white letters, the other is yellow with black letters. Somebody has spray painted them with red

paint that didn't quite stick, so it has slid down in the manner
of movie marquee blood. Right then, I make up my mind. If
it turns out these are signs announcing "God hates Winos" or
"Hobosexuality is a sin," I am not letting him shoot at them. I
don't care if there isn't a picture of Osama or Omarosa playing
The Villain. When you're in the middle of nowhere, everybody knows what you're doing in your backyard. I refuse to
end up on Fox News because John's been shooting holes into
right-wing arguments.

"Where did they come from?" I ask with trepidation.

"My mother picked them up," he answers absently. He's
busy choosing real bullets to put into his gun so he can "sight
in his rifle," whatever that means. I can see the Ruger just fine,
and so can he. I think he just wants me to keep him company.

"From . . . ?" I prod.

"From the road," he answers drily.

"She didn't raid somebody's front lawn, did she?"

"Dunno," he shrugs. He's doesn't care where she got them.
It's totally beside the point. He's too busy getting comfortable
in his chair, twiddling with sandbags used to support the gun,
and lining up the crosshairs on a real target that he plans to hit.

Under the guise of straightening up, I walk up to the lawn
signs so I can read them up close. Much to my relief, they're
just the answers to a pop quiz on prime numbers. The black
sign reads, "No on Question 4." The yellow sign reads, "No
on Question 2." That's it. There's no fine print at the bottom,
no supplemental information on the back, stating "Paid for
By the Committee for Yes on Question Three," that sort of
thing. Looking as official as I can, I smooth and straighten the
cardboard signs, and then I trundle back and resume my place
on the deck. Leaning forward, I check the signs again through
the scope. Then I wait.

And I wait.

Then I wait some more.

Pensively, I fart. Better to get it out now, I tell myself. Otherwise it might slip out at the exact moment that he takes a shot, and then it will spark a fire and make the house explode. This would not endear me to John's parents, who already don't think very much of me.

Phhhhlllttt.

It squeezes out like a question mark with just a little curl at the end. Quickly, I glance over at him, wondering if he heard it. I only care because he tells me I cut the cheese the moment I fall asleep. He thinks it's adorable. I'm pretty sure he's making up the whole "sleep fart" thing just to annoy me, but I also don't want him thinking I'm napping up here.

"You got your ears on?" John interrupts me loudly.

"Huh?"

"Put on your ears," he orders crisply, gesturing to a thickly padded headset resting next to me. Obediently, I smooth my hair and pull on the shooting earmuffs. The world is suddenly silenced.

"Ready?" he asks.

"SORT OF," I yell back. I lower my head and take an experimental peek through the spotting scope, which is basically a large, heavy telescope mounted on a rugged tripod. Through the looking glass, all I see is a greenish blur of grass and trees smushing together.

"We're aiming for the O in the No," he reminds me. His voice is muffled, as if he's inside a jar swallowed by a hippo.

"JUST A SEC!" I holler, leaning forward and adjusting the focus until I locate the first sign. "FOUND IT!" I yell. Then I wait.

And I wait.

Then I wait some more.

Nothing's happening, so I look away from the scope. He's hunched over his rifle, taking aim, adjusting, and taking aim again. This is going to take a while. I resume my ready position, leaning forward and gluing my left eye to the scope, my world reduced to the O in the No. The sun is out. It's a beautiful day to be sitting outside on the deck. Ahh, nature. Ahh, sunshine. Ahh, sparrows swooping in the air and sitting on my head. Go away, bird! I'm workin' here!

O . . . O . . . O . . .

Crack!

"OW!" I yelp. "Hey!"

I am up on the deck. He is down on the ground and a few feet in front of me. His shell casing flew up and hit me on the shin. It stings but not badly. It's more the sheer surprise of being flicked when you're not expecting it, kind of like sitting in first grade home room next to a boy who likes you. Which is more or less exactly what's happening here.

"Did I hit the target?" he calls up, removing his ears and standing up for a stretch.

"Uh huh," I grumble, taking off my ears and leaning back from the scope. "You hit the O in the center," I inform him through the railing. "And, by the way, your shell casing hit me on the leg."

He looks up at me and blinks. "Okay," he replies, sounding completely unsympathetic to my injured dignity. Abruptly, he puts his ears back on and starts readying the rifle again. "Ready?" he calls up.

"YES," I reply, pulling on my padded headset and putting my eye back on the scope, looking again at the O, now with a + in the middle.

Crack! Crack crack! Crack!

"Ow! Ow ow! OWWWWW!" I yelp. I squint at him, annoyed, and then check the scope. There's now a neat little cluster of holes in the middle of the O.

"How'd I do?" he calls up.

"Fine," I confirm grumpily. "Dead center each time."

He reloads. We repeat this exercise until all the Big and Little Os have received his full attention. He is very thorough about things like this, which is why I am very happy with him.

"Okay!" he announces, standing up and removing his headset. "Moving!"

"Good!" I exclaim in relief. "If you go over a few feet I won't get hit by any more shell casings."

"No, I'm mean we're *moving*," he clarifies, as he heads off to start the utility vehicle lounging nearby.

"To where?" I ask in surprise.

"The field!" he hollers back over his shoulder.

"Why? Aren't we done?" I fluster. "I mean, you hit the target. What's there to do?"

In response, he drives up to collect the ammo, the scope, the headsets, and the very heavy gun. "Hop on," he orders, picking me up and plopping me on the seat next to him.

"But . . ."

"We're just getting started! This can take all day!" He grins at me happily as he secures all the stuff to the back of the cart. Soon enough, we're jouncing and bouncing on the splendored grass, driving to the far end of the sixteen-acre front lawn. He parks in a random spot, nudges me out, unloads the cart, and then declares, "You guard the stuff, okay?" He gives me a look, and out pops another one of his maxims: "Never leave a gun unattended."

"Okay," I say agreeably. "Is it loaded?"

" 'Course not," he replies. Then he pauses, gives me another appraising look, and carefully takes back all three boxes of ammo and sticks them in his pockets.

"What's the big deal? I mean . . . ?" I gesture around the large field, surrounded on three sides by walls of woodland off a rural road in Maine, and raise my eyebrow.

"Last thing you want is for someone to swipe it because you just left it lying there. You think you're alone out here."

He gives me another look. "You're not." With that, he hops behind the wheel and prepares to drive off, stranding me out here with the gun and no snacks.

"Where are you going?" I wail.

"I gotta get the table." And off he zooms, picking up furniture so he can turn Nature into his living room.

An hour later, we're at two hundred yards in the big field to the side of the house, seated around a heavy wooden table and shooting at sheets of newspaper stapled to a wooden stand he built for target practice. A spray-painted orange dot marks the middle of the *Bethel Citizen*. At this distance, it's easy to spot the dot but not much else. The edges of the wooden stand disappear into the backdrop of the forest, and when he shoots the paper, the bullets pass right through, leaving tidy holes that look just like typeset. I finally understand why he needs me to look through the scope as he shoots. Without me giving him feedback, he has no idea if he's hitting the target. A man needs his girl to tell him the truth.

Crack!

"TOO FAR TO THE RIGHT!" I tell him through the headset. "YOU'RE HITTING WOOD!"

He nods, clicks a dial on the sight to adjust it, then leans forward on the shooting table, takes aim, and shoots the target again.

Crack! Crack crack!

I search through the sighting scope to find the holes. "TOO HIGH AND STILL TOO FAR TO THE RIGHT!" I finally announce. "BETTER! BUT STILL NOT ON TARGET!"

Sighing, he removes his headset, hops into the utility vehicle, and drives up to retrieve the paper, leaving me to guard the firearm. In the distance, I can see him inspecting the stand for fresh damage, and holding the newspaper up to the light, exposing the small bullet holes that he made in the wrong place. Ruefully, he shakes his head and staples up a fresh piece of newspaper already spray painted with a florescent orange dot in the middle. I watch from the shooting table, then sit down and look through the crosshair sights of his unloaded rifle, seeing what he sees when he shoots. It's not a panorama. It's a pinhole. I can see the target more clearly with the shooting scope, but it's still a very narrow slice of a large range of possibilities. Pointed in the wrong direction, scope and sight will be aiming at nothing.

That's the thing about guns. It takes effort to keep them in perspective.

He drives back and we resume the process, shooting and adjusting, shooting and adjusting, until he starts getting them all on the paper, and then he starts hitting bull's-eyes. Now I understand why he likes me being next to him, keeping an eye on the big picture while he narrows his to a single target in the distance. We have the same goal, which is fresh meat on the table. Working together is much nicer than working alone.

In the distance, on the far edge of the field, a guy is driving up on an ATV. He is making sure that we see him before he approaches.

"Guess it's time to stop shooting," I say, removing my earmuffs and fluffing up my damp hair. "The gun's probably too hot anyway." Each shot generate heats inside the barrels. Eventually, the metal expands and starts affecting accuracy, so you have to let the gun cool, same as you would the engine of an old car in the desert.

"'Happiness is a warm gun'!" John quips.

I look at him blankly.

"You know, The Beatles?"

I shake my head, because I have no idea what he's talking about.

He gives me an incredulous look. "You've never heard the song, 'Happiness Is a Warm Gun'? From the *White Album*?"

"Well, of course I've heard of the Beatles," I crab. But I'm pretty sure he's making the song up, because the Beatles sing about yellow submarines and lonely heart's clubs bands. They don't sing satirical songs about weapons for white people.

He shakes his head in amazement. "North Korean spy," he mutters.

"Me and David Chung," I laugh. David's a diplomat's kid. Last summer, we were the only two people at the karaoke clubs in Seoul who didn't know the words to any of the American pop songs. During David's formative years, he was being carted around places like Jakarta, Kathmandu, and Switzerland. Me, I was in Houlton, Maine, practicing violin. So our childhoods were pretty much the same.

"I sleep with my shotgun when you're off on one of your jaunts," John drawls lazily.

"What!"

"Lots of guys sleep with their guns," he adds earnestly. "Patrick sleeps with one under the mattress."

"What!" I exclaim again.

"Like I said, 'Happiness is a warm gun'!" He raises an eyebrow. "Would you rather that you came home and found a blond hair on your side of the bed, or a little bit of gun grease?"

"Neither, thank you very much," I say nicely.

"Then stop abandoning me," he says pointedly.

To be fair, the only thing he ogles in bed, besides me, is the Cabela's catalog or *Ski* magazine. "Humph," I say. "Humph," I try again, hoping to say something pithy but I can't think of anything. Luckily for me, Norm the Neighbor rolls up in an ATV, rescuing me from having to say something I can be held to later. Norm looks like Gunny the Drill Sergeant on the Military Channel, and he goes to gun shows with Don. He's always neatly dressed in khakis and a button down cotton shirt. He's not a big talker but likes to know what's going on. Out here, the sound of a rifle being sighted-in is

unmistakable. The pattern of crack! . . . crack! . . . crack! . . .
plus the time of year, gives it away.

"Did you hear that we got moose permits this year?" John
asks him.

"Which district?" Norm asks interestedly.

"This one," John answers. "Both Patrick and my dad have
a permit. We're gonna have moosemeat this year!" he crows.

"You mean *if* you guys get a moose," I say pointedly.

"We will get a moose," he says firmly. "That's 1,000 pounds
of meat per moose."

"That's a lot of meat," I agree dreamily, imagining the
sheer bliss of having a literal ton of raw material to experiment with in the kitchen. Cartoon images of moose steaks
dance in my head, along with onions, cabbages, and smiling
stalks of celery.

If a Maine hunter gets a moose permit, he will take the
week off from work, and his boss will understand. If the boss
does not hunt, however, the guy with the moose permit is shit
out of luck. The choice looms: get fired, or go moose hunting. A fair number of guys would rather lose their job than
miss this chance. Because nobody goes moose hunting alone,
each permit holder can add two names to the same permit,
and these people are allowed to carry a gun on the hunt. Don
and John are on Patrick's permit, and Patrick and John are
on Don's. Once a moose is down, that's it. It's one permit per
group, and everybody shares the spoils.

". . . so that's our summer weekends," John says, poking me
out of my reverie. "We have to start tracking!"

"When does the season start?"

"Not until October."

"But we start tracking—"

"—now."

It's June. It's four months before anyone can take a shot, and
the preparations have already started. This is a once-in-a-lifetime

opportunity, John says. His father and Patrick have been apply-ing for permits for decades and never won the moose lottery. This year, they both did. The season in their designated zone lasts exactly six days, Monday through Saturday. No hunting on Sundays. That day God rests. Six days is not a lot of time, because moose hunting is a lot like searching for a really large set of lost house keys: you know where they usually hang, and they're always popping up when you least expect it, but as soon as you start looking for the dang things, they're impossible to find.

Norm nods, clearly pleased by the news. "Been seeing them everywhere!" he enthuses. "There was a bull in my gar-den this morning. He just moseyed on through. Didn't slow down, didn't speed up." He shakes his head, half insulted by the moose's indifference to his beautiful vegetables.

"You should have taken a shot out your window!" John teases. "Moose and potatoes for breakfast, mmm!"

"Ah yup," Norm coughs. "But I stopped applying for moose permits a while back."

"How come?" I ask curiously.

Norm shrugs. "Too old for it. Plus, moose meat—well," he smiles sheepishly, "let's just say that the bowels refuse to coop-erate. Venison is fine. But moosemeat?" Ruefully, he shakes his head. "Nope."

"Oh no!" I exclaim sympathetically. "I *understand*!"

"Don't get her started!" John warns him, because he's not interested in chit-chatting about malfunctioning human digestive systems, especially when he's outside in a strawberry field holding a warm gun on one side and me on the other. It's a beautiful day, and there's loads of sunlight left for all kinds of projects, such as hiking out back and hoping to step in a big steaming pile of poop, otherwise known as "looking for moose sign."

Which is, John tells Norm, what we're doing this afternoon.

"We are?" I say in surprise.

Norm laughs with good humor, and starts up the engine. With a little wave, he zooms away, heading in the general direction of the Big House. I assume he's got a new gun he wants to show Don, as that's the usual reason for him to come by. We watch as he disappears up the hill, out of sight, out of range. The field resumes its quiet.

"Gun's cooled down," John nudges, and prepares to start shooting again.

As I settle back into position, check the scope, and put on my ears, I wonder if Norm knows that *Uncle Henry's* is an excellent *digestif* for the hunter who is strong of will but weak of bowel. Like a fortune in a crisp cookie called "Chinese" but is 100 percent American, it finishes off a meal that won't stick to your ribs or hang around until tomorrow. Confucius say: Here's a gem of Yankee wisdom posted under "Agricultural Equipment," presented in its stark, inscrutable totality:

Red sex link laying hens. Scales can weigh 5 to 20 pounds. $500.

CHAPTER NINE

❦ ❦ ❦

Do Not Feed the Bears

Procrastination is the art of keeping up with yesterday.
– Archy the Cockroach, from Don Marquis,
Archy and Mehitabel, 1927

Weeks later, as fall draws near, the morning sun means that John and I will be bushwhacking up the mountain in back of the Big House. The reason is to look for moose and deer sign, because this is what hunters do. It's also just to get to the top of the mountain, because it's there, and it's a beautiful day. Dressed in hiking gear and ready to go, I start filling water bottles to stuff into our daypacks as John sits at the chair by the door and starts lacing on hiking boots.

"Just so you know," Don says laconically to John from his lounger in the living room, "the McKennas were back there, setting up bear bait."

(. . . bear bait?)

"They quit hunting bears," Don continues. "Now they run a little guide business for tourists who want to see bears. But don't be surprised if you smell something."

(. . . smell something?)

"Err," I say, raising my hand to object.

"Not likely you'll find yourself in the same spot," Don drawls, pointedly ignoring the surprised look on my face, "but no need to worry. Bears get timid as soon as the bait comes out because they know the season's starting. They'll just run away from you."

I stand and blink, processing his words. Heck, even the squirrels don't run when they see me coming. To animals, I'm about as threatening as a helium balloon.

"Some of the guys in Patrick's rabbit club go back there and set up bear traps," Don adds, looking pointedly at John, who nods to acknowledge that he heard, finishes lacing up his boots and straightens up, ready to go on a backyard adventure. "Don't worry," Don says, aggrieved by my foolish yuppie anxiety. "It's too early. There's none up there" he pauses, eyeballing me speculatively, "—yet."

Seeing the look of consternation on my face, John grins wickedly. "They won't trigger when you step on them," he teases me. "They're calibrated for at least three hundred pounds." He guffaws as he wraps me in a hug. "You're not there yet!"

"Good to know," I say, trying unsuccessfully to squirm out of his grasp.

"C'mon, plumpkin," John says happily, as he tucks me under his arm and heads out the door. "We won't see any bears."

But now I have bears on the brain. He sets me down and we start up the side of the mountain, beginning with the familiar logging trails that are wide and worn. As we trudge up, the angle getting steeper with every step, I am thinking there are bears for sure up there—at least three males, Don had said, and probably more. And bear traps. "What do they use for bait?" I blurt.

John snorts. "The kind of garbage you'd find in the dumpster behind a Dunkin' Donuts. Stale donuts and sweet stuff."

"Not rotting fish heads?"

"Nope. They go for the sweets."

An ad in *Uncle Henry's* states it very clearly. *Barrels of bear bait, full of Hostess Pasteries* [sic]. Naturally, this offer appeared in the "Sporting Items" section of the magazine.

We keep trudging uphill. The trail is getting steeper and no longer resembles a logging trail. It's a single track path used by moose and deer. It is very narrow, and barely a trail at all. There are old tracks but no fresh sign.

"Do you think the McKennas have been up here setting traps?" I ask John anxiously.

"No."

"Why not?"

"First of all, they're bear baiters, not trappers. Second, they're not going to hike. They're carrying fifty-pound barrels of bait. You saw the kind of shit they lug around at the Trapper's."

He's referring to the annual Trapper's Weekend held in a big field in Bethel. It's an exciting two-day event full of politically incorrect activities, attended by the sorts of unshaven white folks who think that the federal government is a mind-control plot. I always have a great time, because most of the regulars can't figure out if I'm a New Yorker shopping for a fur coat, or an Appalachian Trail hiker who got really lost. Here, you can buy apothecary jars full of powerful animal scents, antique ammo ("highly collectible," John tells me), Daniel Boone raccoon hats with all of their teeth, and handsome woven baskets that come with leather straps so you can carry them like a backpack. The biggest baskets are the size and texture of trash cans. Fill them up with Twinkies and Ho-Hos, and you've got a redneck buffet strapped to your back.

Out in the woods, the contents of the basket get dumped out in a spot where bears are likely to find it. As soon as their noses lead them to the mound of sticky sweets, bears will stand there and eat themselves into a sugar coma. The idea is to keep on replenishing the feast, turning the bears into the forest equivalent of college freshman at the cafeteria. Determined humans know that a food source is the best place to lie in wait for elusive prey. Eventually, the hungriest ones will show up. Then, when they least expect it—BOOM! They get shot by cameras carried by excitable parents. Everybody goes home happy, including the bears.

John concludes, tartly: "It's not the sort of thing that lends itself to bushwhacking."

"But . . ."

"No," John repeats firmly. "There are no bear traps up here. But," he adds cheerfully, "there *are* bears."

Maine has bears. Many tourists enjoy treating them like pets. When this happens, the bears eat them. However, this mostly happens in Alaska, and the bears are grizzlies. Maine bears are black bears, which are like monochromatic pandas, except they're not from China, and they don't like bamboo leaves. Black bears adore baked goods. As a result, bear talk is everywhere at the Trapper's Weekend, because bears in a sugar coma take skills to move. Every year, you'll overhear snippets of conversations about this guy, I'm not naming names but you know who it is, takin' bears illegally and what are we gonna do about it? In one area, a man will be demonstrating chainsaw sculpting, shaping life-size black bears out of standing logs. A few guys will be watching him, but the chief draw is always the master trapper talking in the main tent. He explains: Mouse traps will catch mice. Ant traps will catch ants. Fly traps will catch flies. They are not interchangeable. Traps that do not trap are unacceptable. Marshmallows will attract raccoons but not housecats. Donuts will attract bears, but also cousin Al. If cousin Al is over three hundred pounds, he's in trouble. Here is a good safety measure to make sure that cousin Al stays away: put up a sign, because bears can't read. A good sign says something like this: *Do Not Feed the Bears.*

John snorts at my citified qualms, and keeps bushwhacking up the side. "And no," he adds for good measure, speaking directly to the thought bubble popping over my head, "tapping sticks will not keep away the bears."

Clearly, this technique also fails to impress flies. Grumpily, I toss my sticks, take off my hat, swat at the flies, and pick up my pace. "Stupid flies," I complain. "Go away!" This has no effect, except maybe it gets the flies to tell their friends to be fruitful and multiply.

"Argh!" I exclaim, and start sprinting uphill in an attempt to outrun my fans. My Flight from the Flies means that I am now ahead of John, who is plodding upwards at a steady pace, without a single fly anywhere near him.

A few yards up, I spot a pile of droppings.

"What do you think that is?" I ask breathlessly when he comes into range. "Bear turds?"

"Nope," he shakes his head, and keeps walking without slowing down. "Old moose poop."

"Those aren't the right shape," I object, swatting at the flies around my head. "Those aren't nuggets. They're *turds*."

"Not turds," he shakes his head. "Definitely old moose poop."

"But you didn't stop and *look*."

"Didn't need to."

I am not convinced. "Do you think it's a good or a bad thing that we're arguing about this?"

"We're not arguing," he says dryly. "We're having a discussion."

"Humph," I declare (swat, slap, swat), but I decide to let the subject drop because it's difficult to be annoyed and bushwhack at the same time.

We go higher up the side of the mountain. We're about an hour in when a new pyramid of slick blackish turds pops up. "There," I say decisively, standing by the evidence. "That's definitely bear." I put my hands on my hips and glare at him, willing him to challenge me.

"Agreed," he says simply, and leans over and inspects it. "Yup," he stands up and nods his head. "He's been eating blackberries."

I lean over and sniff the pile. I can see bits of blackberry stems and the color is right, but I can't smell anything except grass and fruity sweetness. "Blackberries," I echo pensively, because maybe there are some berries left on the bushes, and if there's enough of them, I can make cobbler. "But how do you know it's a 'he'?"

"I don't," he shrugs, and polishes off a water bottle. "But you better hope it's not a mama bear leaving fresh poop around here. If it is a mama bear with cubs, and we run into her, we're in trouble. So keep talking!" he teases. "That'll scare them away!"

"Har, har. Anyway," I add peevishly, "I think a male bear made those turds."

He snorts, because there's really no way to tell. We keep walking, searching for signs of moose activity, but it's deer that seem to prefer this patch of the woods. It's not all that surprising, because moose like swamps, which is the exact opposite of a mountaintop. "Our moose hunting district splits exactly down the Notch," John says, as he thinks aloud for my benefit. This is helpful when I'm not reading his mind but scanning for bears of little brain that prefer "hunny" over humans.

"South side is okay, north side isn't," John adds. "You know that dirt road we drove down the other week?"

"Yes."

"It marks the end of our district."

"So if the moose crosses the road, you can't shoot it?"

"Pretty much. That's a pretty big disadvantage for moose hunting. Imagine how you'd feel if you spent all day tracking that moose, and when you finally sighted it, it had crossed the road."

"Why did the moose cross the road?" I quip. "To get to the other side, so he can go nyah nyah at the hunter!"

"Moose don't go nyah nyah," John corrects me archly.

"It kinda looks like that, with those big antlers, like fat fingers waggling on the side of the head."

John glares at me. He does not have a sense of humor about moose hunting.

Suddenly, up to one side, there's a rustling in the bushes.

"Did you hear that?" I whisper loudly under my breath.

"Hear what?" John drawls in a normal tone of voice.

The crashing noises get louder. They are very close. Something is up there, and it must be a . . . a . . . bear! my brain shrieks. We've stumbled into her den and now she's going to eat us! Goodbye cruel world! In my head I start singing the death aria from *Tosca*, because it's a really good death aria.

"Stop that," John chides. "It's not a bear." He points to an empty spot a few feet in front of us. A split second later, a great ball of feathers tumbles out of the bushes and flops in front of me, landing right in the spot where he's pointing. The bird's making a funny call and it looks like something's wrong with one wing. Abruptly, she starts dancing around in circles, dragging one wing and generally making a perfect spectacle of herself. We stand there, watching the antics with amazement.

"Is she injured?" I whisper to John, relieved that the bird isn't a bear but wondering if she should be rescued. Strangely, it doesn't occur to me to ask him to catch it for dinner.

"Naw," John drawls. "That's a mama grouse. There are babies around. You almost stepped on them. She's trying to draw your attention so you won't go after them."

"Babies? Where?" I whip my head around, scanning the path for chicks, but I don't see any.

"There," he points, indicating a scatter of lumpy dirt near the patch of trees I just passed.

"I don't see anything," I say, and start off in the direction that he's pointing.

THUMP. Behind me, the mama grouse starts frantically dancing and dragging in the opposite direction.

"Maybe move away from there before you give her a heart attack," John suggests dryly. I turn towards the dirt where the babies are supposed to be, and then I turn back to John in order to ask him to show them to me. Just like that, the mama grouse has vanished.

"Hey!" I exclaim in surprise. "Where'd she go?"

"Up there," John points, indicating a spot a few feet up the side of the forest, and takes a lazy swig from his water bottle. "While you were paying attention to her, the babies all ran and hid in a new spot. When you were trying to find them, she flew off."

"So you know where the chicks are?" I ask skeptically.

"Yep." He waves at a shady spot under a nearby tree. "There's a whole bunch of them, tucked under leaves."

"I don't believe you," I inform him tartly, and start heading to the tree to take a closer look.

"Er," John starts, lifting a cautionary hand . . .

. . . and out of the forest the mama grouse tumbles again, a flurry of feathers dramatically playing out her fake deathbed scene. "Who's the diva now?" I think crossly to myself. She circles and drags, circles and drags. She's not really a large bird but her feathers are puffed up. Also, wildlife looks bigger when it's dancing in front of your face. It tends to shrink up when it's on your plate.

"C'mon," John tugs me, because he knows I can play this game all day. "Stop bothering the wildlife."

"Why doesn't she react to you?" I ask curiously.

"Because *I'm* not the one smushing her chicks," he sniffs with an air of superiority.

"I'm not doing it on purpose," I sulk.

"Don't matter. C'mon," he tugs me forward. "You're practically stepping on the babies again."

As we move away, I hear the tiniest of tiny sounds—"peep, peep!"—followed by the whoosh of ruffled feathers. This time, I don't turn around.

෨෨ ෨෨ ෨෨

A few hours later, we get to the top of the mountain, which is maybe not the top, because all I can see are trees. It could be a false peak. Sighing, John gets out the GPS, which decides not to work. So he gets out the compass. It too seems to be broken. I didn't bring any gear because this was supposed to be a quick scamper up the mountain in the backyard. It's turning into The Survivalist Tale out of Chaucer.

I'm not worried. Mostly, I'm peeved. We didn't bring supplies for a daylong hike, it's hot, and I'm hungry. And why, pray tell, did the dancing bird become a grouse as soon as it became a mama? Suddenly, there was no more of this "partridge" business. As far as John was concerned, it was "mama grouse" this, and "mama grouse" that. Given that my bear turned out to be a grouse, it seems only right that I should turn into one too.

"Waa," I complain, as we turn around and start heading back down the mountain. The exit strategy is this: we go downhill. That's it? That's it. Turns out, the hike up didn't follow a path. We were mostly following our imaginations, for what looks like a deer trail from one direction turns out to be a Rorschach test from the other. Humans see patterns because our brains are wired to see them. This is why the face of Jesus turns up on potato chips, because of course the first Sign of the Second Coming would be pulled out of a bag of Original Lays.

We may be lost, but we're still looking for deer sign. He points to a three-toed track on the ground. "Can you tell me what that is?"

"Turkey!" I know this because turkey tracks make me smile. They look like stars missing a point.

"Correct!" he affirms.

Animal tracks have a rhythm. You can envision the whole animal by the nervousness of its toes. John's tracks reveal a steady, firm pace and a body always pointing the same direction. My tracks are smaller than John's and they wander all over the place, exactly like a deer poking around for food.

We keep walking, picking our way down between saplings and stepping over downed trees. I have slipped in mud, my butt is cold, and I am festooned with bug smutch. Several flies have gone spelunking in my mouth. I am now digesting that information.

To my right: a suddenly whiffling, almost like a muffled boom. Another partridge has taken flight. Not a mama. A regular grouse.

"Do grouses roost?" I ask aloud. I am thinking of a wild turkey that was up a tree and glaring at me like a buzzard.

He shrugs and keeps walking, pushing branches out of the way.

"Do you think they like pear trees?" I prod.

"Do you think lords go a leaping?" he responds.

"Yes," I reply promptly. "Besides which, everyone forgets it's twelve lords a leaping, eleven ladies dancing, ten pipers piping . . . they don't get much farther unless they're in the Sunday school Christmas pageant. But the 'partridge in a pear tree,' that's the *punch line*. Everybody knows that line."

He is not paying attention to me because he is moving fallen trees out of the way. "Maybe it has to do with where pear trees grow," he eventually replies.

"Pear trees grow in California," I gabble. "They're not indigenous to France. There's no such thing as a French hen. And a French rabbit is really just a European rabbit."

"Huh?"

"I was reading *How to Raise Rabbits for Fun and Profit*," I explain helpfully.

He gives me a sweaty look.

I give him a look back. "I'm not planning on raising rabbits. I just like reading about them."

He knows me well enough to be skeptical but waves me forward anyway, keeping things moving until I'm keeping pace and trotting next to him. "Pull my finger," he orders.

I pull. He farts.

Apparently, farting frees enough space in his brain to give him clever ideas. He looks at me speculatively. "We should spray you with the scent of 'doe in heat.'"

"Why?" I protest.

He grins happily. "Just to see if it works. You sound like a doe when you're mad."

"Waa," I grouse, making him laugh again.

("Hssss!")

"Did you hear that?" I whisper, tugging at his sleeve.

"No," he replies blandly.

("Hssss!")

"It's just the wind," John says, still walking at a steady pace.

("Hssss!")

"It's just a tree."

("Hssss!")

I grab the back of his pants to stop his forward motion. "Listen," I command. Grumpily, he stops and stands in place, listening just to please me. Together, we stand quietly and hold hands as the forest expands into a soundscape of small noises. Maple leaves clap in the wind. Deadwood barks and creaks. Crows caw, alerting the locals to our presence . . . and in the far, far distance, a rooster crows back with the gossip from his neck of the woods.

Cocking his ear, John listens intently to the barnyard bird reminding us just how close to civilization we really are. "That's not the neighbor's rooster," he informs me. "It's a different one. It's coming from . . ."

("Hssss!")

This time, I know he heard it, because he looks surprised.

"That's not the wind," I declare firmly. "It's a cat." I look around for a likely spot for a den. We're on a ridge with lots of trees and shrubs that provide good cover. "There," I point at a shaded crevice about the right size. "I bet that's a bobcat den."

"Maybe," John nods skeptically as he waves me forward through the brush so we don't get eaten by an unhappy kitty protecting her territory. As an afterthought, he adds: "I know where we are."

I make a face at him. "We didn't come up this way," I say, stating the obvious.

"Nope," he says, looking pleased with himself.

For the great pleasure of bushwhacking is that you can know exactly where you are and still be totally lost. This is true of traveling as well, especially when you go off the beaten path and then try to reverse course halfway through. Even when you try to retrace the exact steps, the way back is never the same.

He starts walking faster, with a confidence born of place. Before long, we're at the head of a natural spring. This part of Maine is the land of Poland Springs: pure, drinkable spring water is everywhere. He promptly whips off every stitch, jumps into the brook, and starts rolling around to cool off.

"Why don't you join me?" he coos, exuberantly naked in the shade.

"No thank you," I say nicely, because outdoor nooky is not really as much fun as the readers of romance novels like to think. Also, John knows perfectly well that fooling around will not happen unless he feeds me first. Laughing, he clambers out and shakes himself dry, looking exactly like a polar bear with a salmon caught between its teeth. Within seconds he's dressed again and perfectly dry. The forest is familiar again.

I follow his lead, knowing that the beaten path is just on the other side of those trees. He pushes through a thicket and scrapes down the steep side of a dry ravine.

"Don't hang on to a dead tree," he cautions me as I slide down into his waiting arms.

A motto for life.

CHAPTER TEN

❧ ❧ ❧

Coyote Mobile

The loudest duck gets shot.
— *Chinese proverb*

"I'm going to kill the chicken," Don announces without preamble. "You want to help?"

"Uh . . . sure," I reply uncertainly. I feel obliged to witness its death since I'm responsible for pointing out its scabrous condition. A little while ago I went out to the henhouse to say hello to the chickens. "Hello, chickens!" I said. Right away they lined up, pressing forward to see if I brought food. They all came over to greet me except for one, the one with the weird walk and the bloated stomach. She looked really bad. Chunks of feathers on her back were gone, and her demeanor was sullen. Worse, she was huddled in the corner where the first bird had croaked. She couldn't smell death, because death smelled like her.

"She's eating," Don remarked, when I returned to the human house and tattled on her. "It's probably not a disease." Dourly, he scratched his chin. He was not particularly interested in deciphering the clues.

"The feathers on her back are funny," I insisted. "Either she's picking them out, or the other birds are pecking her."

After that, Don went out to the hen house to see the sick chicken for himself. And now, thanks to me, her goose is cooked.

150

What does one wear to a beheading? For lack of better options, I throw on heavy canvas work clothes and run back outside. Two hens are standing around in the pen, but there's no sign of Don or the sick bird. I go inside the henhouse and poke around, half expecting to find it already lying legs up and cross-eyed in a corner next to the Eazy-Bake light bulb. All I find is a healthy hen sitting in a laying box. Reproachfully, she looks up at me, but otherwise she doesn't move.

I take a mental count. There are two chickens outside and one in the laying box. That leaves one chicken unaccounted for. "She's not in there," Don yells over, prompting me to stick my head out of the henhouse.

"Where did she go?" I yell back.

"Got her in the bag!" He holds up a lumpy bag in his hand and points at it. It looks like a shrubbery ready to be transplanted.

I close the henhouse door and walk over to take a closer look. It turns out that the hen is head down in a chicken net, a tool that looks like a cross between a pool skimmer and a tennis racquet. Upside down and unperturbed, she blinks placidly at me through the mesh, a Wallace & Gromit claymation chicken in 3D. Her claws waggle comically in the air, but she's not resisting at all. Don tugs at the net, grabs her by her chicken ankles and pulls her free. Dangling limply from his hands, she's about as energetic as a pair of wet hiking socks stuffed with shredded cheese.

"We're going to chop its head off." He points to an old tree stump a few yards from the henhouse. "That's the chopping block."

"But . . . but . . ." I sputter, "that's . . . I mean . . . where the other chickens can *see*?"

"They're not watching," he points out matter-of-factly. With that, he lays the chicken's head on the stump. She just lies there, offering no resistance.

"Where should I stand?" I ask querulously.

"Doesn't matter. There won't be much blood." With that, he draws back the axe ever so slightly and lets it down with a muffled thud.

Just like that, the deed is done.

I feel like I should say a prayer or something, except the dearly departed chicken interrupts my reverie by deciding, *now*, to start struggling. The body careens out of his hands and the head flops over to one side, still attached to the neck by a thin strip of skin. As I watch, it tumbles across the lawn and starts heading back towards the house.

"Hey!" I yell in annoyance. "Come back here!"

Cheekily, it keeps running around the yard. It refuses to listen to me—not out of obstinacy, of course, but because it can't hear. The running chicken should be gruesome but it isn't, because she's already fled this mortal plane. Like Nearly-Headless-Nick haunting Harry Potter's Hogwarts, her head is not quite off and all that's careening around is a body that refuses to cooperate.

Irritated, Don strides across the yard, grabs the chicken again and thok! takes the head all the way off. He lets it go . . . and the chicken zooms off again, doing backflips and cartwheels through the patient grass. There is no blood. The hens in the audience are not upset at all. I notice that Hen 3 has finished laying her egg and has joined the other two, lined up and watching the festivities through the wall of chicken wire.

"Kinda busy for a headless bird," I say, staring in awe at its acrobatics.

"Sometimes they get up and start running around," Don mutters, slightly aggravated by the display. "You have to be prepared for that."

I look for the stubborn head. Somehow it managed to land next to the hen house, traveling six or seven yards away from the chopping block. That's a long way for a head to go on its own. The eyes are closed and the lids are red and pimply. My impression is that the beak is drooling, but that's pure projection. Irrationally, I'd been hoping for a peaceful expression to assuage my lingering guilt, but it looks like the face of a spiteful old biddy who removed her twelve kids from her will and left everything to the poodle. I'm tempted to sketch the decapitated head just to capture its expression, but decide against it. I worry that the neck will sprout little legs and the head will start running away from me, and then I will feel obligated to catch it and preserve it for science. I really don't want to.

Behind me, a faint rustling.

I turn and look. To my surprise, the headless body is wobbling unsteadily toward me, having accomplished a big circle that returns it home to roost. Old habits die hard. As I watch in amazement, the headless chicken teeters forward, a baby out of the bathwater, every slow step threatening to be its last. C'mon, chicken! You can do it! Finally, with a desolate kick, the chicken's body topples over next to its head. Top and bottom reunited, now, in death. I think it's done now. It sure looks that way. But, really, without one of those pop-up thermometer thingies jammed into its butt, who can tell?

Out of an excess of curiosity, I later looked up the thermometer-thingie: turns out that it was invented in 1950 by Eugene Beals and the Dun-Rite Company, otherwise known as the Turkey Advisory Board of California. Here's the interesting part: this marvelous widget was a very hard sell. No agency funded it, the industry rejected it, and everybody thought it was silly except for housewives sick of being yelled at for ruining Thanksgiving. Today, there's one in nearly every Thanksgiving turkey sold at the supermarket, and a fair number of chickens too. The company that won the widget wars now does $100 million of business every year. At ten cents a widget, that's a heck of a lot of birds in the oven.

I glance at the headless chicken. Every once in a while, a toe, a tip, a something twitches. Clearly, a pop-up thingie for done-to-death would be helpful, but I don't see one being invented in the near future. There's no profit in it.

Merely inches away, the other hens can see their fallen comrade through the chicken wire lining the pen, but they take no interest in the fact that she's just lost her head. Nothing in their demeanor suggests distress, just mild hunger at the sight of fresh food. If they're not bothered by it, why should I feign delicate sensibilities? Who am I trying to impress by being all dainty? The chickens don't care. I could waffle on about the majestic indifference of Nature who cares naught for my woes, O the suffering! O the pain! But chickens aren't exactly natural; they've been bred for thousands of years to perform like circus clowns, laying eggs on cue. ("Look ma, no hands!") I take the opportunity to inspect the body more closely. Kneeling down, I grab the legs, which are still churning listlessly, and pull them apart to look at the drooping belly. It is raw and red and rubbed clean of feathers. I probe under the legs and see more raw skin underneath. I flip it over, and look closer at the bare patches on its back, pushing up feathers to see the damaged skin underneath. She was being henpecked to death.

Standing up, I wipe off my hands on my pants. "What do you think was wrong with her?" I ask Don, who has put away the axe, hosed down the tree stump, and walked over to dispose of the corpse.

"Splayed hips, maybe," he replies, taking off his cap and rubbing his head. "The other hens might have jumped on it."

"Cause or effect?"

"Hard to say. By the time it gets like this, doesn't matter. The other chickens will just keep attacking her until she dies." He shakes his head in wonderment at their casual sadism.

I eye the hens with a critical gaze, newly armed with certain knowledge of how cruelly they've behaved. Strangely, it doesn't change my affection for them. They aren't evil. They're birds. It's my fault if I see them through a romantic haze that wishes away the smell, the shit, and the sharp beaks that draw blood. The three of them are no less cute than before, running around in their pen in the afternoon sunshine, scratching for bugs, and clucking softly. They're fluffy backyard hens who lay fresh eggs every morning, and I can't blame them for being cannibals who eat their young and kill their own. All chickens do this, by the way. It's just that they do it when the cat ladies aren't watching.

"Now what do we do with it?" I ask curiously.

"We're going to hang it up for the coyotes"

"I figured we were going to eat it," I blurt. "*Can* we eat it?"

Don gives me a perplexed look. "Layer hens don't have much meat on them. It would take you at least an hour to scald it, pluck it, and gut it, and if you cooked it you'd end up picking at bones. It's just not worth it unless you really need the food." He clears a throat unused to so much talking. "Plus with this one"—he waves in the hen's general direction—"you don't know. It's always a problem eating unhealthy animals. It could have septicemia, diseased portions infected with bacteria . . . the meat might not be good. No sense taking the risk unless you're desperate."

"Oh," I say, feeling very naïve, yet a part of me still wants to practice plucking, scratch and sniff, perform a necropsy and maybe make human food out of the carcass instead of just using it to bait coyotes. Except, of course, that too is a use for a freshly killed chicken, and a good one, too. Coyotes full of chicken don't need to catch Bambi for dinner. Sighing, I remind myself that the impulse to experiment with chickens is what done in Sir Francis Bacon, one of the greatest minds of the Scientific Age and an ex-con who did hard time in the Tower of London. In 1626, he decided to grab a gutted chicken and stuff it with snow to prove that meat could be refrigerated. He caught a cold and expired a week later.

Inadvertently, his early experiment with food preservation merely demonstrated that your mother was right: *Wear mittens outside or you'll catch cold and die*. History does not record how long the frozen chicken lasted.

Don grabs some twine, throws the chicken onto the front of the utility vehicle, and ties it on. Then he settles his large frame into the driver's seat, motions me to climb in the other side, and off we go to hang the carcass for the coyote. As we jounce along through sunshine and daisies, the chicken's legs start churning furiously again. Unexpectedly, instead of making me feel bad, it makes me feel better. It makes me realize how little brains the bird really has.

Don points at a young tree on the edge of the hill, a wooded finger that juts into the middle of the big field, creating a waist and dividing it into two. Seen from the sky, the field would look like the symbol for infinity: ∞. In the winter, the hill is used for sledding; in the summer, it becomes part of a private ATV trail. Foxes keep a den there, and coyotes come by for visits. He rolls up to a sapling tree with low branches and we stop. In no time at all, the headless hen is hanging upside from the tree like a grisly Christmas ornament. Its weight pulls it too low to the ground. The little foxes can get it without effort.

"More'n likely it'll go to the crows," Don grumbles.

Awkwardly, I try to restring the hen so it hangs off the ground, but the sapling is too slight to support the weight of a barnyard bird with wings too weak to fly. What would happen if I hung grapes from the tree? Same outcome, I guess. The insects would gobble it first.

Inexorably, the chicken slips down again—a prize, now, for ambitious ants looking up towards the sky. This hen is afraid of heights, a fear of flying bred into its hollow bones. It wants to return to the earth, to run its yellow feet on the careless ground. There is no chance of that, for it is hanging with cords wrapped around unsexy ankles, a bungee jumper seeking the ultimate thrill. Face your fears, bird! What are you—chicken? But it's already frightened to death. Experimentally, I reach out and pluck a feather off its back, hold it up as high as I can on tiptoe, and then, inhaling strongly for no reason at all, I let it go. It doesn't fall right away. A light breeze picks it up and swirls it through the air, giving the feather the illusion of life.

"Coyotes come by the house at night," Don adds as he pulls the chicken up again and strings it over a higher, stronger branch. "But there's plenty out there for them to eat. Same goes for the foxes." He shrugs philosophically, and ties off a new knot so the bird won't slip down. "A chicken doesn't guarantee their interest."

Silly me for expecting a fast-food freebie will prompt predators to come running. Giveaways only work on humans. The coyote doesn't see "free," it just sees food, and not very tempting food at that. Humans see rejection and insult, because chicken is a precious economic resource sacrificed to the forces of inevitability. Guess what? Even chickens don't find other chickens very interesting. They're only around because eggs are pushy. "A hen is only an egg's way of making another egg," the Victorian satirist Samuel Butler declared. I'm inclined to agree with him, because he was also a preacher's kid, and I'm siding with the egg. I can't fathom what a coyote might think of this meal-on-a-string, let alone Butler, who doubtless would have pronounced it delicious.

In *The Gates of Chan Buddhism*, Jing Hui repeats an anecdote about a group of American schoolchildren who've had a lesson in comparative religion. Asked to summarize the difference between Buddhism and Christianity, they responded by answering the question with another question. To wit: which came first: the Chicken or the Egg? Buddhists believe that a chicken laid the very first egg in the world, the children explain. Christians believe that God laid the first egg.

Why yes, I believe He did.

Looking over, I spot John standing at the opposite edge of the field, on the side where we'd set up the target because it bleeds into the mountain. No houses and no humans. He's leaning on an axe and talking to someone on an ATV. All I can make out is the short white hair, khaki pants, work boots, and plaid shirt.

"Is that Ruth over there, talking to John?"

Don looks over quickly and replies, with just the slightest tinge of amusement in his voice, "Nope. That's Norm."

I squint again, but I can't tell. It would be easier if one of them had a moustache. "What's he doing here?"

"Probably just poking around."

I wave at them. They wave back.

"Huh," I say, oddly pleased. "So what's John doing over there?"

"Splitting wood," Don answers without looking. He's busy fiddling with something on the front of the utility vehicle.

"Kinda busy, this field!" I declare.

"Yep," Don replies laconically, and finishes securing the bungee cords to the machine as I stand limply in the sunshine, staring stupidly into the sky.

I always laugh when city people complain that there's nothing to do in the country, because I've heard the same complaints when Americans move to Paris. The French have a saying, "*On n'est jamais content de son sort*," which is basically "the grass is always greener on the other side." Even a *National Geographic* photographer will get bored with the ho-hum of mountain biking in Costa Rica and boating down the Yangtze River. To her, nothing looks better than a leisurely morning of mall shopping in Wisconsin with an average Joe named Willy. At least this is what Gretchen confessed to me, as she sat down and attempted to fold her long legs under

one of those miniature wooden tables that are everywhere in
Paris. "Just to be clear," she added in a heavy Swiss-German
accent, "it's not Villy vhat's the attraction. It's the idea of doing
something different. Vith cheddar," she adds thoughtfully.

I'd met her at a party held in the cellars of L'Ecluse, a wine
bar off the Champs-Elysées. The guests were mostly Anglo-
phile French and English-speaking expats, which included
New Zealanders, Australians, Irish, Scots, a few Singapore
Chinese, and a whole bunch of fashion models, who repre-
sent their own country. Laura had wandered over from a
photo shoot for L'Oréal cosmetics. She'd kept the makeup
and black jumpsuit from the shoot, but her most striking
attribute was her curly red hair. "It's a dye job for the photo
shoot," she whispered to me out of the blue, because strangers confess random things to me. It's my only superpower.
"My natural color's really dull. They dyed my eyelashes, my
eyebrows, everything." Laura was from Kansas, didn't speak
any French, wasn't planning on learning, and lived with two
other American girls she met through her agency. And that
was about as far as the conversation went before the men in
black suits swept in, flapping their way towards the girl with
hair the color of fresh meat and limbs like soba noodles.

In the wine cellar, the lights were almost as low as the stone
ceilings, making it difficult to get an overview of the room.
But the lilting repetition of the phrase, "What do you do?"
meant the dominant tribe was American. At the wives' table:
four women, all blond, bony, and bored. They were huddled
together as if quilting their napkins into a giant square of
toilet paper, and they were tipsy enough to admit they hated
living in Paris. They wanted to frolic forever in the City of
Light, a city of champagne bars, chocolate dresses, and tiny
cakes shaped like starfish. But they'd been here long enough
to discover that Paris is full of secret doors, and they didn't
want to know what lay behind them. It is F. Scott Fitzgerald

and Ernest Hemingway shivering in cramped attics, escaping the seeping horrors of middle-class morality by embracing their real and frightening poverty. It is alias Jason Bourne, a charming assassin who kills humans for fun, who has no idea who he is, doesn't know his own name, but is certain he lives in the chic 8th *arrondissement* and remembers the door codes to his building. It is Marlon Brando in *Last Tango in Paris*, a minimalist story about a mumbling American expat, a young French ingénue, a big dirty mattress, and a very clean bathroom. In the end, he crosses a line and she shoots him to death.

This is why Carrie Bradshaw went back to New York. She was a sex columnist, not a Soprano.

Sighing, I tug at the headless bird. The knot holds, and the branch doesn't bend. As I watch, the coyote mobile begins swinging slightly in the breeze, making me think of the hours I'd once spent watching Foucault's pendulum in Paris one day when I didn't know what else to do with the thoughts spinning around in my head. Foucault's pendulum is a perpetual motion machine hanging under the dome of a secularized church called the Panthéon. Immense, the gleaming metal pendulum slowly swings and turns across a round circle symbolizing the world. Except the pendulum doesn't turn— the earth does, rotating axis adagio over the course of a day. The pendulum is a lesson in geological time, which swallows humans for breakfast and burps up the next species to take our place. Do we care? No. For by the time it happens, it will not be happening to us. Which is to say, to you. In other words, to me. And that is all that matters, for the ego sees the opposite of truth. This, too, is the lesson of the pendulum. We cannot see the cosmos for the bright shiny object dangling in front of us.

But today, I am staring at a headless hen, her pretty feathers ruffling in the breeze as I stand back and sniff experimentally. All I can smell is oil, sweat, gas, green, and tree. I can't smell blood, chicken, or string. I wish that I could. It is too much like staring at a photograph, too much like the advertisement with Laura that I'd chanced on one day while flipping through a fashion magazine. There she was, a dangling ornament on the page, dolled up in the same red hair and shiny black clothes she'd worn to the party at L'Ecluse. It wasn't an ad for hair dye. It was an ad for shampoo. Somehow, the girl in the ad was more alive than Laura from Kansas, as if a snakeskin layer of youth had been sloughed off and ironed flat, becoming a talisman made just for the garbage can. It's probably why I hate being photographed. Given the pathos of my soul, I must make an effort to keep the little that I have.

"I'm going to go over to the other side," I tell Don, pointing at John, because I want to go where the grass is greener—and no, I'm not making that up, even if I am colorblind. That side of the field gets more sun, more wild strawberries, and thus more turkey poop, which is excellent fertilizer.

"Sure," Don waves me off, as I start trekking across the field, smashing blades of grass beneath wide feet. Behind me, I can hear the engine starting. Don is heading back to the house. I am heading over to John. The chicken has no head. It is staying put.

The next day, I go to check the coyote mobile. The chicken is still there. Untouched, it is still swinging and turning, swinging and turning in the light breeze. I smell grass, wildflowers, and fresh earth. Around me, the birds are singing.

CHAPTER ELEVEN

ॐ ॐ ॐ

Girls in the Man Cave

A man can never have too much red wine,
too many books, or too much ammunition.
– Rudyard Kipling

Back in May 2008, to great rejoicing and fanfare, Cabela's opened a new branch in Scarborough, Maine. John was so excited he started dancing around.

"What's the big deal?" I said. "It's just another store."

"It's *Cabela's*!" John explained by energetically waving his hands over his head.

I still didn't understand what all the fuss was about, so he took me shopping. It was a revelation. Billed as the "World's Foremost Outfitters of Outdoor Equipment," Cabela's turned out to be Disneyland for gun nuts. The décor was vintage hunting lodge, with mounted trophy heads popping out from every wall. There was a shooting arcade, a Gun Library, and a freshwater aquarium, but the centerpiece of the store was an ersatz mountain where taxidermied animals frolicked. To discourage shoppers from attempting to climb it, Cabela's did not sell crampons or guide books for trekking through the Himalayas. The store only sold useful outdoor stuff such as turkey calls and camouflage bikinis, both of which I had to try even though I had no chance of succeeding.

Gobble, gobble! This was pretty much how the camouflage bikini looked on me. Under the harsh light of the dressing room, I managed to turn into a wallflower and a butterball at the same time. I would have congratulated myself for being so clever, but a domestic hen turkey advertised in *Uncle Henry's* pulled off the same trick—with a twist.

She was supposed to be a tom because that's what i wanted, but to all my knowledge toms don't lay eggs and she is laying an egg every other day. im not sure how much she weighs but she's big. she is too stupid to go into her house so she stayed out in the snow all winter and lost the feathers on her chest but they are coming back in. she will eat out of my hand and i have named her "butterball" so if you plan on eating her for the holidays she should live up to her name [sic].

Wild turkeys are notoriously difficult to approach. That's why turkey hunting is its own sport, requiring different doodads from the ones used in deer hunting. Turkey hunters use beards, moustaches, face paint, turkey-shaped decoys, Ghillie suits, hunting blinds, and an amazing assortment of disguises, all in hopes of fooling a tom into coming close enough to be overpowered by their manly body odors. These ruses often fail. Wherefore *tomfoolery*, the tendency of grown men to act like idiots ("in imitation of certain sacred rites of our holy religion," added Ambrose Bierce in *Devil's Dictionary*, 1906.)

If I wear a camouflage bikini while turkey hunting, will the birds be able to see me? What a silly question. Of course they can. But not if I don an entire camouflage outfit consisting of pants, jacket, and magic hat!

Newly invisible to the untrained eye, I slipped out of the dressing room and tiptoed stealthily through the aisles, ducking around the giant stuffed moose and skipping past the fishing lures as I hunted for John. I found him standing rapt in front of a row of chest waders, which looked like headless fishermen standing at attention. To my great annoyance, he didn't jump when I pinched him on the butt, even though I'd managed to sneak up on him like a ninja cat. Somehow, he always knows it's me, even when I am *heavily disguised*.

"There are so many couples being affectionate in this store!" I said breathlessly. "I don't think I've even seen this much hand holding in Paris." I paused and clarified: "*Paris* Paris, I mean. Not the Paris with the Walmart."

"Hur," he snorted, grabbing my hand, and started heading towards the camping gear with me in tow.

"Maybe it's because they're all French Canadians?"

"Hur," he snorted again.

"Are they being nice to their wives because they want them to get them something nice for Christmas?"

"Backwards."

"What do you mean?"

"These men are being really nice to their wives because they're going to treat themselves to a new hunting rifle for Christmas and they're anticipating that somebody,"—he cleared his throat loudly—"is going to be really mad at them."

I gave him a suspicious look. "What are you saying?"

"I love you, plumpkin!" he declared in tones of great sincerity.

"What did you buy?" I prodded.

He shrugged, feigning nonchalance. "Just a new bow."

"What kind of bow? A bow like that lady is carrying?" I pointed to a wood longbow carried by a lithe young woman wearing a self-satisfied smirk and recycled soy shoes. She looked like an Ashtanga yoga instructor who'd mistaken the bow for a specialized piece of Pilates equipment.

"That's an archery bow," he coughed.

"I like that one."

He rolled his eyes. "It's no good for hunting. Not unless you're really strong. Even if you hit your animal you'll just wound it, and that's way worse than a clean kill."

"We did archery at music camp. But my violin teacher objected. She said it ruined my fingers."

"Hur," he snorted again, and started walking faster.

We walked past the guns, the gun safes, and the hunting blinds. Then we sailed by the ammo section without stopping. Now I was really confused. Hunters covet ammo the way that pastry chefs covet butter. For John, it is a great sticking point in action films when the hero doesn't grab the ammo in a shootout. In a typical scenario, the astronaut hero has just escaped his evil captors, the space monsters are trying to eat him, the alien space ship is on fire, and in the midst of the melee, the hero grabs a machine gun abandoned a million years ago by Sylvester Stallone playing himself as president of Earth. Manfully, the hero blasts the heads off the aliens trying to stop him, and runs off to rescue the heroine. At this point, John always shakes me awake and complains, ". . . but that's not realistic at all! He didn't grab the ammo." And then he sulks. Until I met him, I'd been under the impression that stockpiling ammo was like sticking rice in the root cellar. Sooner or later it would go bad, and then you'd have great piles of nasty black grains slowly congealing into sludge.

"You can never have too much ammo," he reminded me earnestly as we hurried past the bulk boxes. "Never." He gave me a look. "If you're ever in a gun fight, don't forget: *always grab the ammo*."

"Okay," I said agreeably. It was incredibly sweet of him to think that I would one day find myself in a shootout *and* that I'd be able to blast my way past the bad guys. He remains convinced that I will one day be a crack shot. It's very romantic of him.

"All the way to the back," he nudged me past the Bargain Cave and into the Archery section. "I got one of those." He pointed to a display of compound hunting bows, the kind that look like really big plasticized versions of a cat's cradle.

"Already?" I asked in surprise. "When?"

"While you were going through the 'Sale' rack up front." He gave me a look. Then he looked at me again, an expression of puzzlement crossing his face. It had taken him a good ten minutes to realize that I was perfectly camouflaged and therefore invisible, but at least he'd finally noticed I'd dressed up just for him.

"You like this one?" he asked hopefully, picking out a small bow blushing in pink camouflage.

"Not really," I said tartly. "Pink camo makes no sense. There must be a lot of French-Canadians who shop here."

"Why do you think that?"

"Because the coffee is terrible and the ATM is in French. It's a stealth machine. It looks like a regular ATM, with one of the stock photos of a happy family all shiny apple cheeky, 'Welcome to Bank of USA' or something like that, then as soon as you swipe your card it switches to French. '*Bienvenue! Vouz êtes bien chez Bank des Etats-Unis!*' And there's no way to change the language back to English."

"Of course it switched to French," he snorted. "You've got a poofty credit union card from the People's Republic of Cambridge. You're at Cabela's. How do expect the machine to take you seriously?"

In French, the word for "automated teller machine," or ATM, is *Guichet automatique bancaire*, or GAB. Which is a pretty good acronym for the French, except the French don't know that. "Well, the bathroom instructions are in French too," I retorted defensively. "What do you make of that?"

In response, he pointed to a door behind the sales counter that looked like it led to the stock rooms. "I'm going to test shoot my bow," he declared abruptly.

I glared at him and adjusted my camo hat, which was now sitting cockeyed on my head. "Are you really going to test your bow or are you just trying to change the subject?"

"Both!" he bellowed happily, and bounced off to the back room, leaving me to stare at the fish in the freshwater aquarium.

"Bloop!" the smallmouth bass told me, their fins waggling eloquently.

"I know," I agreed, sighing, and pushed up my drooping sleeves again. "But at least I know what he wants for Christmas."

Amazingly, two years have already passed since the store's Grand Opening. Yesterday Don chopped the head off the chicken. Today, I'm shopping by myself for arrow tips for John. His instructions are very specific: it's July, therefore the tips he wants are broadhead, not shorthair or wingnut. How difficult can it be, to find pointy things shaped like triangles? I've been to this store before. I know where stuff is shelved. Humming to myself, I wander back to the Archery section. The pink camouflage bow is still on display, flanked by aisle after aisle of archery-related things. I start looking for pointy triangles made out of chipped obsidian or pounded metal, like the arrowheads shown on the History Channel. To my dismay, I find myself facing an entire row of doohickeys falling under the category of "Broadheads & Points," not one of which resembles an isosceles triangle. They look like chess pieces, windmills, and bird claws. One of them looks exactly like a badly bent whisk.

This must be how men feel when they try to buy lingerie as a gift. The permutations are endless. The selection is frightening. Those "training bras" look pretty much the same as the regular kind. Exactly what are bras training those A-cups to do? Sit up and shake hands on command? Just like bras in Paris, the most popular broadhead arrow tips aren't numbered thirty-two and thirty-six inches, but eighty-five and one hundred. When applied to French bras, those numbers indicate chest measurements in centimeters. I have no idea what those same numbers mean for arrow tips, but I doubt they refer to cup size. And yes, the arrow tips come in practice versions that look exactly like the non-practice kind. A screed of panic rises in the back of my head. *Which one which one which one?* I look for the salesperson, but he's busy helping customers who have testosterone in their wallets. After a few futile attempts to get his attention, I give up and call John. He's on a boat in the middle of the lake.

"Why are you answering your phone?" I ask incredulously.

"Because you called me," he answers blandly.

"But you're fishing!" I exclaim.

"You called me. Stop complaining."

Exasperated, I explain that I finally found arrowheads that sort of look like pointy triangles, except they really look more like space rockets, and one of them looks exactly like the Eiffel Tower. One is even called "Shuttle-T," proving that I'm not the only person who thinks these bright shiny objects look like they belong on a charm bracelet. "'Muzzy'," I read to him over the phone. "'Magnum.' 'N-A-P.' 'G5.' I don't know if those are brands, ratings, directions, or what."

There's a long pause as he considers the options. Finally, he says: "I need 100s. That's 100-grain broadhead arrow tips. And the regular versions, not the practice ones."

"But . . ."

"Go ask the guy at the archery counter. He'll help you."

"But I've already been waiting for help," I wail. "He's just ignoring me. Why do you think I called you?"

"Gotta go!" he exclaims abruptly. "Fish!" Just like that, he hangs up.

Sighing, I peek around the corner. The archery guy has moved on from the father and son who were looking at a big bow and little bow. He's now talking to a large dude whose dirty full beard somehow makes it look like he eats because he hunts. I don't shave my armpits. If I flash them at him, will that get his attention?

Ping.

Via text, John has requested "Hornady .22 magnum with plastic tips." I stare at the words as if I've just intercepted a secret spy message sent by James Bond to Q Branch: "The goat eats the left shoe at midnight." Before I started this shopping quest for broadhead arrow tips, I'd thought .22 was a caliber. I also used to think "100 grains" was the number of gunpowder grains in a round of ammo. Obviously I am mistaken, since this "grain" business also seems to apply to arrowheads. I don't understand the "magnum" part at all. To me, "magnum" is mostly "my Magnum," a European brand of ice cream recently introduced to the U.S. by way of an ingénue dancing on cars, which I suppose is the obvious thing for a girl to do when desperate for frozen dairy treats. Maybe this ammo's a hybrid—the cartridge version of a Prius?

Dejectedly, I look around for the archery salesman, who has now disappeared entirely. Even if I find him, he is never going to pay any attention to me, so I head to the Ammo section to look for a different salesman who might take pity on me.

The first person I see is a middle-aged lady with a pleasant face who is standing behind a counter next to the Gun Library. That spot is for filling out all the forms that go along with buying guns in a store. Head down, she's busily scratching out numbers on a pad and completely immersed in her task. Brazenly, I stick my cell phone under her nose. "Excuse me," I say loudly, empowered by frustration, "but is this a bullet or an arrow?"

Startled, she reads the text, looks up at me, scans my face and then she laughs, giving me a smile full of sympathy. "It's a bullet." She looks at my face again, and grins. "Really."

"Do you know where it is?" I ask hopefully.

"You gotta ask one of the gun guys." She gives me a silly grimace and waves at the four aisles of ammo behind me. "I can't tell you exactly where it is."

It tells you something that she works here and she can't point me towards this ammo. There are hundreds of different kinds, but they seem to be the same and yet not the same, like the mustards sold in Monoprix. The boxes come in two standard sizes: "tiny," and "truckload." I wander through the ammo aisles, trying to figure out the ordering system. I'm on the verge of giving up when I finally glimpse a salesman out of the corner of my eye. He's just finishing up with a young man who's also having trouble locating his ammo. As I stand there, waiting, the salesman *finds it*. This is most reassuring. As soon as he sends the guy off to the cash register, I accost him. According to his name tag, his name is "Tom."

Breathlessly, I hold up my phone with the text message still glowing on the screen. "Can you tell me what this is and where to find it?" I demand, all gestures towards politeness gone.

Tom peers at the text message, and a smile spreads across his weathered face. "Oooh, that's a great one," he enthuses. He is missing a middle finger.

"I'm so glad you know what it is!" I sigh in relief. "Can you point it out?"

Tom grins. "Nope."

"Uh . . ." I am suddenly anxious. "Uh . . ." I start again. "Does that mean you can't find it, or you don't have it?"

"We don't have it," he says with certainty.

"You mean you're out of stock?"

"I mean we don't carry it."

"Why not?" I wail.

"Dunno!" he chuckles amiably.

"Is there another brand of ammo that's comparable?"

"To that?" He shakes his head. "Nope."

He takes down a random packet of ammo off the shelf and starts launching into the differences between plastic tips, hollow points, full metal jackets, calibers, cartridges, optimal distances for accuracy, recommended ranges, and all the rest. He clearly loves his job, and he's extremely thorough regarding the details. But he might as well be explaining the arcane mysteries of quantum physics to me.

"I don't understand," I finally interrupt him in small voice.

"Don't worry," Tom says kindly. "My wife can't keep them straight either. Do you know what game he's after?" He explains that the smaller bullets are illegal to use for deer hunting in Maine because they only wound the animal, instead of killing it instantly. Ethical hunters try to avoid causing injury to the animal, a requirement that not only means being a good marksman, but also matching your ammo to your prey. It is also July, meaning that turkey hunting season is over, and it isn't open season for deer for at least another three months.

"Er," I ponder. "I know he knows that. So . . . maybe it's for coyote?"

Thus a discussion of coyote hunting ensues, because yes, this kind of bullet would be excellent for coyotes, *if* Cabela's carried them, which it doesn't, and I'm the third person today to ask him about them.

My despair increases. "Here," Tom waves me forward, trying to cajole me out of my mood. He's clearly afraid that I am going to burst into tears. "Let me show you something you'll find interesting." He hastens me to the "Random Things Related to Hunting" section of the store, and picks up a small electronic device. Much to my surprise, it makes the noise of moose cows and other amazing sounds that defy interpretation. Because we've been talking about coyotes, Tom presses "Rabbit in Distress." The resulting noise doesn't sound like a rabbit. It sounds a lot like me when I'm mad at John.

Tom grins, and presses another button. "Swaaaaaaak!"

I have no idea what animal sounds like that. It is probably the sound a turkey would make when it gets mad at me.

None of these wild animal calls bears any resemblance to the snippets on the Fischer-Price toy, the one that quacks when you press the button with the "duck" picture and pull the attached cord. There is no "rabbit" button on the Fischer-Price toy because rabbits don't bark, moo, meow, or whinny. They mostly just wiggle their noses.

"Does it work?" I ask bluntly. "I mean, does it actually attract animals?"

"Course," he replies, but not with a huge amount of conviction.

He shows me the programmed animal sound cards that can be added to the machine, and promotes the virtues of packaged poop that draws them in. "The smell is awful," he confides, "but they can smell it for up to five miles away!"

I hold the sealed plastic packet up to my nose, but I can't smell anything except for glue and petroleum. "Good packaging," I comment blandly.

He laughs at my expression, and hands me a small plastic kazoo that makes his wrinkled face light up in pleasure. "My friend swears by that thing. He's been using it for decades."

I cast a surreptitious eye at the sticker with the price. The kazoo costs about as much as you'd expect a kazoo to cost, which is to say, a couple of dollars, most of which is probably paying for the hygienic clamshell packaging to keep people like me from tooting.

Tom adds: "You need a call, some bait, and a decoy too if you're serious about getting coyotes." He points to some fake geese lounging over my head. Considering they're 100 percent manufactured out of poly-something, the geese are remarkably convincing. Stick those out in the field with some of that designer poop, and I'd for sure be fooled.

"We hung up a chicken," I tell Tom, by way of explanation for why I'm not buying a decoy. "They're ignoring it."

"Oh?" he says, his face assuming a diagnostician's expression. "Then you'll want a bucket of entrails."

I will?

His head bobs in emphasis. "Every once in a while you'll see someone hop out of their car and scrape a woodchuck off the road. It's not for stew, it's for coyote bait."

I feel weirdly conflicted by this information.

"—And since the chicken isn't doing the trick, you need one of these!" He leads me to a different aisle and shows me an odd looking camera that resembles a small plastic birdhouse. "It's infrared activated," he explains. "You use it to see what critters come visiting at night."

He demonstrates how the camera works. Once you set up your bait, which is ideally very smelly, the trail camera will show you if there's a coyote in the area, or if it's crows, foxes, weasels, or some other predator that's moved in and started harassing your chickens. "As an experiment," Tom whispers conspiratorially, "I bought one and set it up on my patio. Every few seconds, it took a picture of the guy who was mowing my lawn." He nods solemnly. "So I rigged it up and left it up fer a while. Came back, took a look, and it had taken a whole bunch'a pictures . . . of my wife! She was putting birdseed in the feeder!" He lets out a belly laugh. "So it definitely works!"

The trail-cam works on the same principle as those nanny-cams hidden in teddy bears. This time, there's a happy ending for Tom the Husband, who didn't catch his wife with the gardener. Tom the Salesman, however, is not so lucky. Instead of broadhead arrow tips and Hornady ammo, I end up leaving the store with sour lemon drops and old fashioned root beer candy for ninety-nine cents a bag. It may not work as well as the packaged poop on coyotes, but it's pretty good at attracting humans.

I took the bait, and it was delicious.

Gobble gobble!

Chapter Twelve

When Worlds Collide

Your salvation doesn't interest me. Mine does.
– *When Worlds Collide, 1951*

It's my father's eightieth birthday weekend. My brother, his wife, and their daughter are taking a red-eye flight from California and landing early on Saturday morning. They are staying in Wellesley for thirty-six hours, long enough to land, say hello, have dinner, and then they are fleeing back to Palo Alto. We have not been all together since my mother died fifteen years ago.

Am I thinking about this? No. I am trying to organize the freezer. The impending arrival of a thousand pounds of moose meat creates an acute space management problem. In 2000, according to the USDA, the national average consumption was 195 pounds of meat per person. One moose, then, feeds a family of four over the course of a year if you can figure out how to preserve it. One solution is jerky, but I'd really rather not turn good meat into spicy strips of shoe leather.

"If we're lucky, we'll get a moose right away!" John hollers cheerfully, and bounces down the stairs, through the kitchen, and out the front door as fast as he can. He's heading up to Maine. It's Friday night, meaning that he's got Saturday and Sunday to scout. On Monday, the moose season officially starts. He is also trying very hard to disappear before my family gets here. Families are just bigger versions of other people's babies: they're adorable until they start throwing tantrums and screaming. In my case, they're screaming in Korean and sometimes French, depending on who shows up and the nature of the occasion—say, my sister's wedding. Nobody has a clue what the other person is saying, but they're all saying it very LOUDLY.

To be fair, the people in my family hardly ever shout, and the only one louder than me is my *emo* (aunt) Kum Sook, who can shatter the eardrums of a banshee when she gets mad at Mr. Kim, her second husband, who is now as bald as a turtle. But the real reason that John is running away is because Koreans insist on singing at any gathering involving food. This means that a family dinner at a fancy restaurant is a lot like being in a musical, except there's fervent praying instead of coordinated dance numbers. John likes my dad's prayers, because they're really good. But Yankees don't sing for their supper, not before, during, or after. The very thought of having to sit down and join in a harmonized chorus of "Happy Birthday to You" frightens him more than the prospect of facing down an angry hippo in the living room. This is why he's running to Maine, anxious to retreat to the safety of the woods where only the birds are expected to sing.

At midnight, the phone rings. "Are you still up, baby?" he coos. "You're missing all the fun!"

"Well, yes, I'm still up," I yawn. I have finished cleaning the bathrooms and making up the beds. Now, I am vacuuming. "It's like Murphy's Law or something. Smurfy's Law. You saw a moose, didn't you?" I say accusingly.

"Not quite!" he laughs. "Just past the Walmart in Paris, I ran into a bear."

"You ran into a bear?" I repeat stupidly.

"You know how it is," he muses. "You're driving along, listening to the radio, all of a sudden, WHUMP! By the time you hit the brake and realize there's bear in the road it's already behind you."

"You didn't try to look for it, did you?"

"Of course I did," he replies cheerfully. "But without a flashlight, no gun, and no cell phone service, I only went a little ways into the woods. Bad idea for all kinds of reasons."

I sigh. "Are you still by the road or are you driving?"

"The car's got a big dent, but it drives okay. Just think, if I'd killed the bear, we'd have had 300 more pounds of meat for the freezer!" He pauses, thinking. "I guess I'm supposed to call the game warden."

If a large dead animal is in the road you call the cops, it's just like any other car accident. But it's a gray area when the animal is merely wounded and runs off into the woods. Does it count as a hit and run if the victim runs away?

"It's after midnight," I remind him. "I don't think anyone is going to be answering their phone. Budget cuts, you know. No staff."

"I'll ask my dad tomorrow," John says blandly. "We'll go look for it."

I yawn again. "Call me before you go looking for it. With some daylight you should be able to figure out where it went."

"I'm driving up to the house now. Huh," he pauses. "My mother is going nuts with the political signs on the lawn. She must have a dozen out there."

"All for the same guy?"

"Different guys, but all Republicans. What the hell," he snorts incredulously. "You'll see the signs when you get here," he warns me. "Republicans could hold a rally out front!"

"Try not to run over any of those poor helpless political signs, or your mom will be mad at me."

"I'll be careful," he promises nicely, and hangs up the phone.

A few hours later, my sister, her husband, their 8-year-old daughter, and my dad are sitting around the table in my dining room, snacking on brunch food while they wait for my brother and his family to arrive. I'm in the kitchen whipping egg whites for meringues when my brother pops through the front door of the house.

"We're here!" he exclaims, cheerfully stating the obvious. "We got lost!"

"Everyone gets lost in this neighborhood. Why didn't you call me?" I gripe, wiping my hands on a towel and giving him a hug. "I figured your plane was delayed."

He shakes his head. "We landed early, got the rental, and here we are. We got lost about 500 feet from your porch."

With that, he comes inside, his smiling wife and tween daughter trailing behind him as they kick off their shoes. By way of greetings from Palo Alto, my brother hands my father an Xbox. I don't know what that is, but I do know that I can't roast it in the oven, so I don't really care. My father also doesn't know what it is, but he doesn't care for entirely different reasons. Meanwhile, my sister-in-law is trying very hard not to notice the fact that there are ten bikes on the front porch, five kayaks on the lawn, and seven different kinds of fishing poles stashed in the exposed beams crossing my dining room. This house-on-the-pond is not the kind of well-mannered mansion that shows up in *Architectural Digest*. That house went to John's ex-wife. This house is Guy Land. There are bait worms in my refrigerator and ammo in my nightstand. My sister-in-law is struggling to be polite and not say anything. Because I am also trying to be polite, I decide not to mention that there's a fishhook dangling over her head.

"You guys must be starved!" I say nicely, and shoo them into their seats around the dining room table. Before they eat, I must provide the provenance of the food: the sliced tomatoes come from the Wellesley garden. The wild blackberries in the muffins come from berries I'd picked in Maine. The chickens in Don's henhouse laid the eggs that I scrambled. People I don't know caught the smoked salmon off the coasts of Maine. A sourdough round of Poilâne bread arrived from Paris this morning. I purchased it from Wasik's Cheese Shop in Wellesley. The deer liver in my venison pâté came from a buck that Patrick shot in Maine. From Palo Alto, my sister-in-law Insook has brought an Italian sweet bread called *panettone* and Korean sticky rice cakes called *duk*, both purchased in Koreatown, L.A., the day before their plane left San Francisco. She brings the classic duk that look like jelly doughnuts, except they're made of rice paste filled with sweet red beans. They're basically pastry versions of whoopee cushions, complete with farting noises.

The anthropology of this morning's menu reveals the complexities of dining in the twenty-first century. In my version of an ideal world, I'd live off the land: fish, hunt, forage, and cultivate every meal. There are days in the summer where it gets pretty close, with fresh peas from our Wellesley garden and pickerel from the pond. But I am fooling myself. I have to pretend not to notice the details. There is coffee from South America, milk from Massachusetts, rice from Japan, and all the sundries required for home-made pasta, bread, and ice cream: yeast, baking soda, baking powder, cornstarch, vanilla, and vegetable oil. These all come from the great land of Ihni: I Have No Idea. Then there are the staples. Every time I shop for groceries, I think of the household items the wives of grizzled miners in old Western movies were always buying at the general store, namely: flour, lard, sugar, coffee, and salt. Try making any one of them from start to finish at home, from growing the wheat to mining the salt, and no cheating. I have tried. It is exceedingly time-consuming.

And where were the bullets made, the one used to kill the deer? They were made in the U.S. of A. Specifically, on Patrick's kitchen table. John knows how to make them and he's trying to teach me, but I draw the line at making my own shell casings.

As everyone settles into their chairs and starts eating, I am struck by the normalcy of it all. My sister is still pretty. My brother is still a genius. I am still standing in the kitchen with a knife in my hand. And so it will be, until the day we die. When the zombie apocalypse comes, my sister and dad will join me at the Big House in Maine, and Ruth will teach them how to make blueberry jam and John will show them how to make booby traps. They are quite pleased by this plan, because everybody knows that Maine winters are too cold for zombies. But my brother will have to deal with the walking dead on his own, because I expect that California will have been earthquaked to pieces by then.

When I tell him this, he just stares blankly at me.

The last time I saw my brother and his family was in Paris, France, five years ago, more or less by accident. Sort of like the way John hit the bear, which also ran away immediately following the collision.

"We had bear in Brownville," my brother says matter-of-factly, as I explain to them why the boyfriend they've never met isn't here.

"We did?" my sister blurts through a mouthful of smoked salmon.

"Was I vegetarian then?" I muse aloud.

"Not yet," my brother says.

"Did we have bear meat in Brownville?" I ask my dad, who is sitting at the head of the table, glowing with pleasure to see his three kids together.

"No," he answers. "Yes." He scratches his head. "Well. Your brother remembers these things."

"What was I, six?" I ask.

"Around that," my dad says. "It was . . . hmm . . . it was one of your mother's friends," he adds carefully. "She brought over a bear paw."

Random food often showed up at the parsonage, gifts from church people who wanted to do something nice for the minister. Maybe they didn't have cash money to tithe but they had new-dug potatoes or a haunch of venison. We'd open the door and there'd be a plastic pail of crabs or a bucket of milk still warm from the cow, unceremoniously plopped on the porch and hoping it gets taken in without anybody asking any questions.

My father, sitting at my table, feels that way about his son.

My sister, sitting at my table, feels that way about her husband.

My nieces, sitting at my table, feel that way about everything.

And so, I cook for them, using ingredients from around the world right out of my garden. Because everything and everybody comes from someplace else, including me and my vegetables.

Now that he's eighty years old, my dad likes to listen to the Marsh Chapel Choir on the radio, because he sang in that choir while he was a student at Boston University. So on this birthday weekend, because my brother is here, we're going to services at my dad's old church in the city.

"Why aren't we going to Korean church?" my sister hisses in my ear as we drive into Boston, because she goes to a big one in Brookline where the Korean ladies serve up a really good lunch after the service.

"Too political!" I whisper.

"Oh, yah," she concedes, laughing as she considers the ramifications of our dad showing up in Korean church with his whole family in tow, setting off a flurry of gossip because my sister married a Frenchman and I'm an *ajuma* spinster with freckles. Only my brother is 100 percent respectable, because he married a Korean woman from Korea who correctly dyes and perms her hair, produced exactly one child, and kept her tiny figure.

"Marsh Chapel is good," I reassure her. "Just think of it as a Christian music concert."

She snorts, for while it may be true that the BU church choir sings beautifully, it is just as true that one of the great pleasures of small town church choirs is that they're awful.

I like religious music as much as the next person, though when you are six, PBS Christmas specials featuring the Vienna Boys Choir are unacceptable substitutes for Rankin-Bass's classic "Rudolf the Red-Nosed Reindeer." If God is Santa, the church choir is the elf workshop that makes the misfit toys. There is always an asparagus-head soprano, a cluster of pear-shaped altos, a bunch of apple-shaped tenors, and one bald guy who can't sing at all but enjoys being the only man in the group. The whole thing is held together by a twee organist who is absolutely positively not gay, because who ever heard of a gay church organist? My siblings and I would sing with great earnestness, praising God to the highest of holies, and it would be a sort of game to see if the choir could make it to the end of the song without Mr. Veysey's partials falling out. After we finished the song and sat down, I always half-expected my dad to turn to us and say in a weird German accent, "Wunnerful, wunnerful! Tank you, my musical fambilee!" because we watched the *Lawrence Welk Show* every Saturday evening. It was our weekly allotment of television. In retrospect, it makes sense that my sister had to go blonde to play the accordion, because she liked Myron Floren. I liked Bobby and Cissy, the ballroom dancers, a fact I still can't interpret, and my mother liked Norma, the Champagne Lady. After the Sunday service was over, my dad would thank the choir for a job well done, because a small town church choir isn't about making great music. It's about showing up and singing your heart out, even if you suck.

Choir music can also make you burst into the church giggles, which strike when the minister quotes a verse of scripture that's accidentally funny, like the one about the talking mule, or pretty much anything from Zechariah, for example, 5.1–2:

> *Then I turned, and lifted up mine eyes, and beheld a flying roll.*
> *And he said unto me, What seest thou?*
> *And I answered, I see a flying roll.*

For preacher's kids, the church giggles tend to become a Pavlovian response to sitting in pews. I usually do okay if I'm by myself. With my sister around, though, it's not a matter of whether, but when. We're trying our darnedest to behave ourselves and managing pretty well until the scripture reading is over and it's time for the first hymn. It's one of the obscure ones the minister clearly chose for its theme—"forgiveness," I believe—and therefore it has a perfectly rotten tune that stuns the panicked congregation into staring at their shoes and mumbling tonelessly into their chins.

There are hundreds of songs in the standard Protestant hymnal but only five are any good. 1) "Rock of Ages," 2) "Blessed Assurance, Jesus is Mine," 3) "What a Friend We Have in Jesus," 4) "His Eye Is on the Sparrow," and 5) "The Old Rugged Cross," plus Christmas carols, which don't count. Pretty early on, my dad figured out that it was best to ignore the rest, though around Easter he'd toss in one of the "theme" hymns because he felt compelled to find one that matched the theme of palm fronds. The backlash was swift. Phil the Organist and Vern the Lay Leader would corner my dad after the service, conveying the congregation's displeasure, and pretty soon I'd be running next Sunday's programs off the mimeograph machine with the usual hymns put right back in where they belonged.

The whole point of hymns is that the rotation list is the same. Churchy people are conservative. They thrive on routine. It throws everything off when the hymn is such a dud that even the choir can't follow along. My sister gives me a look: ("What's up with the weird hymn?") I give her one back. ("Okay, so it's got no meter and it's homophonic. Like that's my fault?") My sister raises an eyebrow. ("Yes. You homophonic types ruin it for the rest of us.") Which almost makes me laugh because this tune is one that both of us can't sing. Mercifully, the stinker is only three choruses long. The organ stops playing, the congregation heaves a great sigh of relief, and we sit back down with a collective thud, waiting for the plate to be passed.

Purses get opened, wallets come out, and the collection plate goes around as the organist pounds out Bach. All the activity keeps the church giggles from surfacing, until the choir begins singing and an ambitious soprano starts trilling loudly off-key. Oh dear God. She has one of those thick, soupy vibratos that theater girls use. Given the size of her hair, she is surely a refugee from the pageant circuit.

"Glory to God!" she ululates. (*Don't laugh!*) "Glory to God!" (*DO . . .*)— "Gloreee to God" (*NOT . . .*)— "in the HighIIIest!" (*. . . LAUGH! . . .*)

To distract myself, I dig into my purse for a hard candy and hand it to my perplexed niece, who is sitting between my sister and me as a giggle buffer. "Give this to your mama!" I whisper to Sophie, who stares at it in surprise because she's got my food allergies and her diet is strictly patrolled.

"You're just like Mom!" my sister hisses under her breath as she takes the candy with a pleased expression on her face.

"I want one!" Sophie whispers into my ear, and makes an earnest attempt to squirm into my lap and fish around in my purse at the same time.

I hand her a candy. "Just one!" I whisper, holding up a cautionary finger as she happily grabs the butterscotch. The screeching soprano is so loud she almost masks the crinkling sound of the candy wrapper.

"Shush you guys," my sister-in-law pokes me from behind. "What's *wrong* with you?"

I bat her hand away and do my best to ignore her. Out of the corner of my eye I spot my brother, who is sitting behind us with his family in pew 2. He knows exactly what is going on and looks vaguely amused, but of course he is very digni-fied and thus he is trying to pretend he doesn't know us.

Zzzz, my other niece snores. Then she starts drooling. Aww, I think to myself. She looks just like my sister when she was that age.

Around us, annoyed heads are turning, casting offended glances at all the shushing going on in our pew, which only threatens to set off giggles again. If this keeps up I'm going to get the . . .

Hic! Too late! I've got the hiccups. The good part is that it's impossible to hiccup and giggle at the same time. For hiccups, I cannot be blamed. They are an act of God.

With a majestic honk, my sister blows her nose.

Keeping a straight face, I pass her a packet of Kleenex because she never carries extra and I have a purse full of them. The appearance of a Kleenex packet under her nose only makes the giggles resurface, because she knows the fancy packets are upgrades of my beloved rolls of toilet paper. She's trying so hard not to laugh that tears of frustration are stream-ing down her face.

Luckily my dad is paying no attention to us. He's just basking in the beautiful music. "Wunnerful, wunnerful!" his hands wave to the chorus.

Then the music stops, the blonde soprano beams at her adoring fans, the choir sits down, and the minister begins his sermon. He is pretty good at it, delivering a mostly non-sectarian, apolitical message of Christian compassion as—*hic!*—befits a campus chaplain. The sermon puts my brother to sleep, which is to be expected as he is habitually bored by the gibbering of mortals. Sophie and I are playing thumb wars, which gets her to stop pestering me for more butter-scotch. For the rest of her life, she's going to associate going to regular church (as opposed to Korean church) with thumb-wrestling with her *tata*, which is not the worst thing in the world but perhaps doesn't quite strike the proper note of reverence inside God's house.

Or perhaps it does. And I think to myself, this is why my father wanted everybody to come to church to celebrate his birthday. Because there's nothing like getting your kids together and watching them misbehave in pews, even if you've fallen asleep too.

It's 10 A.M. on Monday, my brother and his family have fled back to California and I am cleaning the house in Wellesley. Once again, the phone rings in the middle of vacuuming. It's John calling me from Maine. "So what's the use," he grumbles. "I mean, here we spend weeks, months really, scouting out good locations, looking for moose sign, and for what?"

"It's the first day of moose season," I soothe. "What do you expect?"

"Hur."

"Don't worry, honey. I'll be there soon."

"Too late!" His voice is suddenly full of jubilation. "One walked right up to us on Rabbit Road! We got it!"

"You what?"

"About 100 yards away. Got it right in the neck with the rifle you helped sight in. It was a nice clean shot, instant kill, and no damage to the organs."

From a food perspective, this is exactly what you want, because the animal doesn't suffer, and a swift death means the meat will taste good. John got a young male about two years old, and because it's been unseasonably warm it was still eating fresh greens, not stripping bark off trees. For taste and texture, these conditions are optimal.

"It bled out right away," John adds. "More blood than you'd expect."

I wasn't expecting blood, actually. I was expecting it to expire prettily like one of the good guys in the movies, maybe promising eternal love and leaving behind a magically gifted baby.

"Did you eat a slice of liver warm after the kill?" I ask hopefully.

"That's not a Maine tradition," he growls. "Maine hunters take the tenderloins and do a fry up on the spot."

But you have to bring a skillet with you in order to do this, and cast iron skillets are heavy. Should the hunter be staying in the woods, says the author of *Camp Life in the Woods*, large joints of venison, moose, and bear meat can be roasted on the spot with a green birch branch serving as a spit and resting on two green logs on either end of the flames. It can be propped up in place with a small stick and turned occasionally, enhanced by a sprinkling of salt and pepper stashed in the cuffs of your hunting pants.

"I gotta get off the phone," John interrupts. "My dad is gutting it now. I need to help. You coming?" Abruptly, he hangs up.

A century earlier, it was often said that moose was the most delicious of all the game meats, but hunters were taking moose whenever they felt like it, cows and calves and everything in between, because there were so many of them. In 1864, Henry David Thoreau complained that the Native Americans guiding him through the Maine woods exhibited poor feeling for the forest and no appreciation for God's creations. "What a coarse and imperfect use Indians and hunters make of Nature!" he declared in contempt. "No wonder that their race is so soon exterminated." To make matters worse, his Indians were hunting moose for his dinner. Moose! Imagine! Why, it was like shooting horses standing around in your backyard, Thoreau complained. Where was the sport in that? His sensitive soul was offended by this meat, which tasted, hmm (. . . smack lips, chew thoughtfully, cut off another piece . . .) like a nice side of beef with a bit of veal thrown in, and hand over some more because I'm paying you Chief and this is my food, you savage who can't speak proper English. Because I do not eat, I dine, O Brown Man with moccasins on your feet. This is why the White Man is your moral superior.

In Maine, the female moose and their calves are now off limits, and the season is timed to the rut. Males are more active then, and they will respond to the female's call. She gives off a shrill baaaa! He responds by grunting. Whrff whrrf! It's the balcony scene from Romeo and Juliet, except the balcony is a mountaintop. Like whales, moose will travel great distances in search of their mate. Distracted by desire, they're more susceptible to being hunted, which accounts for the odd timing of hunting season. Lust doesn't last very long. The meat of a rutting male is stronger, tougher, and gamier on the whole, because as soon as they start looking for lady moose the bulls stop eating. Love takes away their appetites and turns them into bellowing fools. This is good for lady moose. It is not so good for cooks.

The solution is mooseburger, which is exactly as good as you expect it to be. It's a mixture of horny moose, store-bought cow, and sometimes scrap pig, the mixture of wild and domestic making a pre-masticated mash not unlike the worms regurgitated by mama birds for baby chicks. It is both adorable and disgusting.

By the time I get to Maine and figure out where everyone is inside this shifting time-space parallax that includes sighting my brother and a moose inside the space of twenty-four hours, the men have gone back out hunting and the bulk of the moose has gone to the butcher. The meat will hang for a few days and then he will cut it up. And no, I cannot help. And no, I cannot watch. And . . . just no. Now go away.

Back at the Big House, I call my sister to complain.

My sister cackles. "I had moose tongue in Houlton!"

"Where?"

"At Anne Ludwig's house. I must have been about nine, I guess." Anne was as cute as a chipmunk and close to the same size. "I'll never forget that dinner," my sister says earnestly.

"Everyone was there, her father, her brother Fred, and her mom. I didn't think anything when the meat was served. They were all taking some and really enjoying it, and so I took some too. Her mom had this really funny expression on her face. She kept on asking me, 'Are you sure you like it? Are you suuuuure?'" She bursts out laughing again. "After I'd cleaned my plate, Anne told me it was moose tongue. And her mom gave me that really weird look again, like she expected me to run out of the room, screaming. I thought it was fine."

I conclude that moose tongue tastes like sushi.

My sister isn't a fan of meat but loves fish, including the kind that's shaped like eel and octopus. Her version of "cooking" consists of growing her own garlic in a flowerpot and eating the raw cloves for breakfast. I'm listening to my sister rhapsodize about her latest health food kick, which involves kefir grains in a spaghetti-sauce jar, when John and Don stomp back into the house and start doffing their woolens. As soon as John spots me wedged into a chair across the room, he starts bellowing something about the moose.

"John needs help," I tell her in a long-suffering tone, and hang up just as she starts laughing again.

". . . I *told* you," John says to me, as he sits down next to me and starts unlacing his muddy hunting boots. "A smaller caliber will kill it but it won't stop it."

"What, like it turns them into zombies?"

John scowls. He does not have a sense of humor about moose hunting.

Blithely stripping down to his underwear in the living room, he repeats telling me that Patrick was high up on the mountain when he spotted a large moose. He took a shot, hit it, and then it ran off. Patrick and his hunting buddy Kevin chased it for hours and finally gave up. It's too dangerous to chase a wounded moose after dark. Nobody wants this, not even Thoreau, who wrote about moose after moose that ran away from him instead falling onto his plate.

The best kill is one that comes so suddenly that the animal never realizes that it's dead. Personally, I would like to die like this. Such a death would be a gift. In modern life, it's just difficult to arrange.

"The plastic bag is for you," John waves at a lumpy sack sitting on the counter. "Go look!" he urges, with a pleased expression on his face.

Carefully, I unwind the bag, and find myself staring at a heart and a liver. I pull them out, set them on the counter, and examine them. The moose's heart is as big as my head. The liver is even larger. Whole, the liver was ten pounds, but a pound each has already gone to two of Ruth's sisters and the lady down the street. The long tapered lobes that remain are as densely textured as the thickest of silk velvets. Resting on my cutting board is not a dread thing: it is a Siamese cat sleeping with its chin on curled paws.

Unexpectedly, Don says to me, "You would've had a great time on the moose hunt. If you'd been there we would've saved the guts. They were perfect."

John grumbles, "I told Patrick to take the urine."

"What on earth for?" I ask in surprise.

"You spray it on your shoes. It masks human smell and acts as a lure. More than one hunter has sprayed that stuff on their boots, only to turn around and find that a moose has been following *him*."

I hate the idea of wasting any bit of the animal, but it would never occur to me to keep the pee. "You're making that up," I say accusingly.

"Nope," he says staunchly. "That stuff costs a lot if you buy it at the store."

"You're not supposed to eat too much moose liver," Ruth says randomly, as she wanders into the kitchen.

"Why not?" I ask curiously.

"Something about the enzymes," she explains vaguely. "It's the old ones that are really the problem." She turns around and wanders out of the kitchen again.

It turns out that moose are herbivores, feasting mostly on swamp plants. As a result, their diets are high in cadmium, a naturally occurring but toxic trace element that ends up getting into swamp water from runoff coming off the mountain. Because moose have to eat at least 9,000 calories of plant material daily to survive, cadmium accumulates in their system, especially the kidneys and the liver. The older the animal, the higher the levels of cadmium, so eating their organs is to be avoided. As far as I can tell, however, eating moose liver for one season out of a lifetime is unlikely to cause problems, because the only documented adverse cases linked to cadmium ingestion were to post-menopausal, anemic, Japanese women.

Er. Hum. "Oh well," I shrug, and begin slicing my prize.

Here is my recipe:

---

1 lb. moose liver, soaked in cold water

1 c. flour

1 tsp. freshly cracked black pepper

1 tsp. salt

Three slices of thick bacon, diced

One medium sweet onion, sliced thinly

A pinch of red pepper flakes

½ cup of lard, bacon fat, or vegetable oil

1 tsp. minced garlic

Remove membrane and arteries from the liver. Slice as thinly as possible and pat the slices dry. In a shallow dish, mix together flour, salt, and black pepper. Dredge slices of liver in the seasoned flour and set aside. Dice bacon, add sliced onions, red pepper flakes, and minced garlic, and sauté in pan until bacon is crisp and onions are translucent. Remove onion mixture from pan. Add lard or oil to same pan, and raise heat to medium high. Add coated liver slices to the fat and fry until edges are golden and crispy; then flip the liver and fry the other side. Do not overcook. Remove slices and serve, topping them with the sliced onions and bacon.

In addition to being poisonous, cadmium is also the stuff that makes red paint look red. Blood red, to be specific, as opposed to rose red, lipstick red, scarlet, carmine, or magenta. It's a reminder that nature is naturally lethal. We kill it, it kills us back. That seems only fair.

For related reasons, contemporary wildlife management sources warn that moose kidneys are not to be consumed, and same goes for brains. Nowadays, the tongue, testicles, brains, cheeks, kidneys, lungs, and blood all seem to be unpopular from the culinary standpoint. I did find one ancient Roman recipe by Apicius that featured the amazing combination of chicken livers, raw eggs, and rabbit brains. But I've looked for rabbit brains, and they don't have any. I've looked for mine, too. I found them in my stomach.

CHAPTER THIRTEEN

❧ ❧ ❧

Don't Shoot the Deer in the Ass

The hunter is not least a subject of song, who brings peace
to our pastures and feasts us with every sort of meat.
— *Synesisus of Cyrene, Letter 148, 1ˢᵗ century AD*

It is 5 A.M., and John is getting ready to go deer hunting. Outside, it's twenty-three degrees in the disappearing dark, and the fields are frozen. By the time I turn over, a shy mist is rising from the land, blending earth and sky. John is using my half of the bed to offload and organize his gear. I am pretending to be asleep.

I open one eye, and see orange. There's a fluorescent puffy vest layered on top of me.

"To keep you warm, baby," he says primly, and tucks it in around me.

"Mmmph," I thank him, and disappear under the quilt.

He tugs on long johns and heads upstairs for food.

Brzzzzzip! goes the coffee bean grinder.

Thump! go the logs in the stove.

Argh! I mutter, pulling his pillow over my head. Something soft lands on me. It's a balled-up sock. I sneeze and count my blessings. This time, the sock is clean.

The lush scents of a good breakfast waft downstairs. A base layer of coffee, followed by last night's apple pie warmed up in the toaster oven. The patter of footsteps signals that the rest of the house is awake. Doors swing open and close, followed by bumps down the steps of the porch. Ruth is taking the truck out to pick up the newspaper from the end of the driveway. She rumbles back up to the house, and shuffles into the kitchen. Male voices discuss the morning's hunting itinerary. As I drift back to sleep, I hear snippets of the plan: John's going to hunt out back today, going high up the mountain where we'd bushwhacked a few weeks ago, and then he will . . .

I'm woken up by the sound of heavy feet thumping downstairs.

"Sleepyhead," John teases me, and starts plucking off the layers that are keeping my feet warm. The hunting outfit consists of thermal underwear, heavy wool pants, wool shirt, double socks, tall rubber boots, duct tape, fleece gloves, fluorescent orange fleece jacket, and fluorescent orange hat. On top of this, he piles on the gear needed for the day: rifle, ammo, hunting knife, compass, binoculars, camouflage tushy-cushion, cotton kerchiefs, a plastic bottle for peeing (*not* to be confused with the water bottle for drinking), cell phone, watch, and sunglasses. No toilet paper, chocolate bars, or thermoses full of hot coffee. His reasons for not bringing these items, in no particular order: "Peeing!" "Too noisy!" and "Don't need it!"

It's daybreak. Such pretty light. It's a perfect day for sleeping.

John kisses my nose, whooshes out the door in a great rush of wool, and then clumps up the stairs with his rifle and twenty pounds of gear.

Clump, clump, clump, clump, clu . . .

His steps stop abruptly. He's on the landing to the front door, the one that nobody uses because it doesn't go anywhere. Just as suddenly the low murmur of kitchen noises suspend, filling the house with silence.

I wait, listening, knowing that something is happening and that moving is a bad idea.

A few minutes later, a high-pitched tiny sound wings downstairs to my ears:

. . . crrrrrrreeeak.

"SHIT!" John roars. "SHIT!" and charges out the door in a great rush of gear, letting the door bang loudly behind him.

Now I have to get up to find out what happened. My feet cringing at the cold, I stick them out from under the covers and ease the rest of me out into the morning air. I run in front of the woodstove, pull on jeans and an old sweater, and dash upstairs to the living room, where Ruth and Don are both looking intently at the frost crystals skating across the picture window.

"What happened?" I ask without preamble.

"Oh," Ruth replies blandly without turning her head. "You missed it. It was a large buck. He was grazing right out front." She waggles a finger at the spot, which is no more than thirty feet from the house. A clear shot, flat ground, no bushes, no trees, and no sun to get in your eyes. "Johnny was standing right at the door when he spotted him. He'd got his rifle out and was ready to take a shot. But as soon as the buck heard the hinges creak, he took right off. Johnny went after him." She waves in the general direction of the mountain.

Don takes refuge in his deaf ear and his tallness to ignore our chit-chat about details that don't matter. Striding to the basement, he returns with a pair of binoculars and starts looking through the picture window again, hoping to spot a crafty deer skulking behind a pine tree.

"Hmm," he mutters inscrutably to himself.

I walk to the squeaky door and peek out, imagining the shot that he'd had on the buck. I can picture John standing at the door, so excited to stumble onto one so close, and then that *sound*, so loud that I heard it asleep under the covers. With a jerk the buck's head comes up and he is off in a flash, bounding with Bolshoi arcs into the waiting wings of the forest. And off John goes, charging at full speed, his camo tushy cushion flapping behind him.

He spends the next six hours trying to outwit the buck. At noon, he stomps back into the house. He is sweaty, tired, and frustrated. "I heard him grunt, twice," he says morosely, as he sits down in the kitchen and reaches for a consolation cookie. "But each time he was too far ahead. I tried heading up the ridge and coming back down, circling around to try and catch him, but no luck."

"You'll get him eventually," I soothe, and make him a sandwich.

"Why didn't you tell me the hinges creaked?" he complains. "C'mon," he says, grimly, through mouthfuls of peanut butter and marmalade. "We're going shopping."

"*Now?*" I yelp in protest.

"Now," he repeats firmly, tucking a sandwich under one arm and me under the other. And off we tear down the road, making a run for Mexico.

In Walmart-Mexico, which is, inexplicably, not nearly as much fun as Walmart-Paris, he grabs a cartful of doodads that somehow relate to hunting. This is the male version of emotional impulse buying. Instead of nail polish, shoes, and a box of chocolates, he's got a bottle of doe urine, one set of antler noise makers, and one packet of scent patches. All that's left for him to select is a bleater, which is a doohickey that sounds like a bleating deer. The most expensive bleater is a lot like the $400 electronic animal call simulator I'd seen earlier in Cabela's, but this machine only plays variations of one animal in various states of aggravation. There's "Buck Grunt," "Sounds of Combat," "Doe in Estrus," and my personal favorite, "Doe in Super Estrus." I can't begin to imagine what a doe in heat sounds like, let alone one that's gone into baby-clock meltdown.

Push a button, the instructions entice.

How can I resist? Let's try "Buck Grunt." I push the black button.

"Whufff!" the machine announces in loud, decisive tones.

Hey! This is fun! Let's try "Doe in Estrus."

"Baaaa!" the machine declares.

A bleating doe sounds an awful lot like a crabby sheep.

The electrical device is a premium widget that needs batteries, which are unreliable in the cold. I prefer the lo-tech version, which is exactly like one of those "mooing" mini-cans found at kid toy stores. It's a small cardboard canister about the height of an adult thumb. The plastic lid is punctured like a salt shaker. Flip it over, and an internal bellows produces a sound that can be interpreted as a "moo." However, "moo" sounds exactly like "doe in estrus." The toddler's version features pink cartoon cows dancing jigs around the sides. The hunter's version comes in camouflage.

"Mooooo!" I mean, "Baaaaa!" I stand in the aisle and turn over the deer bleater again and again. "Baaaa! Baaaaa! Aaaa-aBaaaaaa-a-a-a!"

"Stop that," John complains. "It's not a toy."

"Of course it's a toy," I retort, bouncing up and down like an antsy toddler, making the can jiggle along with the rest of me. "Baaaa-a-a-aaaaaaa-aa-aaa!"

In addition to the moo-can bleater and the fancy electronic sound simulator, Walmart carries a third version that looks like a fat bendy straw with a snorkeling mouthpiece stuck to it. Blow into it, and the tube produces a vaguely mournful lowing. An adjustable string looped around the top makes the pitch go higher and lower according to the age and sex of the deer you're trying to imitate. I am standing behind the glass ammo display case when he decides to try it out.

"Moo," he toots experimentally.

I pop my head out.

"Moo," he toots again.

I pop my head out again.

He laughs, and walks over to me. "I guess it works!"

"Sounds like a handsome boy cow," I say, taking the rubbery flute out of his hands. "Not like a desperate girl deer."

"It's set on 'fawn'," he declares, as if this proves I must be wrong.

"A Shakespeare sort of faun, or a Bambi fawn?"

He frowns. He does not have a sense of humor about deer hunting.

Impetuously, he whisks the flute out of my hands and tosses it in the cart.

"You're buying it?" I exclaim incredulously.

"I'm so mad about missing that buck this morning," he replies, instead of simply saying Yes. That's ten words instead of one. When it comes to hunting talk, he's practically French. "It's so incredibly frustrating to have been RIGHT THERE, with a loaded rifle heading out the door, and if I'd only gone out the back door and circled around, I could have bagged him, no problem. It was an easy shot."

"I'll say a prayer, okay?" I joke. "Dear God," I say aloud. "Since you haven't been very nice to me this year, please send a buck John's way so we can eat this winter. Thank you."

"If it works, you'll owe Him."

"If it works, *you'll* owe Him." I pause. Ahem. "Her."

He gives me a look.

"Realistically," I clarify, "God is an It."

"Realism has nothing to do with it."

"My point exactly," I sniff.

I know perfectly well that God isn't a genie. Or Santa Claus. It doesn't stop me from expecting presents. Does no one else find it peculiar that God and Santa are both barrel-chested white men with long white beards whom no one has ever seen but everyone is quite sure exists, and it's impossible to say out loud, "There is no Santa Claus," without killing five angels, one for each mean word that falls out of your despicable mouth? It's like nobody ever notices that Clark Kent disappears whenever Superman is around. Same goes for God whenever Santa Claus shows up.

"You have an overactive imagination," he growls, and wheels me off in the cart to check out.

"I'm not the one buying a magic flute that summons deer," I remind him archly.

"Hur," he grunts, and pushes faster. He does not sound like a buck. Luckily for him, I'm not a deer. I'm just a pain in the ass.

The next morning, at 4 A.M., I wake to the sound of John leaning stark naked out the bedroom window and bleating with his flute. It's dark outside, and darker inside.

"Baaa! Baa! Baaa!"

"Stop that," I complain, burrowing back under the covers. "It's too cold when you open the window."

"Baa! Baa! Baa!"

"Do you really think that's going to work?" I grump.

"Sure," he replies, turning and grinning impishly at me as I slide unwillingly out of bed, having given up on trying to sleep through the din. "Baa!" he bleats happily, and starts chasing me around the room.

I have to wonder, do deer bleaters work on deer? So far, the only thing that's popped out of hiding is me. On that score, I'd say it works pretty well. But when he toots that flute, what does a buck hear?

"Deer are simple animals, surprised at everything," noted Pliny the Elder in the first century. "They can be charmed by song and by a shepherd's pipe." Pliny isn't necessarily wrong, especially if hookah and bong sorts of pipes are involved, but it isn't as if hunters drag boom boxes into their tree stands and blast Katy Perry tunes, thinking this will attract a curious buck to swing by to see what the fuss is about.

But "music hath charms to sooth the savage beast," the nature lover protests. Can't hunters just sing them to sleep instead of killing them dead? Unfortunately, the line actually reads, "Musick has Charms to sooth a savage *Breast*." It's the first line of the play *The Mourning Bride*, 1697, and Almeria, Princess of Granada, is talking about her own breasts. Her husband died the day they were married, so her lusciousness remains chaste. Her boobies are ungroped. Her heart doth mourn her woe, which is to say, she is mightily pissed off at finding herself a virgin widow. Music isn't quieting her turmoil, and she can't figure out why. "Why do I not have Peace?" she wails. (Modern translation: "I need to get laid!") It should come as no surprise that from this same play by William Congreve, fortunate pupil of Jonathan Swift, comes the eternal line, "Hell hath no fury like a woman scorned." This is also a misquotation, but it more or less gets the gist.

The "beast" version of the line persists because heartwarming anecdotes repeatedly surface about wild animals with a weakness for music. That lasted until snake charmers and dancing bears went out of business, their jobs taken over and outsourced by Disney. In Revolutionary France, for example, two Indian elephants named Hans and Marguerite were celebrated for their devotion to the missionary position and, even more improbably, to Italian opera. At the sound of the bassoon, they'd lift interested trunks and allow themselves to be seduced by its hardwood strains. Inconveniently, the missionary position is anatomically impossible for elephants to achieve. Pooh pooh! What do scientists know? According to the media, the "married" elephants stuck to their Church-approved relations. Under Him, all things are possible. It was literally a fucking miracle.

"Baa! Baa! Baaaaaaaaa!" John bleats with enthusiasm.

I shake my head and mutter, "He's worse than the rooster." I am thinking of making coq-au-vin. It is *not* a happy meal. "Why do I not have Peace!" I wail.

He suddenly stops chasing me as if an Important Thought just crossed his mind. "Are you going to make me breakfast, baby?" He looks at me reproachfully. "Look what happened when you didn't!"

I sigh. "I realize that the only reason you didn't get the buck yesterday was because you ate leftover pie for breakfast." Because, as William Shreiner's *Sporting Manual* of 1840 pointed out:

> It should be one of the huntsman's first considerations, when about starting upon an expedition, to be well supplied with convenient food, as crackers, gingerbread, dough-nuts, &c, and never hunt (as some are wont to do), on an empty stomach, for this organ, like a wild school boy, when not otherwise employed is generally at mischief.

And here he is, a huntsman with an empty stomach, getting himself up to mischief.

"Baa! Baa! Baaaaaaaaa!" he complains.

So I make John a hot breakfast and send him out to hunt. I'm not going with him, and he doesn't ask. He's hot on the trail of a big buck, and I will just get in the way. On days when all the conditions are favorable, he can't waste the chance by dragging me along. Wildlife will not hold still and wait while I adjust my thermal underpants.

"Put on an orange vest if you go out and get the laundry," Ruth warns me as she sails into the kitchen in search of fresh coffee. She nods at my hands, now swathed in white mittens that she'd knitted and given to me when the wintry weather started coming. "A few years back, a woman got shot at the clothesline. She had on white gloves."

"Mistaken for a white tail?" I ask.

"Yep," she replies shortly, and sails out again.

I look at my fluffy white mittens and think . . . naw. I'm just being paranoid. That was *last* year. *This* year, she told me to put on a vest.

Don scowls but doesn't say anything as he lumbers through the living room and goes downstairs to clean his rifles. The hunter should have been prosecuted, but he wasn't. He was old, a pillar of the community. It wasn't right what he did, and it was bad hunting too—even if he saw a deer he should have verified that he wasn't shooting a doe. But to put an old man in jail for a hunting accident? I suppose people were sympathetic because he hit his target, even if it was the wrong one.

When Hell freezes over, it freezes atheists and sinners alike. That's why Hell is hell.

I decide to add bright orange chaps, a bright orange polyester knit hat, and a puffy coat with a bright orange safety vest layered on top of it. I am a giant marshmallow in hunter's orange, clomping forward in heavy boots the approximate weight and shape of small boulders. Even for me, this is an exceptionally frumpy look.

The theory behind wearing bright orange is that deer are color blind. There are two problems with this theory: 1) Some humans (ahem) are color blind too, and 2) bears and bobcats can see color just fine. So while you're out at the clothesline, trying to bend the frozen sheets into submission, the carnivores are watching you from the safety of the woods, wondering if the bright orange idiot tastes like a carrot.

It's a good day for hunting, so Don decides to go out too. Ruth is off to a Republican ladies' lunch, so I'm all alone folding frozen towels in the house. (Dryer aversion is a Maine thing but also a French thing. Instead of clotheslines, however,

Parisians use their balconies.) She's left me with instructions to punch the bread dough down in about an hour, then shape it and plop it into the baking pans. If she's still not back, I am to put the risen loaves into the oven, touching them as little as possible because she's decided that the ingredient that makes my bread fall is me. There is a good scientific explanation for this. When yeast-beasties gobble down sugar, they burp, creating little air bubbles that make bread rise. But yeast-beasties are also like mood rings: when the baker is happy, they eat, and when the baker is grumpy, they go on strike. Temperamentally speaking, Ruth is as calm as a French cow, and her bread is a thing of beauty. My moods swing faster than a do-si-do at a square dance, and the poor yeast-beasties are exhausted by the time I'm finished kneading. This is as good an explanation as any, because every once in a while, for no particularly good reason, my bread comes out perfectly. It also explains why I have a way with meat, because it's already dead. It's got no sensibilities to offend.

Home alone! I take the opportunity to indulge in a long, hot shower. With wet hair and bare feet, I walk out of the bathroom, humming a happy tune . . . and find myself staring at a man who is peering through the skinny glass windows set into the jambs of the front door. Wiry with mild features and thinning brown hair, he looks like one of those overworked guys you see buying beer while filling up his truck at the gas station.

"CAN I HELP YOU?" I shout through the door. Peeping Tom didn't knock and it's pretty clear that he's never been to the Big House before, because he came to the wrong door. I *could* grab a shotgun but I'd rather not. I'm not sure what the rules are about shooting strangers in somebody else's house.

"UH, YES," he replies, his face registering confusion. "Uh . . ." he starts again.

I give him a cross look. No, I'm not going to open the door because I don't know who you are and nobody told me to expect you. Shouting through a closed door is just fine.

"WE GOT PERMISSION TO HUNT OUT BACK, ME AND MY BOY?" He pauses, peers at me again, and blinks. "JUST WANTED TO MAKE SURE ABOUT IT BEFORE WE WENT BACK THERE?"

He stands there, blinking anxiously, waiting for my response.

"Huh. Well, okay," I concede, because what he's saying is not entirely outside the bounds of possibility. "YOU WEREN'T PLANNING ON HUNTING TODAY, WERE YOU?" He's wearing old jeans and a down coat, so I'm guessing the answer is no.

He shakes his head, confirming my guess.

"GOOD THING," I shout through the door. "IT'S CROWDED BACK THERE TODAY!"

He looks mildly surprised, then nods and walks away, his whole body revealing his confusion.

I watch through the windows until he drives off. Shaking my head, I turn my attention to the dough. It has risen forcefully in the bowl, so I punch the puffy dough down, shape it into long loaves, and place them into oiled loaf pans. I'm draping a kitchen towel over the loaves and setting them aside to rise when Ruth returns with a great rattling through the side door. Marching straight to the kitchen island, she lifts the towel with a brusque hand and inspects the bread dough.

"Anything happen while I was gone?" she asks straight-away, as she lets the towel drape back down.

"Some guy stopped by," I tell her. "He said that he has per-mission to hunt out back?"

Ruth stares at me blankly, but as soon as she hears my description of him, her expression clears. "Oh yes, that's Mark

Farmer. Talked to his boy yesterday about the hunting. He's got permission, but he's supposed to let one of us know before he goes back there." She pauses, thinking. "He's divorced now. I don't know what happened with their divorce, but in the middle of it, his wife put up a big sign up on Route 9, saying 'Mark Farmer is having an affair.'" She shakes her head in bafflement at the crazy way people behave, adding. "It was gone the next day."

"Did he?" I prod.

"You mean, did he have an affair?" She shrugs the question off. Either way, she doesn't care. This attitude is pure Yankee: she inhabits a universe of minutia, not gossip. "I've got to go out again to run errands," she announces. This is somewhat obvious as she is still fully bundled in her hat and coat. "You okay being in charge of the bread?"

"Yep," I say with a great show of confidence, trying to maintain positive waves to keep the dough from spiraling into a bleak state of depression.

Ruth laughs. "Okay then!" And out she sails again.

The dough likes the dry wood heat permeating the house. In a matter of minutes, the loaves are fully inflated again, so I pop them in the preheated oven, sighing with jealousy at their fluffy optimism, and set the timer for 30 minutes. Settling into a sofa, I entertain myself by reading *The Cook Not Mad, or Rational Cookery*. Published in 1830, it advocates "good republican dishes" ranging from "ARROWROOT, prepared for sickness," to "WHITEWASH, excellent." As usual, I start with the end and go backwards, because I'm contrary and like to know how stories end. It doesn't ruin the plot because *The Cook Not Mad* isn't a whodunit. The big revelation at the end isn't the name of the killer, but an old-fashioned index to useful skills such as "DYING," on which there is an entire section. These how-to instructions make more sense once you realize that the "duties of the wedded life" and the "mysteries of the eating department" include:

> BEEF, to corn
>
> BEDBUGS, to keep clear of
>
> COOKIES, nice, that will keep good three months
>
> FEMALES' DRESS, to put out when on fire
>
> MEAT, red, and vegetable flavours

This book aims to please the American palate. Thus, the anonymous author explains, it's pointless to introduce the English, French, and Italian manner of rendering food "indigestible," as their saucy ways are for city palates corrupted by "loathsome objects." Good cooking is plain cooking, resulting in health and happiness for the family. Take recipe 266: "To expel nameless intruders from your children's heads," which involves boiling larkspur seeds in water and then, presumably, inviting a priest to complete the exorcism using your homemade holy water. This is very plain and wholesome cooking.

"Calf's Brains—Turtle Fashion," requires the whole head and the hooves. There are two versions of this popular dish, which pop up after a recipe for smothered fowl with oysters. So, *The Cook Not Mad* is really a relationship advice book for the modern frontier couple. For new husbands, the advice isn't subtle: keep the missus happy, else risk being shoved into the stewpot by a very rational, extremely angry woman who knows how to brain cows, make poisons, and expel demons. It also warns the single girl to *learn her yeasts*. A wedding was ruined, the cookbook relates, because the prospective bride used brewer's yeast instead of distiller's yeast in her wedding cake, and so "the cake was spoiled and the wedding postponed." I imagine the hungry groom ran off with a gal who knew that what he really wanted was a corned beef sandwich and a pint of homemade beer.

Ping! the timer rings. Obedient to the sound, I rise from the sofa, open the oven door, bask in the heat, and pull the loaves out. Then I pop them onto cooling racks and slather the tops with butter.

Suddenly, a tingle runs up my spine. Dashing to the kitchen window, I look outside. I don't see anything but the chicken coop and the trees, but it's late in the afternoon, and the light is swiftly dimming.

Two shots ring out. It's coming from out back, far up the mountain.

The phone rings. It's Don. "It wasn't me," he says right away. "If John calls the house, and he got a deer, tell him I'll be right up with the four wheeler. Then call me." He hangs up.

Instantly, the phone rings. It's John. "Tell my dad I'm right by my tree stand," he blurts, and hangs up.

I ring Don, convey the news, and I'm still standing by the phone when Don comes through the door, carrying a rifle and a fold-up canvas hunting chair.

"I thought you were way up out back?" I ask in surprise.

He chuckles. He was by the edge of the field in the front yard, hoping to get the buck that escaped the other morning. "I was in my chair, arms folded across my chest, just thinking how nice it was to be out here, and I'd just nodded off when I heard those shots. And when I heard two, I was pretty sure Johnny'd got one."

"You were right. He did!" We are both grinning like crazy people. I am on the verge of tears. I'm not sure why, a potent combination of happiness, pride, and proximity to a killing. A life was not lost but taken. And so we will eat well for supper.

As Don grabs a prepared pack of field dressing supplies, I pull on my orange gear, and off we go up the trail. By the time we set out, it's twilight. The path through the forest is familiar, but the headlights darken the sides of the trail even as eager branches and ambitious saplings cast strange shadows in the headlights. At nightfall, the forest becomes the playground of four-footed beasts and wanton creatures with wings. We are interlopers in a generous realm we pretend to understand. Riding through the falling dark on the back of an ATV, I duck behind Don's enormous frame in order to keep branches from slapping me. There are new ruts, deep puddles, and fallen trees blocking the trail. This is normal. It is the forest. Bears shit in the woods, and trees fall too.

The machine sounds louder when daylight fades, coaxing shy animals to feed and quiet to come out and play. The familiar becomes uncanny: we are entering the land of Need, for the animals are in charge when the light drains. On either side of the trail, indistinct shapes form a grisaille of high expectations and slow, hard truths. Up and across we go, higher and higher up the land's inexorable rise until we reach a short section of flat trail. I know where we are. Don does too. My eyes scan the darkness. The ATV growls in warning. Don is driving slowly for fear of me falling off the back without him noticing. An oddly exposed mound gleams high on one side of the rising slope. We putter by in low gear, heading toward the tree stand, when a deep voice rings out, "Hey, stop! Hey! HEY!" the voice bellows. "Over here!"

"We just passed John!" I yell in Don's good ear. "He's right behind us!"

Nodding, Don stops the ATV. I hop off, run back, and scramble up the side of the hill, dragging the heavy field dressing pack along with me. Vest flapping and knees buckling, I am tumbling up the uneven ground, the dark earth a quagmire of branches and leaves that slip on the tongue. Threadbare and reedy in the cold, the forest canopy blocks the starlight as bony branches beckon me forward. My nose leads me to the spot. I'm right next to John before I can make him out. The weird whitish shape I'd spotted is a buck on its back.

"Did you bring a flashlight?" he asks without preamble.

"Yah," I reply, wanting to throw my arms around him and cover him in embarrassing girl kisses. Instead, I dig around the pack for the flashlight, pull it out, and shine it efficiently on the buck. As I stand there, holding the light, John adjusts the carcass, positioning the blade for the first cut.

There is a moment, a balking, before the body. It always happens, even to experienced hunters. The first cut is an irrevocable act. But it is something else, a primal activation: the sight of the incommensurable. It is to look Medusa in the face, and thus be turned to stone.

We are frozen in the dark.

Holding a large hunting knife in his right hand, John suddenly slices open the belly and goes up through the peritoneum, a membrane under the skin that holds the innards together. Humans have one too. Our inner jellyfishes. As John kneels by the carcass, carefully working the knife under the hide, the ATV rumbles up the side. John, the buck, and I are illuminated in stillness, caught in the headlights and forming a makeshift backwoods nativity scene. Steam rises from our mouths, from the deer's supine torso, from the engine making heat. The ATV sounds like a generator. In my head, we are working in perfect silence.

With effort but not difficulty, John splits the ribcage, so now the belly cavity is fully open. To me, this feels like surgery, a repair of a psychic imbalance resonating across the universe and crash landing on this lonely planet. What means the death of one animal in the forest? Is God watching? What are the sparrows thinking? I could recoil out of fear. But of what? Make neither more nor less out of all this than what it is. And what *is* this? The skeptic in me demands to know, squinting malevolently at the blood, the body, the bones gleaming in the artificial light. Oh, but it is life, and death, and life again. A miracle pretended into oblivion when I shut my eyes, and painfully real when I open them again. This meat will be eaten with gladness, rejoicing, and juniper berries.

But that is the future. Do not ignore the present.

Packed into the belly, the viscera is white, pristine, except for a small portion where the chest area is messy. "That's where the bullet went through," John tells me. I lean forward with the flashlight and look, but I can't see what he means. He points at the lungs, directing my gaze. The bullet went between the ribs, piercing the lungs and taking some of the liver as it exited. That trajectory explains why the lungs are full of blood and a thin line of blood trickles from the deer's mouth. "It ran, even after I'd shot it clean through," John explains. "It didn't drop right away, and I had to chase it. That's why I wasn't at my tree stand. In thirty seconds, a deer can get amazingly far." He snuffles away mild embarrassment. "I almost couldn't find it, especially after it got so dark."

"It's incredible that it didn't drop right away," I mumble, just to have something to say. "A man would have gone down instantly."

"The adrenaline surge that goes through a buck is really something," John says in wonderment. "This is why it's best to get it through the heart." He rummages around the body cavity, and when his hands emerge, they are holding the heart. It's perfectly intact. A beautiful sight. Along with the surviving lobe of the liver, it's going to be eaten tomorrow for dinner. He hands them both to me. I drop them in a plastic grocery bag, and carefully tie it shut, trying my best to keep leaves from getting in.

Next, he tips the stomach, lungs, spleen, pancreas, and small intestines onto the ground. Covered by a light blanket of frozen leaves, the entrails will stay where they are. By tomorrow, they'll be gone. Tonight, the forest will feast. Waste not, want not. The suet will do the chickadees good.

The testicles come off, along with small loose pouches of white fat. "Can't we use that fat for something?" I ask hopefully.

"Indians used to eat that fat right away, just reaching in and eating it out of the fresh kill," Don says, lumbering forward with another flashlight. "They'd cut the long bones too, and suck out the warm marrow."

"Don't give her any ideas," John mutters.

"No," Don says dryly, "we're not keeping the fat."

"Can we make soap? Or candles?" I ask hopefully.

No, the men shake their heads. Not tonight. It's too late to deal with those kinds of details. Not if we want to conserve the meat.

Nudging John aside, Don goes to work on the large intestine, bladder, and anus, all of which must be removed carefully, to avoid corrupting the flesh. I can watch but must not touch. A mistake here can ruin everything.

But the deer's bladder is empty, the intestines nearly voided, and the anus isn't visibly different from any other furry bit of the deer—say, the ear. There is no odor except that of fresh blood, which is a distinctive scent not unlike the smell of good sex, a fistful of salt dissolved in the air. Other predators will soon be coming, attracted by the sweet smell and the lure of an easy meal.

At night, the forest is lightless. It is not frightening, though the air is thick and shadows layer the land. Out here, the moon becomes a moth fluttering inside a child's bedroom. The woods are a sieve. Through it run desires that civilization loathes to admit. It is why animals live here and humans cannot. Society cannot survive the end of all charades. Too many people can't stand themselves. They will die out here.

The work proceeds quickly. A few more cuts and the field dressing is done. The three of us stand around the deer, standing silently with hands balled and heads bowed. I take a deep breath, inhaling the forest into small lungs, and feel myself suddenly weary. The earth is tired.

Without asking for help, John lifts the carcass to the ATV, its headlights still shining steadily, and ties it on the back with bungee cords. I pick up the field dressing kit and put the tools back in. With a wave, Don drives off with the prize, taking the light with him. He'll meet us back at the house. John and I will walk.

The ATV drives off, pulling the human sounds behind it. The forest resumes its quiet. Overhead and underfoot, small birds are gathering anxiously, hoping to be fed first.

"Greedy bastards," I say lightly, wondering who else is out there with empty stomachs and strong beaks.

With a flashlight in hand and nothing to pack out, the trundle back down the mountain is easy. John's whole body thrums with fatigue and pride. He takes my hand as we walk, as he always does. I don't mind that his hands are covered in blood, because mine are bloody too. My other hand clutches the bag with the offal. The coveted. The grotesque. The perfect. Mine because he gave them to me.

"Did you use your new gizmos?" I ask him curiously as we slip down the trail.

"Yes!" he nods happily. It's too dark for me to see him but I can feel his head bobbing up and down.

"Did you set up the scent patches like the instructions said?"

"Yes!" he says again, waggling the flashlight so that shadows dance in our path. Then he flicks it off, because the harsh light illuminates a narrow path but that only makes it more difficult to see where we're going. Eyes adjusted to moonlight take in the entire forest. "I sat upwind, created a little triangle with the scent patches, then went in my tree stand and started calling, Baaaa! It may just be a coincidence, but the buck just came right up and stood right in the middle of that little triangle I created."

"I'd say that's pretty suggestive."

He squeezes my hand. "Mmm. Nice and soft," he comments appreciatively.

Deer fat is a great moisturizer.

"You're going to get the wrong impression that bagging a buck is like going out for groceries." He squeezes my hand again because he's pleased with himself. "You send me out to get meat for the table, and I come back with meat for the table!"

I squeeze his hand back, because I know better. This buck represents weeks and months of effort forgotten in the moment and the mind playing tricks. John loves to hunt, but he also hunts because he loves me. Primordial, he exults in his ability to feed me, to share the unseemly beauty of the fresh kill. The size of the rack doesn't confirm his prowess. The supper table does.

What matters, always, is the nearness of the life being consumed. This is food. Everything else is bullshit.

By the time we get close to the house, I can hear the sounds of running water. Don is out back and rinsing the cavity with a garden hose. "We'll hang it tonight, take it in for tagging tomorrow," he says as we trot forward to join him. "It needs to cool down. It's not really cold out tonight."

"Are we going to take the tenderloins?" I ask anxiously.

"There's a few more steps," Don says patiently, "but yes, we'll cut out the tenderloins."

John doesn't give any indication that he's heard, but I am literally twirling for joy. If it wasn't already so late I'd start up the fire pit. But a fire means hours of waiting, and I'm already blinking away sleep. The men start preparing the deer for hanging, wiping the sacrificed body with care. I'm no help here. As my hands flap uselessly, I realize that I'm still clutching a bag of offal, and I bring it to my face, staring at it with a sense of déjà vu.

Back inside the warm house, I place the heart and liver in a large bowl of fresh water, trim off the fat, and remove the arteries. In the light, the organs look enticing, their health evident in every aspect. There is blood, but not much. It's less than a child's nosebleed, and more than a paper cut. The sight of them makes me hungry.

They get rinsed a few more times, and go into the refrigerator. I peek through the kitchen window to check on the men's progress.

John, Don, and the deer have vanished.

Rattling noises and flashes of hard light give away their location.

Wiping my hands dry, I head out to the henhouse, pop inside, and close the door quickly behind me to keep the heat from escaping. Inside the small space, John is holding the deer, hugging it tightly to keep it from twirling as Don throws a heavy nylon rope up and over the rafters. The deer's hind legs are notched into a heavy metal hanger that keeps them from flopping together. This step speeds up the cooling, which keeps the meat from spoiling.

"Er, but won't the chickens mind?" I ask in surprise.

In reply, Don hands me a portable lamp and gestures for me to hold it up as high as I can while he ties the hanger to the rope and pulls steadily. On the other end, John is lifting the deer: an ice skater hoisting up his reluctant partner. A few more tugs, and the carcass is hanging a few feet off the ground. In the background, the chickens cluck softly. I wonder what they're thinking about their new roommate. They can't see the deer, but they can smell it. Sniffing, I smell human sweat and chicken feed. The deer smells like down feathers.

Head down, the buck hangs gracefully from the rafters, its curving antlers grazing the floor.

Now, finally, it's time to take the tenderloins.

Until you take actual tenderloins from a carcass, they don't make much sense. According to Wikipedia, the word, "tenderloin" refers to "the psoas major muscle anterior to the transverse processes of the lumbar vertebra." This is precise but not very helpful. Tenderloins are difficult to envision because they don't seem to have a purpose. They're on the underside of the backbone where they're just kind of riding around, giving moral support to the deer but not much else. They're as soft as pillows because they're rarely used. The muscles on top of the backbone, also called the backstraps, are the ones that do the heavy lifting. When humans pull their back muscles, the backstraps are the ones that hurt. Nobody pulls their psoas majors, not even yoga instructors.

Now that the carcass is hanging upside-down, the tenderloins are easier to see, because they're the only bits of visible muscle inside the belly cavity. A glistening hollow lined with a silvery skin, the cavity appears to be empty, because it is. A small sharp knife, applied carefully, will take the tenderloins off the spine. They're thick skeins of meat as long as my arm and so soft I can shred them with my fingers. In cold hands, the flesh feels warm. But that could just be my imagination.

I take the first tenderloin. Don takes the second. I hold them both, cradling them as if they were a two-headed snake, in olden days an omen of miracles portending. It's my job to tend after the meat, to turn it into a dish that evokes the richness of this day and all the days that came before time stopped forever. The deer deserves that. Outside, the trees rustle. Inside, the hens cluck. The night's work is almost done. Tiredly, the three of us leave the coop, bungee the door shut so the coyotes don't get in, and head back to the house, carrying tenderloins and two freshly-laid eggs for good measure.

While we were going about our business, the hens were busy too.

Stomping back into the warmth of the living room, the men suddenly look much too large for the house. Grunting, they take off their boots, brush off their pants, and disappear to wash up. I change quickly into clean clothes, give my hands a soapy scrubbing, then march into the kitchen, slice off a few chunks of the tenderloins and sear them quickly in very hot oil, crushed garlic, and a pinch of salt and pepper. A deglazing with red wine and butter, and they are passed to the plate, served with fresh homemade bread to tired men waiting expectantly at the table.

Take, eat, this is my body which is given unto you.

On communion Sundays, I used to think it was really funny to kneel at the altar as my dad served grape juice and white bread, calling it the blood and body of Christ and God bless us every one, in the manner of Tiny Tim. No matter how hard I tried it was always just gummy Wonder bread that I'd cut up before the service into crustless white cubes, and Welch's grape juice I'd poured in those little thimble glasses that fit into the special stacked round trays used for communion service. My mind rebelled. The prayer didn't match the taste in my mouth.

Now, I finally understand what the ritual means, because this morning, the "white bread" was walking around on four hooves. And once again it was me who sliced it up with a big knife standing all by myself in the kitchen, turning the bread into a body, and serving it to weary souls in need of comforting.

If religion is ever going to find its way back into this world, it will have to go through the taste buds first. I'm tired of hearing politicians invoke the Lord's name while talking out of their asses.

The meat is meltingly tender, the flavor mild and sweet. That note of sweetness is one I never taste in farmed meat. I am tasting blueberries, I think.

John looks ready to burst with pride. His entire body is beaming.

"It's from our land," Don says gruffly. He is happy.

CHAPTER FOURTEEN

☙ ☙ ☙

Blood and Guts

Lawyer Amanda Bonner: "And after you
shot your husband . . . how did you feel?"
Defendant Doris Attinger: "Hungry!"
– Adam's Rib, 1949

*P*atrick lost another one in the dark and rain. He was
very high up the mountain, where the terrain is steep
and treacherous. He'd been tracking a buck and took a shot.
The hit was fatal, but the kill wasn't instantaneous. Running
after it, Patrick found bone, blood, and hair before the pound-
ing rain washed the trace away. A weaker animal would have
dropped in its tracks. Five friends came out the next morning to look for it, and all they found was the gut pile left by a
stranger who'd stumbled across it.

Is it poaching to take another man's quarry? It's not unusual
for hunters to lose their animals in the forest. Humans stand
out. Animals blend in. Within seconds, the wildlife can vanish, even if you know exactly where they are going. So if a
hunter stumbles across a buck felled by another man's bullet,
the right thing to do is to dress and hang the carcass, alert the
game warden, and have a nice day. To walk off with the deer
violates an unwritten code. It's the hunter's version of the girl
crush. A nice girl never steals a boy that her girlfriend likes.
A tramp would hit on him just for fun, and steal him if she

could. It's one of the ways you know she's a tramp. Sure, all's fair in love and war—but in real life, it's not exactly true.

In Maine, a lot of men are veterans. My dad is a veteran of the Korean War. John's dad is a Vietnam vet. Patrick served in Iraq. From WWI to the war against terror, each conflict has been getting a little bit blurrier between right and wrong, good and bad, us and them. Morally, the entire world has become a wilderness. Soldiers don't expect civilians to understand. But a hunter ought to know better. There is a community, and there is a code. Every community has its laws. Each group has its rules. This guy violated a big one.

He shouldn't have taken Patrick's buck.

Angered by the betrayal, Don calls the tagging stations and figures out who took it. Only one deer tagged that day, and the buck that was brought in—a really big, beautiful specimen—fit the description. It was stolen by a man who lives a ways down the street. "A bottom feeder," Don says in disgust. "He advertised a .22 in *Uncle Henry's* for a good price. Went over there to take a look. The gun was a piece of junk. Turns out he'd no intention of selling it. Carl was just trying to get people to come over so he could sign them up for Amway." The really infuriating bit is that the deer thief knew that Keith and Norm were up there, helping Patrick look for his buck. He walked right by them and waved hello but didn't stop to talk, which is the usual thing to do when you run into someone you know in the thousand-acre woods. His silence cemented his guilt.

"Word will get around," John says grimly. "He stole the buck. People around here don't tolerate that."

Prissily, I snip: "Your mother says he doesn't have permission to hunt out back."

"Oh?" John says in surprise.

"He asked years ago if he could. But he hasn't asked since."

"Well," John responds, scratching his head. "Well."

"If someone catches him out there hunting illegally, can they shoot him?" I ask hopefully.

"No," John says sternly. He doesn't have a sense of humor about the law. "But it's criminal trespassing. He can be arrested."

"A guy like that will probably try to submit the rack for a trophy," I ruffle indignantly.

"Well, there's not a specific trophy for large racks around here, but if you get a buck over a certain size you become a member of a Big Buck Club, and you get a patch. Kind of like the patch I got for getting the moose," he adds proudly.

Morosely, I sag onto the sofa. "I'm sad we won't have moosemeat next year."

"You never know," John replies optimistically. "My mother can still enter the lottery."

"She has a hunting license?" I say in surprise.

"Sure," John says easily.

I've seen Ruth in hunter's plaid but I still can't imagine her hunting, even though it's from her that John gets his hale constitution. Then again, I'm sure that none of my French friends can picture me perched on a boulder high up on a mountain, trying very hard not to freeze to a rock while smelling like a doe in heat. *'allo, sexy!* Like war, hunting is still a man's business, even if it always includes women and children. Increasingly, we live in a world of gray zones, of cats in the dark, and round women trundling through the Maine woods, hoping to spot dinner lurking in the bushes. Impending doom prompts movement, which is why war forces migrations. It's why my parents ended up in this country, why they married each other and had just three children instead of nine. War catapulted my parents toward a life they never imagined, living quietly among aliens that looked like the palefaces in Western movies speaking cowboy in Korean.

Around the world, war makes humans move. And when humans move, animals do too. The reasons don't matter, except when they do, but they don't change the outcome. It is always happy, because everybody dies in the end.

Once the deer is dead, it becomes a compendium of resources not to be wasted. It is a potlatch of potentials, a mystery box of maybes. A blanket, a G-string, a pair of gloves? It is all and none of these things. We only know what we hope it to be. We cannot say what it is.

Can we eat it? This is all I want to know.

Of course, the men mutter.

Ah, but the hunter always thinks his venison is good, even if it's not. Pride is a wonderful seasoning.

The deer has been to the tagging station, and now it is back. As a carcass, it is having Great Adventures, going places it would never get to go if it was on its own. It is now hanging in the garage, partly because it was just weird to keep it in the henhouse. The temperatures dropped overnight. Today, it is freezing cold outside.

"You can't skin a deer wearing gloves," John points out in amusement. His hands are bare. He's not concerned about his fingers going numb.

Scowling, I remove my fuzzy gloves, and go back inside the house. I return with a bucket of steaming hot water and a stack of kitchen towels. Entertained by my preparations, John arches an eyebrow but he doesn't say anything. "Okay," I declare, rolling up my woolen shirtsleeves and grabbing a skinning knife. "Ready!"

John gives me a look.

"No," I answer his unspoken question, "I didn't put on hand cream."

There are a number of ways to proceed at this stage. Traders will skin for the fur. Trophy hunters will skin for the head. Our objective here is to create food. Thus the wisdom of long, clean cuts that slide between follicles and bypass knobby knees. The skinning begins at the top and descends all the way down. Because the deer is upended, this means we start with the butt. I am short, I point out. To reach this part of the anatomy, I need a stepstool. Don smiles grimly, reaches over my head, and starts the cut. The first slice goes up the inside of one hind leg, followed by a hard yank to separate skin from flesh. It yields, but not easily. The skinning knife slides between them, cutting away membranes working very hard to hold them together. Whitish but not white, this layer reminds me of rubber cement without the gooeyness.

I love that word, gooeyness.

To peelers of oranges, the action is familiar. Dig in with your fingers, separate with your thumbs, yank firmly until the skin yields, and then marvel at the world within a world that lies excavated before you. There is the membrane, and the pith, the white strings connected to fruity condoms sheathing each ripe wedge, preventing promiscuous rubbings. Skinning a whole deer is the kind of work that goes from hand to mouth, a labor with discards lying in fragrant shards. In the form of a knife, your will imposes between skin and flesh, and muscles must obey. Raw is raw. The exposures lack grace.

Imagine leaving a scraped house unpainted. What would the neighbors think? They'd think: that looks awful. The wood will rot. Rot will stink. Your ugly house makes us look bad. Fix it now! The woe is not for the suffering wood. The work is condemned for revealing the banality of violence. And so the job must be done, and quickly.

The trick to skinning a deer is to make as few incisions as possible. Efficiency is elegant. A hacked-up pelt is not only useless for leather, it sheds. Those fine little hairs float around thicker than parachute seeds from dandelions, getting in your eyes, going up your nose, and eventually landing on the naked, shivering flesh where they will cling with the stubbornness of a thousand mules. The fuzz gunks up the blade and sticks to probing fingers, because mules really are stubborn, and they don't like you.

Don't poke holes. Don't puncture the membrane. Don't slice the hide. Pull hard but not too hard, or the muscle will rip in the wrong place. In some places the skin is fused to flesh. In others, the hide pulls off in slabs. The older the deer, the harder the skin. Suppleness is not a word associated with age.

As I slice and pull, slice and pull, tugging the pelt off the leg, I think of sagging skin, paunchy knees, frown lines, and jowls. If I had fur, none of this would show. If I clasp my right hand around my left arm and twist, the skin slides and ripples into orange peel.

Because the fat girl is not young. Perhaps she never was.

All those years of sewing come in handy here. Starting around age five, I used to take apart clothes from the church thrift shop to figure out how they were put together. Painstakingly, I would remove the zipper, waistband, buttons, and clasps, lifting them out and removing them intact. Then I'd attack the seams, picking out each stitch one by one so I wouldn't ruin the panels. Once all the gores, shirring, and darts had been undone, I would take the pieces of cloth and iron them flat. Then I'd lay them all out on the living room floor and study the mosaic of shapes, marveling at these abstract cutouts that used to be a dress. Strewn all around the floor, there would be snippets of thread balled up like cat hairs, tumbleweeding past desolate piles of rotted silk linings and intestinal coils of seam tape. It was all an experiment in the end, a three-dimensional puzzle made of soft pieces draped on the bias.

The bias changes everything. It's important to know about it.

One Christmas, I was given a seam ripper. I was delirious with joy. I had no idea what it was, but it was exactly what I wanted: a blade like a bird's beak.

Cutting the cloth is the only way to make a garment, but folks who routinely wear clothes will cringe at the thought of taking shears to a rippling length of silk. What is the fear? It's not the fear of exploiting those poor Chinese silkworms laboring away in some dark palace, small minions living out their numbered days and laid to rest in unmarked graves. It's the fear of ruining something of great worth. It is the fear that you don't know what you are doing.

In war, wounds cannot be repaired with soft words.

The three of us tug, slice, and pull. Tug, slice, and pull. A pair of pliers comes out to grip the hide. Metal fingers don't slip the way that flesh fingers do. We work our way down the torso until three-quarters of the hide is hanging down. I stand back to survey the job: the deer looks like a kid hanging from the monkey bars whose head got stuck in a turtleneck. This is as far as the skinning goes. Now the head gets cut off. The turtleneck becomes an executioner's hood. A regular hacksaw does the trick. There is no blood. The sound of the saw is dry and crisp, the feel identical to good cordwood. The head goes into a homely plastic bucket along with the hide. With a final "oh, shit," the slender forelegs come off, cut off at the knees with a heavy utility knife. I pick up the felled limb. It feels like a hand weight. The bone is full of dense yellow marrow. Next time, I will take the hooves and boil them to see if I can make Jell-O.

The pelt is thick in my hands. I want to bury my face in it, comb it, make it shine with love. It's taken the three of us about an hour to skin the deer. "Patrick could probably have done it a couple of minutes," John says to no one in particular.

We stand back and assess the work. The meat glows darkly. A single drop of blood stains the concrete floor. There is one more step left. As John holds the body off the floor, gripping it tightly in a wrestler's hug, Don saws off the back shins. A headless, skinless, limbless, gutless wonder swoons into John's waiting arms. The deer is now dressed. In this state, it was good enough to be presented at court and served to Elizabeth I. It is, however, too unrefined for civilized folks snorting

Cheetos and washing them down with Nyquil. For the deer carcass to become proper food, it must be cut into recognizable chunks with titles such as "Sir Loin" and "St. Eak."

It is time to dispose of the body.

The sun is out. It's just above freezing now, but I can still see my breath. I huff experimentally, to prove to myself that, yes, contrary to popular belief, humans are mammals. The operation moves to a wooden picnic table covered in tarp outside the garage. It is next to the hose, on top of hard ground. John carries the stiff carcass and lays it across the short end of a long wooden work table. More knives and saws come out, along with paper towels, a bucket of warm water, some large stainless steel bowls, and another homely plastic bucket. Under the winter's sky, the sclera of a baneful deity, the three of us begin the process of transforming the deer into dinner.

Using large knives and saws, the men start the quartering. All serious hunters know how to make their kill into food but it doesn't make a good story unless it's getting chunked up and fed to the lions. But the hanging, the gutting, the dressing, the butchering, the cooking, and finally, giving thanks to the Lord for this food we are about to receive—this, too, is hunting. I don't know anyone who hunts purely for the rack, and I don't know anyone who doesn't pray before eating their kill. I always do—but I don't thank the Lord. I thank the deer. That's what wrong with me, I guess.

In this very spot, a few years back, Don butchered a buck taken by a poacher off his land. The poacher was caught by the game warden. The warden gave the deer to Don, because the buck belonged to him.

It is a curious thing, the ownership of a wild animal. Until the moment it drops in its tracks from a bullet or a bite, it flees predators and forages for food, shivering in the cold and bleating for sex. It belongs to no one but still it is not free, for its every action is driven by need. Its movements embody the geography of hunger. Its death marks the spot. It dies dispossessed, stripped of authority over its own existence. For the executioner recreates it in her own image and thus the body belongs to her, whether she is called Sickness, Stupidity, or Starvation. In the modern imagination, however, the animal is no longer the child of Mother Nature, but a tamed thing sitting quietly at the supermarket. This is why human language distinguishes between the living and dead states of certain creatures that matter. Alive, we are human. Dead, we are corpses. Deer is not venison. Pig is not pork. Man is not meat. The body bears witness to the means of its end. The dentures define its destiny.

With death comes a claiming, but only for the fortunate.

Don was a field medic taking care of wounded in Vietnam. There is nothing to fear in flesh. There is no pain here. Now, it is about preservation. Venison is valuable.

As the sun rises overhead, bringing warmth with the light, the men saw the deer in half, going across the middle, parting it like the lady in the magic box. In southern climates this halving isn't done, out of fear of exposing the meat to compromised fluids lubricating the spine. This far up in Maine, it's too cold for wasting diseases, so folks don't worry about it. The haunches will become steak, the shoulders become roast, the shanks are ground for burger, the flanks cut up for stew, and the neck made into mincemeat. The fat that pads the butt looks like glue paste, the kind that came in small plastic bottles with lids used as applicators. They're still used in grade schools because this glue is cheap and can be washed out of clothes. In theory, you could eat it. I tried once, and convinced myself it tasted like stale coconut. At home, we didn't use store-bought glue. We made our own glue out of rice. I ate that too. It tasted like rice.

My hands are cold. I dip them in the warm soapy water and lift them out again. I think of fingerbowls and baby baptisms, of watching my father dip his hands in holy water and placing them on soft heads. Then he rocked the babies in his arms and blessed them in the name of the Father, Son, and Holy Ghost, and the congregation welcomed them into the community of the church. Everybody clapped. The families always wore their best church clothes for the occasion. All by itself, this was usually pretty entertaining. The young men wore suits handed down from their fathers. With their hair slicked back and feet in work boots, they'd look proudly on their wife and child with love and terror shining from their eyes. The babies were festooned with baby hats, shoes, tiaras, and sometimes Christmas ornaments, a random assortment that mostly displayed the devotion of the grandparents. Usually, the little ones slept through the whole thing, but every once in a while, a baby would unload a big stinker into his diapers, or take a leaky whizz and promptly start wailing. When this happened, my father would joke, "Well, I guess my job is done!" and hand him back to his weeping, mortified mom. You'd think loss of bladder control would ruin the solemn religious occasion, but it always made it better.

As the Ghost in today's proceedings, my job is to take the large chunks and trim off the excess rind, silver skin, and membranes. A large knife and a small knife serve these purposes. The trick is to follow the natural massing of the muscles, and to only cut where it's absolutely necessary to free meat from bone. In France, butchers hold competitions for this skill approaching an art. I'd studied charts of cows that illustrate where the cuts come from. But these two-dimensional cartoons convey little of the logic of the cuts, or the fact that my cold damp hands freeze where they touch. The muscles have an integrity the fingers respect. The tongue can taste what eyes can't see. I spot my breath rising in soft, desultory puffs. As I pull and tug with determined fingers, I'm amazed to see familiar cuts of meat starting to emerge out of twining skeins of muscle, as if just waiting to be discovered underneath the chaos of the carcass. With a tug, pull, and a slice, I've created a lovely roast for Sunday dinner.

"Look!" I point, waggling an excited finger at my find. "It looks just like a roast!"

"You'll be wanting a meat saw soon," John teases me, pleased by my joy.

Don grunts. This means he is starting to think I am not completely useless. I am now only partly useless.

The large cuts get carried into the house, where the men will wrap them in butcher's paper and put them in the freezer. One haunch stays intact for the future pleasure of feasting. The other stays behind for me to cut up. Alone, I stand outside at the table, working at my own deliberate pace, silently scraping off fat and tugging at silver skin. It is too cold for ants, and the chickens are paying no attention. I tilt my head up: the sky is clear. I concentrate, and cut, and cut again. The worry is the knife will slip. After a while, my hands begin to ache, so I pause, breathe in, and contemplate my work. Looking at the raw meat and red bones scattered across the table, it's an effort to remember how they used to fit together. In my mind's eye, I reassemble them, spooling the reel backwards and remaking the deer out of the parts in front of me, and it's a fascinating exercise to recall that those roasts are plucked from the body of a wild animal. The imagination resists. It does not want to go there. To reverse time invites a curse. Blinking, I see the deer that used to be, a creature tilting gorgeously through the mud and the green. Then I refocus, and see rump roasts and steaks popping up like mushrooms out of the silt of the forest. A movie director walking into this scene would see a horrorshow of bloody knives and meat saws. A starving soldier would see a dream come true. The air snaps and crackles as it goes up my nose. I will need a snack soon.

"What about the ribs?" I ask Don, as he comes back out to collect the latest batch. "Can we eat them?"

Don gives the ribs a half-hearted poke. "Not much meat there," he declares, stating the pitiful obvious. These ribs are long and skinny compared to the brawny heft of beef ribs or the robust fattiness of pork. "You can cut them apart and take the bits in between for mincemeat. But that's a lot of work."

"I'm going to make ribs out of the ribs, then," I announce. "If they come out lousy, who cares?"

Don shrugs indifferently, and heads back into the house with another roast in his hands.

One side of the ribs sports a big, messy hole where the bullet passed through. "You'll want to clean that up," John reminds me as he comes back out to collect the largest bones.

"Okay," I agree, because shot-up meat isn't any good. It has something to do with the way the blood pools. If you've ever split a lip, you know what raw blood tastes like. It's salty, rich, and not exactly bad but somehow too flavorful. Shot-up venison tastes a lot like blood, but bad blood. And thus it's best avoided.

John gathers up an armful of venison and heads back into the house. Alone again, I cut through bones and crack the spine, a modern-day Sweeney Todd mincing my neighbors into meat pies. My little knife slides between the ribs, but I need a heavy blade and a cleaver to cut out the bullet hole. Meat shears would be good, and a bone saw too. Despite the cold, I'm perspiring lightly. It's a lot of work for little meat but I hate to waste it, especially when I have a fifteenth-century British recipe for "rbbys of Venysoun," which I have to consider just for the pleasure of the word, "rbbys."

Take rbbys of Venysoun, and wasshe hem clene in fayre water, an strayne the same water thorw a straynoure in-to a potte, an caste ther-to Venysoun, also Percely,

Sawge, powder Pepyr, Clowys, Maces, Vynegre, and a
lytyl Red wyne caste there-to; an thanne latte it boyle tyl
it be y-now, & serue forth.

Take venison ribs and wash them in fresh water until
clean. Strain the same water through a strainer into a
pot, and put in the ribs. Add parsley, sage, ground pepper, cloves, mace, vinegar, and a little red wine, boil it
until it's done, and serve.

Middle English recipes are the cooking equivalent of a
trip to IKEA, which is like shopping inside the mind of Doctor Seuss. Somehow, IKEA combines the shopworn Latin
alphabet into painfully cute new words. A long, skinny sofa
called EKTORP. A table lamp called KNUBBIG. A door mat
called TRAMPA. Every Wednesday, the in-store cafeteria
serves Swedish meatballs in a cream sauce with lingonberries.
Strangely, the meatballs are not bouncy, though this is how
the Swedish Chef makes them on *The Muppet Show*. He is
Swedish, and a chef. He is also a hand puppet whose Christian name is "Tom." Surely his recipe for Swedish meatballs
is authentic? When he makes meatballs, he serves them with
tennis racquets. This culinary flair explains why he has his
own cooking show, which is a fairly impressive achievement
for a piece of felt.

I have never tried to cook using athletic equipment, and
thus I cook in obscurity. I have, however, attempted some of
his other culinary techniques using an assortment of lethal
implements. Because he endorses the use of very fresh ingredients, the Swedish Chef is constantly trying to clobber his
dinner over the head. He shoots his Brussels sprouts with a
blunderbuss to make "salad à la boom-boom," uses a "caken-
smøøsher" (a baseball bat) to overpower his feisty chocolate
cake, and shakes a red squirrel out of a tree so he can whack it
with a cleaver. He hopes to make it into a stew. "Cøme døwn,

squøørly!" he cajoles. But the squirrely doesn't want to be stew. Instead, the nutty creature runs off to fetch his friend Mister Bear, and they end up chasing the Swedish Chef out of the "great outdøørsy" with a rousing "børk børk børk!" for good measure. Since nobody, not even Swedes, can understand what he's saying, the Swedish Chef Show was originally graced with subtitles. They were in Chinese.

七嘴八舌,七嘴八舌,七嘴八舌! (børk børk børk!)

IKEA's cafeteria also serves Swedish Ribs. Shouldn't they be Swedish RBBYS? It used to be that "y" was in venysoun, vyngre, and wyne. Where did it go? In French, *y* is a whole word. It means "there." In American, Y is an entire organization. It's short for YMCA or Young Men's Christian Association.

Nowadays, "i" has replaced the "y" in just about everythyng. I'm not sure that's an ymprovement.

I want ribs, not RYBBS, and so I proceed accordingly. The first step is boiling the long bones until the meat is soft, about an hour. The next step involves the preparation of the sauce. Like all wild meat, venison is very lean, so the sauce has to be thickly applied. The ribs go in the oven at 300 degrees for an hour. Remove the tray from the oven, let the ribs cool enough to handle, and then move them onto a butcher's block and chop them up with a meat cleaver. The ribs are not as soft as pork ribs, and not as thick as beef ribs. Cooked, the thin meat stretches tautly over narrow bones. Truthfully, they don't look promising.

Now it is time to take an experimental bite. I get a good grip on one end of the skinny rib, bite down hard with my teeth, and rip the meat off the bone. It's quite enjoyable to attack food in this way. It feels like eating a Popsicle with strong opinions. The meat isn't tough or stringy at all. "Hey!" I exclaim in relief. "Come try some," I tell John, gesturing to the venison ribs piled on a large platter. Without stalling, he rises from the couch, pads over to the kitchen island where the platter is lounging, grabs a rib, takes a tentative bite, and then he tears in, eating three before yelling downstairs: "Hey Dad! You want a rib?" Within minutes, the entire plate is gone. There's meat stuck between my teeth.

CHAPTER FIFTEEN

✣ ✣ ✣

A Long Winter's Nap

If skill could be gained by watching,
every dog would become a butcher.
— *Turkish proverb*

Home butchering makes a lot of sense if you're committed to understanding the nature of meat. It means that you know exactly what odds and ends go into the grinds used for burgers, and every bit of usable meat gets taken, according to your time and inclination. It also means you can take the other bits of the deer that have odd but practical uses, such as strips of membrane for bowstrings and the tarsal glands off the legs to use as scent lures. I want to take the intestines for natural casings. It can be done. It's just the unpleasantness of dealing with yards of entrails, the idea of which is off-putting because human beings have strained relationships with their own guts.

Deer hunting season begins at the start of winter during the rut, so the bucks are padded with fat. It's too early for them to be starving to death. The hunger phase doesn't begin until February, after the earth is buried beneath snow and they've stripped all the bark and buds off the dormant trees. The external fat is a mixture of oily fat—the alluring, sexy kind you see on the rinds of T-bone beefsteaks—and suet, which is fat so hard and crumbly it looks and feels like dried

spackle. Suet can be made into tallow, baked into British pud-
dings, or stuck in a bird feeder to plump up the chickadees.
When a deer dies in the forest, even songbirds join the feast.
Compared to a domestic cow or pig, a whitetail doesn't have
a lot of suet. But it's there. It sticks to everything, smearing
your fingers with a tacky layer of grease that coats the knife,
gumming up the blade, prompting that awful wiping motion
across stained pants legs.

Butchering a deer is a lesson in physical wellness. Once you
start rummaging around a body cavity with a sharp knife, it
suddenly becomes blindingly clear what surgeons mean when
they say they're performing exploratory surgery. There's a
feel, a look, and a smell to health that simply is, and when it is
not there, it reveals itself through the negative. This buck was
in perfect condition, fatted for winter but not fat. Every muscle, organ, tooth, and bone reinforced its robust good fortunes.
The knife helps your hands understand what surgeons mean
when they say that certain tumors can't be removed. In some
cases, the thick sheets of opaque and flexible fat will pull away
from the flesh, leaving behind a smooth surface still encased
nicely in a membranous sheath. Other times, the same kind
of fat adheres tightly to the surface, and there is no way to
remove it unless you dig into the flesh. And if that fat clings to
a vital organ, that cutting sometimes leaves virtually nothing
behind. You have to make a choice.

It was a Christmas Eve when my mother went to the
hospital. She died a year later on Christmas Day. This happened long before I'd met John, but it might as well have been
yesterday.

My mother was feeling poorly, but she'd been that way ever
since she'd returned from a mission to Russia with a group
of church women a few months earlier. On her way out of
the country, her passport was stolen by the passport control
officer. He simply took it from her, stashed it someplace safe,
and then started yelling at her for trying to board a plane

without the required documents. There was a small international incident. My Russian friends chuckled cynically when I asked them how this could happen. An American passport for an Asian woman was the most coveted passport on the Russian black market. The passport control official probably thanked his lucky stars when my mother stumbled across his path. That day, he became a rich man. She was traumatized by the incident, as much by the confrontation with ordinary corruption as for the shocking reaction of the church ladies who boarded the plane without her, rolling their eyes at her stupidity. How could she forget her passport? How dare she inconvenience them? My sister and I chalked up her droopy demeanor to depression. For trusting souls, it can be hard to accept that good Christians can be lousy human beings.

She complained about feeling sick, and we went about preparing for the holiday. She complained about feeling sick, and we didn't listen. She complained about being sick, and she was not believed, for unhappy women are unreliable witnesses of their own bodies. Medical sexism is so ingrained that women who die of heart attacks will go to their graves thinking it was just a really bad case of gas. None of us expected bad news from the family doctor. We were thinking she had the stomach flu, maybe an ulcer from the stress of her trip to Russia. She'd get meds for her depression, and this would be good. It's good, we agreed. *There's really nothing wrong with her. She just hates us. Her stomach pains are all in her head.*

But the diagnosis wasn't "ulcer." It was . . . nothing. She needs more tests, the doctors intoned. For that, she needs to go to the big hospital.

Why?

Bye-bye, have a Merry Christmas!

And off her rocker my mother went, trailing us behind her in a cloud of confusion.

As we sat, waiting, in the hospital lobby, the new doctor came out and read us the sympathetic script with professional

crispness. *Cancer . . . chemotherapy . . . not a good candidate . . .*
But the small muscles on the sides of his mouth were saying
something else. *She should have come in earlier. It's her fault for
not self-advocating. Sick people always wait too long to see a doctor. What the hell is wrong with them anyway?*

Asshole. Go away.

For reasons I didn't understand, the doctors felt compelled to perform exploratory surgery. So they poked around
and stitched her back up, then delivered the usual line: "The
tumor is too big to remove. She's got three months to live."
None of us cried, mostly because we didn't believe it. My
mother was never sick. She had the constitution of an ox. It
was my father who was always teetering, frail, his body suffering from pains that came and went, sometimes worse, but
always threatening to undo him, forcing him into isolation
whenever we came home with the mumps, the flu, the pox
in the house. Women think that if they take care of a man, he
will love them for it, and reciprocate with undying adoration.
This is a mistake. It's nobody's fault, really. (I blame romance
novelists.) As she aged, it was only her heart that ached, not
her knees and hips. As years slipped away she glowered in the
kitchen, eating donuts as her dreams dissolved in the harsh
light of reality, protecting her wounded soul in a layer of
battle fat, her discontent erasing the last traces of that beauty
grudgingly bestowed on my baby sister because the youngest
is the last best chance of living forever. I'd watched as the corners of her mouth turned down, one side twitching like a sec-
ondhand clock as her hands knitted neuroses together. She sat
in her rocking chair in the living room and read the Bible in
English, mouthing the alien words aloud. She never became
comfortable in the language of sermons delivered from the
pulpit, and it made her angry that my father was venerated by
the congregation just for walking on withered legs that carried him through the processional and up to the altar every

Sunday, but could not take her on long romantic walks on the beach or strolling through Paris. One of these days, she was going to walk out. With that, she'd reduce him to something merely mortal, not just human but lesser: a man.

Even in the best of circumstances, it's a challenge being a minister's wife, because there's nobody for you to talk to. You can't gossip, you can't complain about your husband, you can't do or be anything but a pure paragon of pacified virtue, going to all the ladies' circles, prayer groups, Bible study groups, and choir practices, saying nothing and smiling always as you dress demurely in clothing that would have not been out of place on a nineteenth-century schoolmarm, as befits the wife of a Methodist minister. I don't care how strong your faith is or how happy you are to know God's love. One day, you wake up, and you realize that you're horribly vulnerable to the ficklish gaze of judging women, cluck clucking under their tongues. It's worse than the social gauntlet of high school, because there's no graduation day to free you. It's just the endless grind of piety because gossiping mouths never shut. The bitter pill was learning that decades of being the good wife had earned her nothing but Brownie points in Heaven. On the practical plane, she got nothing. No pension, no Social security, and no health insurance. Her this-worldly worth as a wife added up to zero. Even as she sickened, a lifetime of resentments gnawing at her guts, she couldn't complain about it. The dying have epiphanies and enemas. They do not have hissy fits.

That would be petty.

And small.

Cluck, cluck.

She lived on the earth like a migratory mammal, and I thought to myself, I wish her death could be merciful. In nature, sick animals are taken swiftly by predators. Starvation takes the weak. When people romanticize nature, it's a sure sign they're tourists of their own lives. Give me a reason, I used to ask her. Why is the sky blue? What makes snow fall? Why do people lie? She could not answer. So I asked God. He didn't have good answers either. My father just sat, and repeated, All the great theologians start out just like you.

He accepts God's will in all things. This is intensely aggravating.

Faced with her death, I loathed the fact that a fatal tumor still didn't make her the master of her own reality. No, the doctors had "discovered" the tumor, the way that Columbus had "discovered" America (by mistake, and let's pretend that the indigenous peoples already living there are sort of like a new species of bear). Surprise! Even though they couldn't do anything about it, wasn't it grand that the men could go exploring? I had nothing to say to them. I had nothing to say to her. Talking doesn't change facts. Stomach cancer is fatal. I knew it, and it is not in my nature to pretend when the answers mean something real. But for her sake I lied, and said the medicines had potential, that prayers would help, that she was in God's hands and He is loving and kind, but I thought it was both cruel and foolish to offer psalms and platitudes to a woman being eaten, slowly, alive.

Following her diagnosis, I flew back and forth between France and the U.S., ping-ponging between Paris and Maine on cheap student fares, bearing exotic gifts of caftans and turbans for her balding head. I changed her sheets and washed her nightgowns. I helped her to the bathroom, helped her back, fluffed her pillows, and brought her sad liquid dinners in sadder little cans, then went back in the kitchen and cooked a proper meal for my crumpled sister and dad. Then I sat down at my father's large, messy desk where he wrote his sermons, and dealt with all the paperwork that accompanies the big business of lingering death. I asked her once, just once, because I wanted to make sure, "Do we have things we need to discuss?"

"No," she said, not looking at me.

"Okay," I said. "I didn't think so." I watched as she pretended to drink her dinner, and then I took the can away.

The difficult part is waiting.

Death will come, of course. It always does, yet it is always a surprise. For hours, days, weeks, and months we'd been holding our breath, playacting normalcy as the invisible clock wound down. The anticipation infused every moment with morbid wakefulness as the chickadees chirped outside the window. Shut up, stupid birds! One month, two months, three months passed and she was all better, yes she was praise Jesus and it can all go back to the way it was. But the miracle didn't last very long. She pottered around outside in plastic sandals and white socks, the rest of her draped in a fuzzy pink robe and mismatching turban, and she'd sit on the steps in the sunlight like an oversized plushy won at a carnival, sitting with big bright button eyes staring at dug holes. She poked at the dirt but didn't plant new bulbs. No next year, no next spring.

I cried, then.

Because I hate gardening.

Her body wasted on narcotics as the tumor swelled like a pregnancy. My new friends became men twice my age. Men my mother's age and still they weren't nearly old enough, so they became older and grayer until they were finally old enough to know something about parents dying though they assumed mine were both living. I suppose technically this was true.

Sometimes I wonder if the condemned just want to get it over with, already. The only people who whine about the immorality of euthanasia aren't the ones lying twisted on a hospital bed and suffering horribly. My father isn't afraid to die. Neither am I. Because either there's heaven on the other side—a place that, honestly, I would be very interested to visit—or the Bible is wrong and there is no heaven, at least for the likes of me, and that leaves my soul to haunt the earth, going BOO! to all the living people who bugged the hell out of me. No matter what, it's an adventure and I'm curious. God made me this way, didn't he?

Exactly, my dad agrees, ruefully.

At the very end, as the silent snow fell and fell, it took her a week to finish dying. She did it by aging in reverse. "She looks like a little girl," the nurses murmured in horror. She was mummified by morphine, a peculiar little smile on her drug-addled face. A vegetable with blood in her veins. She was lost in strange dreams that I could taste. Her tumor was her beloved infant, the center of her universe and the center of ours and so we orbited around her, feeding her with love as she swelled with pride and loathing of our pathetic little lives. We lived at the hospital because it was a hard December in Maine and driving was dangerous. There was so much ice on the roads and my dad was also very sick and we were stupid with fatigue. My sister developed pneumonia and crater-sized zits. She looked so bad that I couldn't help laughing at her, the two of us collapsing into hospital hysterics at the sight of our sad sallow selves. There were giant black bags under my sister's eyes so huge she looked like a character in a cartoon.

In my mother's mind her tumor was her baby boy, just hers and you can't have him, a sweet soft baby in her belly, filling her with the pleasure of giving new life to the world. I was glad for her fantasy, glad that the morphine was messing up her mind, glad that powerful drugs had given her refuge from the betrayals of the flesh. The fantasy is fatal, of course. She was merely food for her tumors. I could hear them too, hissing like barn mice. In grim amusement, I thought to myself, if I ever ran for political office, the negative ads would scream: "Not just one but *both* of her parents were drug addicts! She's practically a crack baby!"

In truth, the greater lie.

Her belly was a landscape of violence. Beneath her ribcage, the newest scars blushed prettily in pink, slicing across horizontally where the specialists had gone spelunking for tumors. Below, a mad-scientist's seam marked the three cesarean sections that she'd had, a procedure that used to involve making a vertical incision about five inches long—virtually the entire length of her torso because she was a hipless wonder then, and very small. The surgeons had cut into the same place three times, once for each child, splitting and re-splitting the scar and leaving behind a thick, knotted, black rope of flesh that seemed to grow longer, thicker, and darker with every year that passed. "*This* is where you come from," she used to tell me, showing me her scar so I could touch it. My baby sister turned white and recoiled in fear. I would study it, a doubting Thomas sticking his finger in the wound in Christ's side. "After your sister," my mother said to me, "doctors warned, *No more*. Next one will kill you."

I looked over at the little woman lying stupefied on bleached sheets. She was cradling her swollen belly with a sweet smile on her face.

"Where is your brother?" the nurses asked with concern. "She's waiting for him. She won't let go until he's here."

I thought to myself: she's not yet given birth to him.

She curled on white sheets, luminescent, a body drinking our energy like a vampire from the moon. Mindless, she'd become a succubus sucking at plastic tubes. Her body was scorching hot to the touch, as radiant as a log in the fireplace, steadily crumbling into dying embers still capable of burning down the house. Hour after hour, day after day, the bedside vigil continued. But, you know, limbo can get boring, because it just goes on, and nothing happens. Nothing at all, not even television commercials.

Plump and kindly, the nurses started shooing us away, because our presence was keeping her alive. The nurses knew what doctors couldn't say: our emotions were feeding that flesh but she was already dead.

"Don't," the nurses reprimanded us as we tried to hold her hand. "You feel better. It just makes it worse for her."

Eventually, you figure it out. *She's* the one suffering, you selfish jerk. She's done mothering you. Let her die in peace.

Every day the doctors would ask me, "Is it today?" And I would listen to the whispers in her head, listen to the stories she was telling herself, and reply, "No." And they would nod and leave, because there was nothing left for them to do. Until the seventh day, and I said: "Yes." They nodded, and they left. This time, we left too.

My sister and I went to the cafeteria and ate raspberry Jell-O with canned whipped cream on top. We sat and stared out the window, and watched the snow fall in silence. Snow is very pretty. It's soft and fluffy and hides all the dirt. Then the plows and salting trucks come through, and the world is ugly again but it's the only way for humans to resume normal life.

Because humans are ugly and mother is dying, you selfish jerk. Look out the window, and see what is true.

We ate more Jell-O, even though my sister prefers pudding. Actually, I do too. After a while, we took deep breaths and tiptoed back in her room, peeking shyly around the door the way that little kids peek when they know they're not supposed to. She looked like a pregnant teenager, her taut skin glowing with the otherworldly shine of the addict, and her belly ballooned. Baby wants to be born! As we watched, awestruck, circling the bed, her happiness flared like a firecracker and her labored breathing finally stopped.

Tick tock.

The next moment, the phone next to the bed rang. The sound was loud and demanding. Robotically, my father answered. It was my very old grandmother who was calling.

"She's gone, isn't she," my grandmother said in Korean. "I just saw her. She came to say goodbye. "

"Yes," my father replied without surprise, because all of our watches had stopped.

"*Aigu*," my grandmother wailed. "*Aigu, aigu*. For her sake, I'm glad."

"Yes," my father repeated, compressing a lifetime into that word. Then he hung up, because my mother's mother already knew too much about life and death and death again, and was not in need of comforting. My grandmother had already outlived her husband, two of nine children, and a war that tore her country in two. Nothing surprised her, especially not ghosts, holy or otherwise.

I was glad too, because what my grandmother said was true. And so we prayed and sang the way that Korean people do, holding hands in the hospital room to celebrate the birth of Jesus Christ.

Merry Christmas to all, and to all, a good night.

CHAPTER SIXTEEN

☙ ☙ ☙

Fish Heaven

[Pliny] fashions the name of "good mother" to the Earth,
because having compassion for us, she instituted poisons.
– *Pierre Gassendi,* Concerning Happiness, *1647*

The first Sunday of No Hunting after the winter snow has
melted, John wants to show me where he shot the buck.
"Look," he points at the ground. "You can still see the blood."

Except I can't. There's just leaves and more leaves layered
thickly over moss.

"Look," he points again, and waves his arms around. "It's
all over the place."

I shake my head. Nope. The earth has drunk deeply. He is
seeing a memory.

Exasperated, he kneels down and starts jabbing at an oak
leaf, one of maybe a hundred oak leaves I could grab if I just
stood in one spot and started raking with my hands. "There,"
his index finger waggles. "*Now* do you see?"

Myopic, I bend over and squint. There's some blotches that
could be a stain from spit-up baby food. "Well, yah," I agree
peevishly. "Now that you're pointing right at it, I can see the
blood," I lie. "But it's just a drop!"

He stands back up and gestures operatically around the
clearing. A sudden beam of sunlight pierces the clouds and
the trees clap deliriously, demanding that Macbeth deliver his

soliloquy. "There's blood *everywhere*," he utters dramatically. Out here in the forest, in front of the tree stand where the king of the mountain sits, it's our own little Globe Theater. "The blood trail goes over that way," he points over to a little rising that moves away from the clearing and back to the safety of thickets. "There's a path the deer have been making." He heads off, following the path, looking for deer sign higher up the hill.

Now that he's pointed it out, I can see the trail the deer have made. I still can't see the blood. It makes sense that Patrick could have lost a moose in the woods, because the ground is tangled. Even when blood is freshly spilled, it's difficult to see, for the living ground stirs restlessly in the light. Visually, it's very busy out here. It looks a lot like a color blindness test in 3D, what with all those pale mottled leaves wherein hides a symbol. Or so the optometrist claims. I do not believe her.

"Out, out, damned spot!" takes on a whole new meaning out here.

Experimentally, I crash willy-nilly through the underbrush, and then circle back around to my starting point. In the movies, the Indian tracker would spot the indentations in the ground, the overturned leaves and bent blades of grass, and he would be able to determine my age, height, and astrological sign from all the evidence I've left behind. I *tried* to leave a trail. I *tried* to be obvious. I *know* exactly where I'd passed and still I see nothing. I smell nothing. It is embarrassing. I am, however, quite able to hear John, who has returned to find out why I was running like a crazy person through the woods. There are bears around, and it's not nice to wake them.

"What are you doing?" he asks crossly.

"Nothing," I say innocently.

He looks around sharply. "Where's the rake?"

"I put it down."

"Why did you do that?"

"Because I couldn't find the tree stand."

"Don't put anything down. Ever," he scolds. "It's amazingly easy to lose things out here."

"But I know exactly where it is!" I protest.

"Oh?" he says skeptically. "Where is it then?"

"It's in the clearing, right before I turned around and headed back up to follow the deer trail. It's perfectly obvious! I made sure to prop it up and everything! It's right . . . uh . . ."

The rake has disappeared. The thought crosses my head: naughty fairies are playing games with me. Naw, I tell myself, that's just silly. They'd never be able to carry off a rake. Not unless there were hundreds of fairies working together as a well-coordinated team. There's no way that would happen. Fairies don't follow directions. There had to be a better explanation. Like maybe I set it down and lost it.

"I told you it's easy to lose stuff out here," John repeats, and starts walking around, searching for the lost rake.

"Speaking of which," I pester, "where's the tree stand?"

"It's right over there," he replies, and points up the hill at a clump of tall pines.

"I don't see it."

"Over *there*," he points again. "You're too short. Go closer."

Annoyed, I start walking in the general direction that he's indicating but I'm pretty sure he's winding me up. It's just a clump of . . . "Oh!" I exclaim, as the perch of the tree stand suddenly comes into focus. "I see it! Wow, it's really obvious," I complain. "Isn't it kinda conspicuous? I mean, if I'm a deer coming from this direction, you'd be sitting right at eye level."

"Deer don't look up," he says bluntly.

"Whaddya mean, 'deer don't look up'? That's like saying 'bunnies can't cook.'"

"Well," he shrugs, "bunnies can't cook."

I scowl. ". . . but they can dance?'"

"Uh, yep," he bobbles his head. "Pretty much."

Bunnies can't milk cows. Bunnies can't play with fireworks. Bunnies can't vacuum...But they...can...DANCE! That line is from a series of cartoons linked to "Rayman Raving Rabbids," an animated Wii game from France, where it started as *"Rayman contre les Lapins Crétins."* I know about the "rabbids" thanks to John's twelve-year-old son Baird. When he comes over, he enjoys showing me funny YouTubes about Marcel the Shell instead of doing his homework.

We walk around some more, searching for the rake. After a while, he spots it. It is nowhere near the place where I left it.

Tomorrow, Patrick and Christy are going up to Greenville to get married by a notary public. They're driving out on a Thursday night after Patrick gets off work, staying overnight at a motel, getting married early the next morning, then heading up north to the cabin on a remote lake. There's indoor plumbing but no phone. They've got the cabin and lake to themselves.

"Are they nervous about getting married?" I ask Ruth.

"Nah," Ruth replies stolidly.

"Is Christy wearing a dress?"

"She's wearing a skirt." Ruth nods to herself, seeing it in her mind's eye. "She bought a lacy top to wear with it. I'm altering the top a bit, taking out the dickey to make it prettier." She pauses, and then adds, "It's nice."

I can't quite picture a lace top with a dickey. However, and more importantly, I can't picture Christy wearing a skirt. "Has Patrick ever seen Christy in a dress?" I ask curiously.

"Sure," Ruth replies dryly.

"I wasn't sure if it was a matter of principle—not wearing dresses, that is."

Ruth squints at me. "Well, I've never seen *you* in a dress," she says matter-of-factly, and resumes kneading her bread.

"I only wear dresses in other countries," I explain limply. "What's Patrick wearing?"

"Patrick?" Ruth repeats, slightly amused. "He's wearin' something dry."

". . . wearin' something dry," John echoes, as he walks through on his way to the garage. He's decided to go fishing since Baird is with us for the weekend. "You wanna come with us?" he asks me, an expectant look on his face.

"Yep," I reply.

"Okay!" he nods, pleased. "But we'll be fishing. We won't pay any attention to you. And you're going to need to stay away from the brook."

"So I don't fall in?" I ask curiously.

He waggles his finger at my nose. "So you don't scare the fish. All that swatting at flies and dancing around, dodging bugs—that'll spook them."

"I can't help it if I'm a bug magnet," I sulk.

He snorts and walks out of the kitchen to look for his chest waders.

There are lots of theories why some people are living fly strips—too much carbon dioxide exuded by the pores, the wrong blood type, B-12 vitamin deficiencies, etc.—but the most entertaining explanation I've run across blames the smell of your politics. "I have fished from a canoe at night fall," wrote Sewell Newhouse in 1865, "when these insects rose like clouds." Otherwise known as the unofficial state birds of Maine, the mosquitoes didn't bother Newhouse at all, whereas his fishing buddy was a mess of bug bites. Served his friend right for being a Copperhead, Newhouse joked. Who knew that Civil War mosquitoes could not only sniff out anti-government, ultra-conservative, pro-states' rights Copperheads who hated "Abraham Africanus I," but they also found him—the Copperhead, that is—to be magically delicious! Newhouse himself was a "radical" pro-Union bastard who supported that nice President Lincoln, and the mosquitoes

left him alone. Which may or may not have meant that Maine
mosquitoes were Republicans.

Politically, Newhouse and his buddy were chalk and
cheese, but these two went fishing together because they both
loved the kind of Great Outdoors that comes with stingers
and teeth. "Your delicate, metropolitan dandy, who adores
champagne suppers, and warms himself with brandy, had
better keep clear of the North Woods," Newhouse warned.
Naturally, the North Woods is exactly where we are going.
Some would say that the North Woods is where we already
are. Personally, I don't think this, but I've lived in the part
of Maine where Canadians go shopping for peanut butter
and half the town is named Pelletier, a French name meaning "fur trader." We jounce along back roads and end up
at a spot I've not been to before. It's more than a few miles
from town and sort of remote, but you're not really very
far from civilization if somebody already built a road to get
there, even if it's a road less traveled and mostly made of
dried mud.

The sound of rushing water provides a soundtrack to our
fishing expedition. John pulls the truck over and abruptly
parks, letting the truck tilt into shallows. Eagerly, boy and
man hop out. Rubberized in waders, they land with both
feet in careless puddles. There isn't an obvious clearing so
we just plunge into the woods, pushing forward through
the leafy dark until the babbling brook appears, sparkling in
the sunlight.

"This looks like a good spot," John says, pointing at the
brook. Under a heavy canopy of trees, the two of them throw
their gear down and begin to set up their fishing poles. I help
them untangle fishing lines and untie microscopic knots. Hats
on, they stand side by side with arms raised and eyes shut tight
while I spray them with bug repellent, giving myself a few
booster puffs for good measure.

"Done?" John asks through clenched eyelids.

"Done," I affirm.

Their eyes blink open. Rushing with anticipation, they grab their gear and nimbly scramble down steep banks and stride into the water, one setting up downstream, the other upstream, not close together but close enough that I can still see both of them from the banks. They cast lines and stand quietly, watching and waiting for a hungry brook trout to bite.

Slap! I whack a mosquito that's landed on my head.

"You're scaring the fish!" John bellows across the water.

Ah yes, the man adores me.

"I'm going to look around," I announce loudly to the frightened fish, and head off into the woods.

It's a horizontal journey over slippery slopes. Walking by the brook, I can imagine how Newhouse's fishing buddy felt. I am dipped in bug spray and my hat has been soaked in DEET, but the mosquitoes still hover around me like my own personal black cloud. Does their unhealthy attachment to me mean that those Republican mosquitoes are now Democrats? The switcheroo that would make sense if they'd migrated to Maine from the Dixiecrat South, but I don't think mosquitoes do that, even if the ones around here are the size of swallows with appetites to match. There are also butterflies galore and moths fluttering around, along with some insect that buzzes very loudly. It is neither a grasshopper nor a cicada. Obviously, it is a Libertarian.

Looking back over my shoulder, I can still see John and Baird standing in the narrow brook, positioned by boulders that create thin rushes of water. I wave at them from the embankment. Baird looks up and grins. Like all kids, he loves it when adults pay attention to him.

Then I turn, and go exploring for real in the woods. But it's my version of the woods, which isn't poetic in the least. Here I am, a Weeble wobbling along, doing my best to enjoy

nature in the correct attitude of reverence, impressing myself
with my sense of adventure as I clonk along in store-bought
hiking shoes. I admire ripening berries. I inhale pine-scented
air. Nature is so natural. It's amazing! I should take a picture of that bright orange mushroom and put it on Facebook!
Then something starts itching. I sprout a mysterious rash. A
bird poops on my head. A frog craps on my shoes. It's a sym-
phony of bodily functions, most of which aren't mine, and
none of them are lofty or sublime. They're various shades of
vomit. Planet Earth is God's baby, and the adorable infant is
upchucking all over me as I pick it up and burp it. Does this
mean I'm mother to Nature? And if I am . . . *mon Dieu*! What
might this mean?

I know what I'm supposed to be thinking about the Great
Outdoors, namely, inspiring thoughts about God's visible
hand—not to be confused with the *in*visible hand of the free
marketplace. God reveals himself in the acorn, growing into
an oak. His face is the symmetry of leaves and His breath
forms the veins in every butterfly's wing. Yah, they're gos-
samer and all that, but if you watch the butterfly for long
enough, you'll also see it squeeze slimebutter out of its tiny fly
butt. If that isn't a miracle, I don't know what is.

The forest floor is covered with moss, pine needles, and
poison ivy; I look up, and find myself facing an enormous
spider web. Glittering, it is several feet wide and hangs
between two tall trees, spinning a doorway to another world
I cannot join today. I've probably walked through several
spider webs without noticing, because the thing about bum-
bling around in the woods is that you mostly don't look at
the woods. You look at your feet, lest you step into a big
heaping pile of deer sign. This is undesirable, because stepping in it means that you've ruined your evidence, making it
loads more difficult to determine whether the poop is from
a creature worth tracking.

Before long, green strands of goo are clinging to my clothes, and small white bug balls are stuck to my shoes. I am coated in forest life. For a while, camouflaged in insect crud, I sit under a friendly oak, hoping that a pair of porcupines will start having porcupine sex in front of me. It is one of my fondest wishes to someday experience this. It's my idea of a threesome. But it's midmorning and daylight: not even squirrels are interested in playing sunbeam peekaboo with me. So I get up and resume walking, going nowhere in particular, letting the butterflies lead.

I walk, stop, and listen. Walk, stop and listen. This is not hunting. This is walking in the woods. The idea is to lift your feet high and place them carefully on the ground, trying to sound as much as possible like a deer rooting for a noontime snack. There's an oak tree looming nearby: three branches at the top are growing vertically, turning it into a giant wooden dinner fork. Nearby, there's a small hardwood tree that managed to grow up and back down into the ground, making a perfectly formed arch. Stripped of bark, another tree stands as weirdly naked as a streaker on skis. Other trees bear the marks of antlers rubbing, and a fir has been nearly cut in two by the energetic assaults of a woodpecker. "The tree will die," I say aloud without thinking.

When a tree falls in the forest, it becomes a rhetorical question. But when a tree gets chopped down on purpose, its noisy death catapults it to new life among men. It becomes all kinds of useful things, such as toilet paper, toboggans, pianos, and coffins. Amazingly, not only can all these items be custom-ordered on the Internet, they can also be purchased at your friendly neighborhood Costco. Coffins for sale also pop up occasionally in *Uncle Henry's*, under "Senior Section." I found an ad for a "front-loading coffin," which I can only assume doubles as a washing machine, as well as a little one sized to fit "small dogs and most cats" but for the exceptionally obese tabby. I've yet to turn up any ads for coffins in the Wanted section. I suppose it's in bad taste to post, sort of like putting up an ad for a used parachute ("tried once, never opened!").

My mother didn't want her remains returned to Korea. Instead, we buried her in the Eliot cemetery. Hundreds came to pay their respects, including her siblings now living in Canada. After driving all night from Windsor, my *emo* Kumsook came barreling through the door, waffling between sorrow at her baby sister's death and delight to see her American nieces and nephew again. "Why your mother stay in America?" my eldest aunt clucked mournfully, shaking her head at that fatal decision. "She should have come live with us." Luckily, the fact that her husband required feeding temporarily overrode her other reason for making the journey, which was to take over my mother's job of getting me hitched. My stubborn commitment to being a bachelorette was holding things up for my younger cousins. We were supposed to get married in order of birth, with the oldest cousins going first. Because they knew better than to try and cross their mother, Kumsook's two doctor sons each married a lovely woman from Korea. Then it was my brother's turn. He married a Korean woman from Los Angeles. And here I was, next up in the queue. Well then. Following the pattern, shouldn't I marry a Korean woman too?

"미쳤어," my eldest aunt hacked in disgust, and stomped into the kitchen to start chopping up chickens. I would have helped my *emo* but she was scary even when she wasn't holding a cleaver. Also, I had shopping to do. In the middle of everything, I had to go to the mall. My mother's favorite outfit would no longer fit her correctly, and the only solution was a new blouse.

Try explaining to an eager salesgirl that you, a red-eyed, disheveled shopper redolent of old-man smell and bleach, are just looking, thank you, and don't really feel like talking. No, I am not homeless. I am . . . er, that's not quite right. I am in fact *shopping* for my mother, who is not able to try things on because she's a corpse. She needs a new blouse to go with her wig, which has fallen off her head because dead skin dries up faster than people expect, you know, and then there's kimchee I need to chop up before the chicken goes bad because it came all the way from Canada and the smell of *doenjang* is following me everywhere and . . . Oh look, a blood-red blotch of the stuff is staining the front of my ratty sweatshirt with a hole in the armpit. Idly, I started picking at the crusty bits.

High on *doenjang* fumes, my brain had somehow failed to register that the salesgirl had been backing up with a frozen smile the entire time I'd been rifling through racks and scowling at the lousy selection of blouses for bloated middle-aged women. Abruptly, she screeched, "Security!" Blearily, I looked up, wondering what kind of idiot would bother to stick-up a J.C. Penney's at the mall. To my amazement, she was pointing a hysterical finger at me.

Hey, what did I do?

". . . somebody call Security!" she repeated.

And now a small group was starting to gather. Time to skedaddle! I tossed a fistful of twenties behind me and ran out of the store clutching a white blouse as the soothing strains of "Raindrops Keep Falling on My Head" oozed deliriously through the PA system. With glazed eyes and erupting zits, my sister was waiting for me in the getaway car, where she'd stayed rather than risk going among the masses and being mistaken as a plague victim. "Did you find something for her to wear?" she asked dispiritedly as I climbed into her car and slammed the door shut, perking up when it dawned on her that I was foully peeved. Like a cat with its fur rubbed the wrong way, my piques usually meant that she was about to be entertained. "Just go," I sulked, sinking down into the seat and defiantly eating a contraband cookie as she started up the engine and my throat began to swell.

The new top and the old dress went to the undertaker, who whisked the outfit away along with fresh pantyhose, favorite shoes and—worst of all—her toiletry bag. A lifetime of inconvenient beauty summed up by a bottle of prescription pills and a caking lipstick tube. Soon enough, my sister and I found ourselves inspecting the dressed body lying peacefully in the coffin, trying our best to remember our mother even as we stared at the mummy. But Virgos can't help but notice the stupid details. Such as the fact that the stockings weren't on straight, her wig was ever-so-slightly askew, and the made-up face seemed weird, because in everyday life her face was bare. "She looks . . . nice?" my sister said uncertainly, just to have something to say, and I knew she wanted me to wipe the lipstick off but didn't want to do it herself. She gave me a look. I gave her one back. The both of us started laughing so hard with the church giggles that we burst into tears.

By the time I resurfaced from my little expedition, Baird and John had disappeared from the spot where I'd left them. I'm not worried. All I need to do is follow the brook upstream. This is a simple idea somewhat challenging to execute, because the slippery banks aren't designed for feet. After a while I tire of slogging over uncooperative terrain and whack my way back to the dirt road, trudging gratefully on cleared paths, until suddenly the truck roars behind me and John scoops me up.

"Where have you been?" he growls, as I buckle myself into the seat. "We needed snacks."

"If I didn't have the food, would you have left me?" I ask rhetorically.

"No," John huffs.

"Yes!" Baird laughs.

"Here," I say, reaching in my pack and handing them sandwiches.

"He knew where you were," Baird declares happily, completely unbothered by the fact that he's caught no keeper fish today.

"Only a few little fish in that brook," John explains through mouthfuls of peanut butter. "We're trying a different spot."

We drive a few more miles until a turnoff appears. The side road leads to an exceptionally beautiful spot. Seems we're not the only ones who've come out here to appreciate it. A family has set up camp out behind the big sign that announces BOAT LANDING ONLY. They are three men and two dogs drinking cheap beer.

"Hello," I say neutrally, keeping my distance. A few yards behind me, John is still twiddling with the fishing gear in the truck. He doesn't know there are other people here.

"Yus," the patriarch replies, talking with an unlit cigarette butt dangling from his mouth. He is smiling with thin lips but he is missing a front tooth, and his eyes are wary. He is wrung out in a way that comes from drinking all your calories. His two adult sons are sitting side by side in ratty lawn chairs, their faces unmoving, stoic, knees apart with one hand on a can of Coors. A white pit bull sitting between them resembles Suds McGee from the Budweiser commercials, except this dog looks miserable.

"You doing any fishing?" I ask in my best non-accented English, trying very hard to look like I might be Michelle Malkin without makeup.

"Naw," he replies carelessly, and gives me a mean smile, as if there's something funny about the question. "But this mornin' I seen fish jumpin' around the point." He gestures lazily a long way down the marsh. I get the distinct impression he'd like it if I removed myself to that spot.

"Thanks for the information," I reply, gazing again at the water. This place is beautiful. I just wish there weren't any humans here ruining the view. I imagine he was thinking the same thing about me.

"Yur first time fishin'?" he asks politely, but his neck is tight. I am conspicuously unencumbered by a fishing pole, net, rubber boots, and vest, all of which adds up to a tourist from flatland who thinks that "fish" are chewy sweets from Sweden.

"First time in this spot," I reply truthfully.

Behind me, John walks up and stands protectively in my space. I can feel the men looking each other over, sizing things up. John nods at the man but doesn't say anything. Behind me Baird keeps his distance and watches, waiting for the adults to make up their minds about something kids aren't supposed to know about. John is a large man who looks like he belongs in the woods, which means he looks like he carries a .22 to handle surprises.

The spot is big enough for all of us, I think to myself. We came here to fish, but we're all just travelers lost in this land.

A beagle breaks the stillness by moseying into the picture, emerging from somewhere in the forest where he was entertaining his bowels. All heads swivel to the dog. The dog doesn't look up but keeps on sniffing the ground. The two sons hold back the pit bull, which has started to sniff butts. His tail stops wagging when he gets shoved down. So we stand, and wait as the air thickens and the birds sing and the beagle casts wistful glances at Baird, because all dogs want a boy for Christmas. It's our own little version of the "Three Billy Goats Gruff," and we can't cross until the trolls give us their permission.

"Good luck," the patriarch burrs abruptly, and lights up another cigarette.

John nods curtly. The conversation is over.

We pass them, walking deliberately in silence, splitting into two groups that puts me on the side with the boat landing sign and the dogs. A small man-made dam serves as a bridge to the other side of the marsh. I don't have on chest waders. John already knows that I won't follow them across. Instead, I walk down to the water's edge, which offers a sandy strip of soil good for sunning, and find a comfortable rock. Briskly, John and Baird cross over the dam and begin wading through the sucking edge of the water on the far side, going up to their ankles, and then their knees. They cast and walk, cast and walk, following a slow, graceful rhythm that synchronizes their movements. They are not doing this on purpose, which makes the coordination a lovely thing. Out there, in the water, they are two fishermen—one tall, the other taller—the similarities in their stances reflecting the father in the son.

"It's really slippery!" Baird yells to me in delight as he waves and teeters joyously in the water. "Whoops!" he announces happily. He regains his balance as one hand flies to the top of his head to keep his hat from escaping, doing a Chaplin dance in the water. The water isn't deep or fast. John doesn't turn his head. The yells of a happy boy are like the caws of crows or the splash of fish jumping high into the air. It's only a problem when they go silent.

They cast and walk, cast and walk. From my rocky perch I watch them fish, moving together but not side by side, Baird feeling his independence but knowing that his father is close and I am watching. Today, there is no sketchbook. I look out at lush trees, blue sky, and limpid water, and it looks like a painting by devout hands, invoking a sense of harmony between earth and sky. We thank artists for letting us believe we are benevolent stewards of God's green earth. A vastness hardly begun to be explored despite travels on paths well worn. How much sees the glowing green inchworm crawling up my big toe? I watch it move, wondering what it's looking for as it pleats slowly up my foot, my ankle, my calf, its whiskers tickling slightly as it meanders over my knee, impudent, ignorant, tickling up my thigh until I decide it's gone far enough and I brush it off.

It lands lightly on the rock and resumes inching along. I suppose it was looking for food. But it's an inchworm. It tastes the world through its whisker toes.

If it lives long enough, it won't become a butterfly. It will become a moth. Recently, scientists discovered a moth that looks exactly like a long-haired sheepdog. Were it not for the fact that it doesn't live very long, this moth would be an ideal replacement for Pikachu, because it's about as close as a real creature can get to being an animated Japanese cartoon.

When she was seven, my niece loved Pikachu, a ninja mouse-like creature inside a video game called Pokémon, but such love falls strangely on my old-fashioned ears. I'm the last generation to grow up without video games, though it was mostly because I refused to cooperate with my brother when he asked me to play them. I liked my toys lethal. My sister liked hers to taste good. For years, she lugged around a stuffed animal named Dogie, which is "doggy" with a Korean accent. It was a yellow snoopy dog that lapsed into filth, but she refused to let my mother wash it. She loved that threadbare doll with every fiber of her being, loving it the way that children love, lavishing it with drool and affection, scenting it with baby sweat and careless smoochie kisses. One day, mom threw Dogie away, making sure to do it on Garbage Day so there was no chance of rescuing it. My baby sister cried and cried as if her heart was breaking, wounded to the core by this heinous act of betrayal. It upsets her to this day.

My talisman was a stuffed polar bear that had no name. Its great usefulness was that it had a hard plastic face that was excellent for hitting things. I disliked its crazy clown grin, but I enjoyed thwacking my brother with it. Its face was indestructible. Even as the rest of its body disintegrated into a vile heap of fuzz, that pink plastic grin remained stuck in place, stoic, regardless of all the insults I heaped on it.

My sister wanted a real dog. I wanted a real bear. Neither of us got our wish. Koreans of my parents' generation didn't keep pets. For them, the American habit of keeping animals inside the house was deeply weird. Dogs have accidents on the floor. They don't wipe their butts. When you walk the dog so it can go doo-doo on the lawn, do you wash its paws when you let it back in? "Dogs are naturally cleanly animals," wrote Sir Peter Beckford in 1781. "They seldom, when they can help it, dung where they lie." Ah, but seldom isn't never. Such are the semantic somersaults of shit. Predictably, I was massively allergic to anything with a tail, but I was willing to sacrifice breathing if only I could please, please have a pony? *Aniyo?* No? But all my friends have ponies! I thought I was being quite reasonable for giving up on the bear. Obstinate, my parents refused. But the main reason why we didn't have pets was because my father worried they'd trip him. Because he had to wear special boots and sometimes braces in order to walk, our household did not enforce the Korean custom of removing footwear before crossing the threshold. Ironically, his handicap helped us blend in with the locals. When parishioners came to see him, they took off their caps but not their shoes. It never occurred to them that they could.

As a concession to my pet-keeping impulses, I received some real fish. That experiment lasted for one night and two days. The angelfish ate all the other fish in the tank, ten little minnows then there were none: the shiny silver angelfish croaked within hours of polishing off the last one. Fish-tank fish are domesticated. They've never lived in the wild. They no longer depend on fishing to survive, and so they have no clue how to live without four walls and manna falling from the sky. They're also cannibals. Fish flakes are made of fish. Given the chance, they will eat themselves to death. When this happens, it's not suicide. It's called "overfeeding." No matter. Fish-tank fish don't go to fish heaven when they die.

Did my mother go to heaven? What happened to her soul? Here is what I know:

We'd sung "Amazing Grace" at her funeral, which ended up mutating into a large and stately affair where hundreds showed up to pay their respects. In the late '80s, she'd been Maine Mother of the Year, and in that way had contributed to a small slice of history. Both she and my father were naturalized U.S. citizens and Republicans who liked that nice Bill Cohen. Politicians were always coming around, hoping for some sort of endorsement, which merely confirmed that they had no clue why so many church people loved my parents. The pews were packed with familiar faces, and it filled my father's heart with gladness that so many folks and one stray son had showed up for church that day, even if it was for a funeral.

Then the service was over and my brother raced back to California. Now what?

Turns out that my mother had gotten the last laugh. She hadn't walked out on my father but she'd left him just the same, sucking away his spiritual resolve and leaving him a little man with two stick legs. It wasn't a good look on him. His health was in alarming decline. Nothing new was wrong with him. It was just reality cutting him off at the knees, reminding him that he wasn't supposed to be able to walk in the first place.

For days, he sat alone in darkness, enfeebled by loss and the deafening silence. If you ask God "Why?" and God doesn't answer, it's much worse when you're used to hearing that still, small voice in the wilderness. Instead of words of comfort from the Almighty, he got mindless chatter from me and my sister as we cleaned up the residue of our mother's last year on earth. Stomach cancer is not a pretty disease. It's not Greta

Garbo dying gorgeously of tuberculosis in *Camille*, or even the picturesque rot of your average war movie. It's a smell. It's bedding stained with vile fluids and the sickly-sweet odor of puke permeating the curtains. It is the truth of a body that never gets spoken or seen. You get used to it. In any case, I had no cause to complain. I was a guest in the sickroom. My father had shouldered the burden of counting pills and draining catheters, honoring his vow to be there in sickness and in health, tenderly caring for her until the bitter end. Now she was in the ground and he was exhausted. It was up to his girls to finish the task.

In the flabby, shapeless weeks that followed, the U.S. postal service would deliver random junk addressed to her. Throwing out her mail felt like a betrayal, because there was so little, and yet that little was too much. Sighing, we cancelled her magazines and ripped up obscene credit card applications. Her personal things were more difficult to discard, for even rectal thermometers and soiled underwear turned into relics intimately infused with her essence. Not only did it feel wrong to throw these things away, it seemed positively sacrilegious. Some part of you insists on believing that if you just put all of it in a pile and cast a spell, a magic force will descend and the pieces will return to life. Never going to happen, especially not in Maine. When Yankees hang on to weird shit, it's not called hoarding, because that's what dragons do. Yankees are merely frugal. They just keep crap in the barn, with no expectation that all those lidless jelly jars and busted chainsaws will one day, after a hard rain and a lightning storm, rise up as an autonomous collective and start putting food by all by itself. They might, however, come in handy if extra people show up for supper and you need more juice cups and steak knives.

We stuck the rubberized sheets inside garbage bags, and kept cleaning.

Next, we tackled the closet, making the depressing discovery that her wardrobe mostly consisted of the nightgowns that had swaddled her sickness. The rest was winter coats, scarves, and mittens. Maine winters are long. Grimly, we gathered up armfuls of woolens, emptied out sock drawers, and opened unwise windows, numbing our nostrils with cold air. We cried a lot, wringing our hands and worrying she'd be angry if we tossed out her girdles. Then we laughed at ourselves for being so silly. Plucking at dresses, we sorted through memories for days and days until we were giddy and hungry and suddenly my sister and dad were back in the kitchen, sitting at the table, and eating my cooking.

Life was becoming normal again.

Until the nineteenth century, the mourning period after a major death would be a year, maybe two. Nowadays, most people only get a few days to process their emotions and move on, already. My sister had to go back to work and my grant was running out, so we reluctantly left our father inside a cloud of Korean ladies fussing over him. He'd complain, but he'd be fine. My sister drove back to Boston, and I flew to Chicago, where I would remain for three months before starting another impoverished year in Paris.

The weeks passed quickly, and before I knew it, I was packing up my suitcase and getting ready to leave the country again. Since I would end up routing through New York on my way to Paris, my then-boyfriend thought it would be nice if I extended the layover and spent a few days with him in his temporary home. He was living in a luxury hotel in Manhattan. This was his idea of heaven, and my idea of hell: an ultramodern suite that looked like a magazine spread and smelled like essence of lavender. At 3 A.M., my boyfriend was fast asleep, which irked me because I was wide awake and staring into the dark. Restlessly, I twisted and turned, debating whether I should just give up and read until I remembered that I don't travel with books. So I lay in bed, twiddling my thumbs, staring up in the general direction of the ceiling. Then I closed my eyes in a futile attempt to fall asleep. That's when I saw her.

By "seeing" her, I mean that I knew my mother was in the room and looking down at me. Who else could inspire in me a combination of surprise, horror, and embarrassment that I'd been caught in a hotel room with my boyfriend? (Look, ma! *Not* a lesbian!) What I saw was nothing at all, but in my mind's eye it translated into a hazy formless presence glowing near the ceiling. Opening my eyes and staring nearsightedly into the dark, I did my best to make sense of this energy blob beaming love . . . yup, love, but also mild amusement at my emotional thrashing. It was most definitely my mother and not some ghost-impersonator come to yell at me. How the hell did she find me? What, do ghosts get some kind of special haunting GPS device, like the owls in *Harry Potter*?

I'm fine, the apparition said serenely inside my head. *You don't need to worry about me.*

What, no lecture about my haircut? No *aigus* and wailing about my unladylike penchant for spinsterhood? I'd love a few clues about what you've been doing for the past twelve weeks, Mom. Could you please describe what Limbo is like? Pretty please?

No such information was forthcoming even though I screwed my face up and beamed questions from my brain as hard as I could. All I felt back from her was a kind of amazed bafflement, but bafflement free of fear and thus strangely pure. I turned my head, wondering if my boyfriend was getting any of this. It was too dark to see him, but his breathing was the deep, steady puffs of a man enjoying his REM sleep. Useless, I muttered to myself. Just useless.

So I poked him. He grunted, but didn't wake. My motions stirred the strange energy in the room, and she began to fade.

Before she disappeared for good, I heard her add with a small, surprised smile that felt like a tickle: *You're doing what you need to do.*

Now she understands me? Figures that I only make sense to the dead.

Then she was gone.

When I woke up early the next morning after a brief but curiously refreshing sleep, my boyfriend had gone to work out at the gym. Yawning, I ordered a big breakfast from room service, unfolded his fresh copy of the *London Times*, plumped my pillows, and used the landline to call my sister.

"You saw Mom last night, didn't you?" she said right away in an accusing tone.

"Yup. A little after three in the morning."

"I did too!" she exclaimed. "So did Dad. Same time for all of us. *Halmoni* called Dad right after she saw her. Dad says they—he and *halmoni*, that is—talked for hours last night. He's feeling much better now." She paused. "Did she say anything to you?"

"Just that she's fine, and not to worry."

She sighed. "Same here. I'm glad she said goodbye. I feel better now too. Where are you?"

"New York. Leaving for Paris soon."

My sister didn't think it strange that we saw her ghost. Same goes for my dad. It seems that Methodists are okay with the paranormal. Who knew? It turns out that John Wesley, the founder of Methodism, believed there was an interim period between death and Judgment, so the fact that her spirit hung around for three months was entirely consistent with his eschatology. Also, Methodists don't have a Heaven or Hell. They just have Resurrection and the Life, plus eternal Damnation for the wicked. But whereas my sister, my dad, and my *halmoni* felt a sense of peace after seeing her spirit, I felt something different.

I was annoyed.

My friend Chan, a Korean *p'ansori* singer, explained it very simply: if you see ghosts, and don't speak for them, they will not let you alone until you do. She thought I was lucky. I was pissed.

This may be a cultural thing, but Koreans don't insist on a bright line between this world and the other world. I have tried to figure it out in a way that makes sense, and the explanations are always lamer than just admitting your *umma*'s ghost saw your boyfriend's bits and pieces. For example, the fact that four of us saw an apparition at the same time can possibly be explained by an idiopathic parasympathetic connection negotiated through the limbic system. In other words, we all experienced a traumatic loss together, and our subconscious minds, having processed her death at exactly the same rate, translated the emotional epiphany into "ghost." The problem is that my grandmother wasn't in the hospital room with the rest of us. She also ruins the popular "mass hypnosis" hypothesis, because my *halmoni* is over 100 years old, and she's lived that long because she's exceptionally unimaginative.

I don't believe in ghosts, but they don't seem to care. Shoo! Shoo! This works about as well as it would with hopeful cats following you home. They make no sense at all—ghosts, that is—especially the Hollywood ones that wear clothes. The best I can come up with is that ghosts are glitches in the First Law, which is the Law of Conservation. In physics, this Law states that energy can neither be created nor destroyed but it can change forms. That's the lesson of the maggot, which starts off as a mealworm and ends up a housefly, buzzing around with the bees until the fish gulp it down. These fish get eaten by bears, which have a great time frolicking with the bunnies and pooping in the forest until they get run over by lawyers going moose hunting. Because only some lawyers are maggots, they don't get wings when they die. Instead, like all humans, they end up as pure energy, to be reformed where and how God and the cosmos see fit.

Here is where physics parts ways with religion: if a soul is consciousness, and consciousness is energy, humans don't get to choose what happens when the soul gets released. The universe does. Maybe your soul will come back as a bolt of electricity, a thunderclap, or the warmth of sunlight. Maybe you'll get lucky and become a fungus, a virus, or the mold growing in a shower stall. But if you're kormically confused without a sense of direction, this means you've spent your whole life doing one thing when you think you're doing another. Why should death suddenly change how you live? Instead of going straight to Heaven, you hang around as a ghost, thinking that it's totally normal to be baffled and slightly lost before you dissipate into the cosmos, singing the music of the spheres as you make the planets wobble.

Or, ghosts don't exist and seeing them is just a side effect of having allergies. Which, in my case, more or less get blamed for everything.

A tickling restores me to the present. Persistent, the inchworm has returned to my foot. I think it likes the warmth. I don't think it likes me.

I look down at the worm. It lifts the front of its body up and bobbles stiffly back and forth, waving to get my attention. Obediently, I put my hand down next to it, waiting and watching as it inches forward onto my finger, and then I lift the fleshy perch up to my nose to stare at the green bug, its entire body wagging like a judgmental finger at me.

Hi, Mom.

When I finally look up, a woman hovers near the water's edge. I don't know where she was before, but she's a few yards from me. Far enough to keep chatting at bay but close enough that I can see the lines on her face. Crouching down, she dips her fingers in the water as she glances over at me, her gaze incurious yet seeking solidarity. The light is gone from her eyes. In the curve of this woman's back I can see shadows of my mother sitting blankly at the kitchen table, just sitting there, listening to conservative talk radio stations and picking at cake donuts until the whole box was gone. She looks like a wild animal raised in captivity, well fed and growth stunted. She dips her right hand in the water, feeling its silk soothe her skin. I feel bad for her, but I'm not sure if I should. She wants to shuck off her socks, stick both feet in the lake and play the way children do. There will be trouble if she does. She is already too close to me.

Instead, she waits at the boundary between lungs and gills, coaxing herself to take the plunge into an altered state. I do not think she planned on swimming with the fishes, because she is still wearing shoes. But she is a camper person. I do not understand their shoe rituals.

On hot days, my mother used to scuff around in Korean sandals made for Flintstone feet, the rubber kind with a single wide strap. These were always paired with cropped polyester pants and thin white cotton ankle socks that polished the floors if you wore them inside the house. The three of us kids zoomed in and out of the parsonage wearing sneakers with tied laces. Aggrieved, my mother followed behind us with a waggling finger and a broom, but she didn't insist we take our outdoor shoes off, not even in the kitchen. It never occurred to us that we should.

The gunk on my feet was the least of my mother's problems. I tracked in chaos on my soles and carried it around in my pockets. In warmer months I dragged home turtles and frogs caught in the gully, a muddy river bed in the forest that was an inexhaustible source of kid fun. I'd plop my little friends in the bathtub and feed them bugs, as my little sister peered anxiously over the rim, deeply uncertain if frogs could leap up and bite off her nose.

"Yes," my brother said with a straight face.

"No," I peeved back, and reached for my stuffed polar bear to thwack him upside the head. It goes without saying that I used my Barbie doll as a hammer.

Inevitably, the turtle would relax its bowels, the frog would disappear, my sister would shriek, my brother would get bored, and I'd go outside, catch a garter snake, and put it in the tub with the turtle and the flies. And so on until bath time, because my sister would refuse to get in the tub until I removed Mr. Turtle and Mrs. Snake and all the twitching Fly children left over from the buffet. I'd have to gather up the lot, put them outside, and start all over when the next-day sun rose in the sky again. It was a relief when I moved on to ants, because I'd just lie on my belly and study their anthills outside. Since I did the laundry, she couldn't complain about grass stains.

After I moved in with John, I got my stuff out of storage. A few diaries had survived my periodic purges, and I hadn't looked at them since I'd begun writing them, starting at age seven. I sat down to read some pages. Here's the entry for January 4 when I was nine years old:

> Mom was in a grumpy mood. First thing she said was, "You look so stupid, and silly." So I started to do an English book. I played with Blue Royal [my parakeet]. I would pick her up on the chopstick and she'd mangle the bell. It goes "ting" every time she hits it. I went to the post office. I washed my hair. While I was drying it, Blue Royal got tangled up in the bell string and was hanging upside down! We went outside. We had an icicle fight. We went to the choir Christmas party. The Thomas's came for supper. Mom told me that I was getting fat.

The next day, January 5, I woke with pus oozing from my belly button. It smelled like rotten bananas.

As I thumbed through scrawled pages, I read that my mother had told me to "work on my charm," as I was clumsy and lacking grace. Pretty girls do not get festering sores. They do not play with snakes. I burned my fingers cooking meals, and got yelled at for ruining pots and pans. My mother never bought me clothes because I was too fat. Then she took money I'd earned by giving piano lessons and bought cute outfits for my sister. If my sister got mad at me, I was punished. If I didn't do my brother's chores, I was punished. Nearly every day I did the laundry. On sunny days, I'd hang it on the clothesline and then take it down. On other days,

> I ironed the sheets and clothes and folded them. I put the sheets and clothes away. Then I vacuumed. I gave "B" a bath. I made rolls. Then I cleared off the tables. I dried the dishes. Then I ironed and starched the collars for our choir robes.

Basically, I come off like a chubby Asian Cinderella without the backup chorus of singing mice. Still, it came as a bit of a shock that my mother was so mean to me. I don't remember the insults. I also don't remember all the housework. But there it is, the nasty comments and the litany of chores, day after day after day.

So it happened. But is it true? For what I recorded, and what I remember, don't match up at all. Am I to believe myself or my diaries? It's easy to explain the discrepancy. Early on, I'd developed a tendency to treat myself as an anthropological specimen, and thus my diary records my activities but not my feelings. When she conducted her career-making study of adolescent sex in Samoa, famed American anthropologist Margaret Mead was so clueless that it never occurred to her that girls make things up, especially when foreign grown-ups start asking questions about stuff that is none of their damn business. Her book did a better job skewering her own understudied tribe, the Episcopalians of New England, than it did explaining Samoan attitudes to mating. Mead was twenty-four years old and didn't speak a word of Samoan, Tokelauan, or any other Polynesian language. She talked to the teenagers (through her interpreter), and observed them (when they felt like it), so what she ended up with was the kind of meaningless stuff that went into my diary. Factually true, and completely irrelevant.

All the mean things my mother said to me sound important, as if my restlessness could be explained by growing up a charmless child ignored by both parents. As a kid, however, I lived inside my head, and what I was feeling was nobody's business, not even mine. My mother was very good with kids, and she was excellent at being a mom. I don't remember her being a saint. That was my father's job.

My father believes that human beings are basically good. I believe they are gullible.

The woman next to me pleats forward again and splashes her face, a terrible thought fluttering down the back of her neck. Then the thought passes and she unfurls slowly, stretching her spine like a pissed-off cat.

"Whooorf," the beagle whines in the distance.

"Shurdup," a male voice slurs behind me, followed by the hiss of a can being cracked open.

After a while, she turns and shuffles slowly back to her family.

The light lengthens. On the other side of the water, man and boy cast and walk, cast and walk. Do they want to catch a fish? Yes. What will happen to the fish if they do? They will conk it on the head, and I will cook it for them. I am allergic to fish. It doesn't change anything.

Hours pass. As I watch, Baird catches two brown frogs and loses his hat. Stumping along, he fishes the hat from the bottom of the marsh, sticks it back on, and waves at me, grinning. I wave back. The frogs are forgotten, and so they hop off. By now, the sun is nearly down, making it difficult to see through the alarming thicket of blackflies.

Bloop! Bloop! Hungry, the fish jump and rise.

My hell, their dinner.

Eat, little fish, eat! Remove this scourge that plagues me!

But they've got no reason to bite. In the distance, two shadows slog through the marsh, disappearing briefly into the trees, and reappearing again as they tromp silently across the bridge.

And thus they cross from one world to rejoin the one that they'd left.

Chapter Seventeen

✿ ✿ ✿

Ham Supper for 227

I like pigs. Dogs look up to us. Cats look
down on us. Pigs treat us as equals.
— *Sir Winston Churchill*

"Ow," Patrick announces, as everyone sits down to Sunday supper at the Big House. "I just bit on something."

"Buckshot," John says calmly.

"But I'm eating potatoes," Patrick protests.

"Buckshot," John repeats, and reaches for another serving of venison chop suey.

"So tell me about the wedding!" I prod Patrick.

"We got married," Patrick shrugs, still chewing with a slightly puzzled expression on his face. "Then we fished at the lake."

"That's it?"

"Yep."

"You still doing the pig roast?"

"Yep."

"What about the pig?" I poke him. "Have you got one yet?"

"Nope," he replies. "If I bring a pig home early, Christy will start cooing over it and before you know it, it will be another Bucky. And then I'll just have to get another pig to roast."

Just to be clear, Bucky wasn't a pig. He was a dog stuck in the body of a goat.

It is a truism of animal husbandry that certain animals come in pairs. The dove is one of them. The goat is another. Even if herds of other friendly animals are around, a single goat will not do well on its own. The specifics of the pair don't matter: It can be girl-girl, boy-boy, boy-girl, old-young, big-small, or black-white. They just both have to be goats, preferably two of the same kind, and not an Archy and Mehitabel kind of pair (a cockroach and an alley cat, in case you were wondering). Bucky thought he was a dog. So did all his friends. Wagging his tail, Bucky followed Patrick wherever he went. Begging to be petted, Bucky lived inside the house and shed on the couch. But one day, while nobody was home and he was all alone, he died. Death deprived him of his amazing powers of mind control, and behold! Bucky was returned back to being a goat. It was very upsetting.

In the weeks of bereavement that followed, it came out that Christy didn't much care for Bucky's habit of chewing on the curtains, and had no plans to replace Bucky with another dog. For her next pet, Christy wants a miniature donkey. Patrick has no opinion about this.

"What about the pig?" I repeat, because Patrick has resumed ignoring me.

Patrick takes a large forkful of venison chop suey and chews pensively. "Last time I got a pig from this guy who runs a pig farm. He's got hundreds. I'm not worried."

"I'd call him now and get one tagged," Ruth mutters, as if talking to herself.

"What fer?" Patrick asks loudly. "Last time we did a pig roast, we just went over the day before and got two."

"*Two* pigs?" I exclaim in horror. "How many people were you planning on feeding?"

"Just me and him," Patrick deadpans, jabbing a fork at John, who is too busy eating to pay attention to this conversation. "T'weren't on purpose," he clarifies. "We only wanted the one, but my friend, he shot the pig in the head and it went clear through and hit another pig. The farmer made him buy the other one." He takes another forkful of venison and chews energetically, adding, "The room was full of bullet holes from bounces."

"Why didn't he use a stun gun?" I ask, aggrieved.

"Bullet's quicker," Patrick replies through a mouthful of mashed potatoes. It also requires more skill, and bullets are expensive, which is why they're not used for large-scale slaughtering of livestock animals. Obligingly, Patrick ploughs on with the gruesome details, accompanied by graphic hand gestures. "They stick the carcass through a machine that takes all the hair off," he explains. "They're these wire coils that turn round and round and pull the hair right out. They're fast but they don't work that well. Better to do it by hand." He nods firmly.

I've never hand scraped a pig, but once I tried using a lady shaver on my legs. It had three round pivoting heads made up of wire coils that worked on the same principle as the pig scraper. The attempt was both painful and silly, as most efforts at hair removal are. The experiment was never repeated.

The phone rings, and Ruth rises to answer it. "Wonk wonk wonk wonk?" the phone speaker asks.

Ruth hangs up in annoyance. "One of those phone surveys," she grumbles. "This one wanted to know if I believe that marriage is only between a man and a woman. Why do those people always call during dinner?"

"Because they know you'll be home," John says briskly.

"It's a good way to make sure you won't answer their questions," Ruth snips, and sits back down at the table.

Lots of things come in pairs, such as socks, scissors, and pants. A pant on its own has no purpose, except to make the wearer look foolish. John's parents think that people should be married. However, they do not think that people should marry their pants just to make the flies happy.

I think that lots of people come in workable pairs, just not the molded plastic kind that gets stuck on top of wedding cakes.

Take Archy and Mehitabel. Archy the Cockroach has the soul of a poet. Mehitabel the Cat used to be Cleopatra. (Somewhat obviously, Cleopatra couldn't claim to be the reincarnation of herself, so she insisted that she used to be the goddess Isis.) Before they became best friends, Mehitabel tried to eat Archy. He objected to this. After they got to know each other, however, she left him alone so he could write, which is about as high a compliment as a cat can pay to a cockroach. An ardent social- ist, Archy lobbies for insect rights. Mehitabel reminisces about her romances and sighs for the good old days—"*toujours gai*," she repeats melancholically. They don't have much in common except a disdain for rats, a love of living freely, and a firm belief in transmigration of souls. For in their heart of hearts, they are still human. That much they know. I envy them their certainty.

An outdoor tent party presents a logistical challenge requir- ing months of advance planning. Add a pig, and the mission turns into a small-scale military operation complete with large men in camo. To keep the mayhem in check, there must be sufficient jeeps, targets, and exploding rockets to entertain the troops. First aid must be available for the wounded, and yes, there must be food. Not just lots of food. Parking lots of food.

I may not know much, but I know how to cook for the masses, thanks to spending my formative years helping out with the blissful weirdness that is the church supper. Not to be confused with Easter Sunrise breakfasts (fried eggs and bacon!) and Sunday school picnics (bologna sandwiches on Wonder Bread!), the church supper is a competitive cook- ing event of epic proportions. A light meal of bread and wine before a big hike? That's not a church supper. It's the Last Supper, which also happened to be Christ's last proper meal but it's never called the "Last Meal," because that's what pris- oners on Death Row get served. Curiously, the theory behind the church supper and the Last Meal is the same: when you accept food from strangers, the rules say that you can't haunt them after you're dead.

Church ladies are at their finest when they roll up their sleeves and start cooking for Jesus. Over the years, I have roasted enough beasts to feed a small army, so I have learned a few things about commandeering home refrigerators in the name of God and food safety. This is why a page from one of Ruth's cookbooks catches my attention. It is a recipe for "Ham Supper for 227":

---

48 lbs canned ham

24 potato salads (solicited)

5 lbs coffee

1 pt cream

45 strawberries

6 pkc Bisquick equals ¾ in. biscuits

2 qt. milk

1 lb Crisco

5 to 6 c. water

48 pkg. peas

8 qt. milk

6 qt. heavy cream

1 pkg. Starlac

1c. sugar, add to Bisquick

That's it. There are no explanations or instructions, because it's a grocery list. Why 227 servings? I don't know. *227* was a popular television show in the '80s, but it seems unlikely that the number was meant to pay homage to a sitcom starring Florence the Maid from *The Jeffersons*. The list itself would suggest a church supper at Easter, but I've yet to work out

why a pig would be the centerpiece for a feast meant to celebrate the Resurrection. I've sifted through various explanations for the Glorification of Glazed Ham, ranging from the
pagan roots of Christianity, to the food calendars of colonial
Americans: slaughter hogs in fall, cure haunches over the
winter, enjoy ham in the spring. None are entirely convincing,
because the Bible frowns on humans eating cloven-hooved
beasts. Then again, what better way to defeat the Devil than
by drowning him in honey?

This list illuminates an entire way of life, even as it demonstrates how much gets lost in translation. Like presidential
speeches, it seems to make good sense until you try to put it
all into action. Best I can figure, the side dishes will be potato
salad and green peas. For dessert, there will be strawberry
shortcake topped with whipped cream, washed down with
hot coffee. But "5–6 cups of water . . ." What for? To add to
the "5 lbs. of coffee," or to boil "48 packages of peas"? There's
enough dairy on this list to send a lactose-intolerant reader
rushing to the bathroom, and yet there's no butter, because
there's no bread. Given that this list of ingredients is designed
to feed over two hundred adults, the portions seem very far
off, breaking down to a skinny slice of meat and 0.2 strawberries atop a very short piece of shortcake—"¾ inch." A normal
biscuit is ½ inch thick before baking, and rises to thrice that
amount after being baked. From a cook's perspective, the list
is just plain confusing.

The only part that makes sense is the line, "24 potato salads
(solicited)." It absolutely cannot be store-bought potato salad
from a deli, and no, it can't all be made by Mrs. Zinc, even
though everyone agrees that hers is the best. No, that would
entirely miss the point of the church supper. Each potato salad
must come from two dozen different households, each bowl
proudly displaying its quirks. I can see them now, one bowl for
each hour of the day, mounded white and creamy, and made
with potatoes brought up from the root cellar. Some will be

amazingly good. Some will be lethal soups of creamed phlegm sprinkled with cat food. And nobody will complain, because Mrs. Cooper is ninety-seven years old and smells like mothballs. When she sneezes, every member of the Church Supper Committee will say, "Bless you!" as they fish her dentures out of the Meow Mix® and whisk her out of harm's way. Her smile of gummy bliss is a beautiful sight to behold.

This list comes from the *Bicentennial Cookbook of Woodstock, Maine*, a spiral-bound collection of recipes sold to benefit the Woodstock Fire Department Auxiliary. It's possible that the ham supper list was meant for a fireman's fundraiser, but those dinners are always chicken barbecue. The cookbook is undated, but it was published in the late 1950s because Starlac is on the list. Once a very popular brand of powdered milk marketed as "the heart of milk," Starlac was the first convenience food ruined because of a public health scare, known to the annals of history as The Borden Starlac Incident of 1966. The Borden Company survived the discovery of salmonella in its powdered milk, but the bad publicity doomed the Starlac brand. The company pulled Starlac off the market before anyone became ill, but the entire powdered milk industry suffered from the fishy taint of disease. Five years after The Borden Starlac Incident of 1966, a man with the wonderful name of Hersey Benn sued Borden because he claimed plain Starlac without chocolate had made him sick. Unfortunately for him, Benn was an inmate in the state of California system, and the well-preserved Starlac had come from the prison's canteen. Was drinking milk flavored with salmonella more cruel and unusual than being forced to eat boiled lobster? In nineteenth-century New England, inmates had protested because they were being served disgusting sea bugs fit only for pigs. The inmates won. Today, lobsters are still eaten by pigs, only now the pigs are rich. Hersey's Starlac lawsuit was tossed. Powdered milk is now the food of fallout shelters and missionaries.

The advantage of powdered milk is that it travels *and* it keeps, especially during summer months when icebox real estate will be at a premium. Because the wedding feast will be in August, the menu will be roast pig, bean-hole beans, and strawberry shortcake topped with whipped cream.

After weeks of perfecting the recipes, finalizing guest lists, and organizing supplies, the Three Days of the Pig are about to begin. The countdown starts with a day of picking strawberries in Wayne, Maine, about an hour's drive from the Big House. Stevenson's Strawberry Farm is a well-organized operation with staff members stationed at tricky intersections, steering tourists away from fields being ploughed by free-ranging pigs. Impatiently, John wheels the truck onto the grass next to the other vehicles and jumps out, stretching like a bear just woken up from hibernation. As Baird and I follow suit, an employee quickly approaches us and tells us where to set up. "Go . . ." he scans the fields, shading his eyes from the sun, "over there," he instructs, pointing at a corner spot, and rushes off to direct the next batch of unfashionably dressed people. Swinging into action, John and Baird each grab a strawberry flat out of the back of the truck and head out into the field without waiting for me. They know better. I will need to 1) adjust my sun hat, 2) put on gardening gloves, 3) spritz on bug spray, 4) layer on sunscreen, 5) apply lip balm, 6) drink a bottle of water, 7) go find a port-a-potty, and 8) rest before repeating steps 1–5. If I don't finish the beauty regimen, I freckle in the sun. Then I pass out.

There are few activities as satisfying as gathering strawberries, even the farmed kind that are bred to be couch potatoes. I love that tiny tug of resistance before the ripe berry releases into your hands, surrendering with a sweet sigh as it joins its overweight friends in the sunny flat I've set up for them. I manage to pick about a dozen fat victims before payback starts. First, my arms start to itch. Next, the hives pop up.

Then, my eyes begin to turn red and . . . so far, it's all very predictable. Wiping sweat off my face with the back of my gloved hand, I keep picking strawberries, adding a few more fruits to my basket until—ayuh, that's wheezing. The final symptom before I achieve suffocation by strawberry. Grumbling, I stomp back to the car, reach into the glove compartment, and grab a bottle of liquid Benadryl to top off my regular antihistamine cocktail. Then I lean against the truck, watching the bucolic scene in front of me as I wait for the diphenhydramine to kick in.

Since before we arrived, a nosy man draped in long-lens cameras has been hanging out in the patch. Spotting me red-faced and weepy, he walks over with an air of concern.

"You okay?" he asks with a certain note of hope that he might have stumbled into a scandal. He is, he says, a photographer getting local interest shots for the Augusta paper.

"Yah, fine," I reply distractedly, as I rummage in my pockets for a fresh packet of Kleenex. "I'm allergic to strawberries, so I'm itchy."

"I have alcohol rub!" the photographer volunteers brightly. Without waiting for an answer he dashes to his car, pops the trunk, grabs a bottle, runs back with the useless stuff, and holds it out with an expectant look on his face.

"That's not—*atchoo!*—going to help," I inform him politely, sneezing again for emphasis.

He stares with horrified wonder at the hives bubbling up my arms, exposed now because I am coating them with anti-itch cream. "Wow, you're really allergic to strawberries!" he exclaims in surprise.

"Yep," I snarf.

"Can you eat them?"

"Nope."

"All that," he gestures prissily at the pink eruptions decorating my skin, "happens just by being around the plants?"

"Yep."

Skeptically, he eyeballs my gloves, long pants, wide-brimmed hat, and an overall level of protection on a hot day that would not be out of place on a beekeeper. "Then, uh, why are you picking them?"

Is it really that difficult to fathom why I am in a strawberry patch? As if it isn't perfectly obvious that you can't make strawberry shortcake without strawberries.

"Because—*atchoo! atchoo!*—I like picking strawberries," I shrug, blowing my nose and re-rolling up my sleeves, which insist on unrolling just to spite me.

He stares at me with a look of puzzlement on his face. "But you're allergic!"

"Extremely allergic," I agree cheerfully, as I head back into the patch, but not before turning around and shouting, "Thanks for the alcohol!" just to see heads swivel in hopes that they'd lucked into a tailgater. Standing limply in place, the poor fellow looks utterly baffled.

Between delicious sips of liquid Benadryl, I locate my abandoned strawberry flat lying crookedly on the ground, pick it up with two gloved hands, and then go looking for John. Thanks to his bulk, he is easy to spot even when he's doing the strawberry squat.

Honk. I blow my nose delicately, and wait for him to look up. "Take them," I order him nicely, handing over my stash as he reaches for the sorry tray of strawberries I've parked on his head. "I'm going to head over to the pea patch." Squinting into the sun, he takes in the rash spreading up my neck, philo-sophically plucks a strawberry off the plant, and eats it while shaking his head and sighing heavily. This is his way of telling me, I Can't Take You Anywhere. I give him a cross look. "Just come find me when you're done, okay?"

He sighs again. "Okay," he agrees, and resumes his task with a martyred air of resignation. Baird is AWOL. He is pos-sibly bothering the cows. What with me getting the farmhand version of a Section 8, it is now left to John to manfully pick enough strawberries to feed a few hundred guests before the sun goes down.

It is nearing two in the afternoon, and the skies are still blue. It's a glorious summer day. As I walk to the next field, I wave friendly-like at the photographer, who has resumed pointing his camera at happy families engaged in a wholesome outdoor activity. He waves back with a vexed expression, as if I must have made up the allergy story, and I'm really a humanoid science project grown from toadstools.

The farm is large and I am easily confused, so it takes a while to find the pea patch. To my surprise, I spot John's Aunt Nancy wading among the bushes. "Nah, it can't be." I dismiss the thought, because she didn't tell Ruth she was going pea-picking. It's just another tanned lady with cropped white hair who doesn't wear a hat in the sun. I squint, shake my head, and revise my opinion. That has to be her, because the state of Maine is one big small town. "Hellooo!" I call out, waving to get her attention.

Peapod in hand, Nancy straightens up and looks around to see who might be scaring the birds. "Why, hello!" she waves back when she spots me heading her direction, a pleased expression crossing her round face.

"How're the peas?" I ask in greeting.

"Too late in the season," she says crisply. "They're mostly picked over. You'll find some if you look."

Nancy is picking peas with a friend from church. Between the two of them, with a century of expertise in their hands, they've managed to scavenge several bags of peas but that's not even close to being the forty-eight shelled bags needed for the pig roast. I find a few pods, but they're either overripe or immature. By the time I hear John honking impatiently for me, having picked fifty pounds of strawberries plus a few extra for snacks, I've managed exactly one robust pea.

Which more or less sums up today's outing for me.

"Bye Nancy!" I wave, as John scoops me up and we roar off in the truck.

Taking backroads on the way home, we drive by rolling hills and working farms. The land up here is lush. In the back seat, Baird is working his way through a pint of strawberries, singing Beatles songs to himself while he eats. He smells like cow. So I sneeze.

Abruptly, John slams on the breaks.

"What are you doing?!" I exclaim in surprise.

"Look!" John hisses, pointing insistently at the middle of the road. "Not at me. At *them*!"

"Them . . . ?" I start to object. Then I spot the doe and fawn blinking at us, so close that they're practically nuzzling the hood.

"Take a picture!" John nudges under his breath.

Precisely in hopes of such encounters, a compact digital camera is hanging off my neck. For once, I am at the right place, at the right time, with the right equipment at hand. It is a *sign*. But by the time I take it out of the case, power it up, and point it in the general direction of the doe and fawn, they've become bored and shuffled off into the woods, strolling at a leisurely pace, in no hurry at all.

"Did you get it did you get it did you get it?" Baird asks from the back seat, bouncing with strawberry-fueled excitement.

"No," I say crossly, turning off my camera and zipping it back in the case.

"Why not?" he whines, just to be annoying.

"Oh, shush," I pout, making Baird laugh.

John starts up the truck and we resume the ride home. He doesn't tease me at all, because he knows the answer to Baird's question. Even with a camera at the ready, deer are a challenge to shoot.

Day Two: It's the day before the party, and the strawberries are washed and cut, the shortcake is baked, the tent is up, the bean-hole beans are baking, and all that remains is the star of the show. I've been waiting all day for the pig to arrive. "Look over there," Don says dourly to me, pointing through the picture window. "The pig's here."

In the distance, I can see Patrick's big blue pickup, parked by the far edge of the field. Clapping my hands together like a little kid, I dash out the door and run down the front lawn to greet the guest of honor.

There it is, the whole pig, lying in a cardboard coffin that's been slit open with a box cutter. The sow has been dressed, scraped, and gutted, giving her a svelte waistline and smooth pink skin. Her eyes are open but they look fake, as if made of melted wax and colored in with a crayon. The joints move easily. There is no blood and only the faintest trace of an odor similar to wet wool.

"How much does it weigh?" I ask, poking it lightly, in the manner of a car buyer kicking tires.

"About 125 pounds," Patrick shrugs. "It's pretty small."

A group of Patrick's hunting buddies materializes to help with the pig. The boyish one, Luke, is a professional hunting guide. He jumps up in the trailer bed with the pig, holding it steady by its legs. Sporting a moustache to hide the bald spot on the top of his head, Kevin is on the ground next to the truck, and starts to clear the area for trussing. The Preparation of the Pig is officially starting.

Kevin leans over and peers intently into the pig's mouth, checking out its molars like a wily horse-trader. "That there's the best bit," he comments sagely, pointing at the tongue. He straightens back up with a satisfied expression on his face. All the men nod in agreement.

"Hate the liver," another hunting buddy adds, with a philosophical air regarding the vagaries of taste. "But my wife loves it. Me, I like the heart. Deer, that is," he adds for clarification. "Nuthin' better."

"Sure," the guys agree. Their wives like liver too. They all look at me. Apparently, a taste for liver is a chick thing.

It takes two men to maneuver the pig. Each end of the rod gets closed up with giant prongs that stabilize the body, creating a sort of trap that comes apart in the middle. As we stand around watching, the pig's head and spine gets wired to the rod. Kevin is cutting short lengths of heavy wire with a pair of clippers and handing them to Patrick, who shapes them into a U, shoves them through the belly cavity until the ends poke out the back, and then twists the wires together with a pair of pliers. I think of the croquet gates poked this morning into the front lawn.

"Frankenpig," Kevin chortles, underscoring the XXX of the crude sutures traveling the length of the torso.

Patrick huffs and puffs and wrestles the front legs apart, wires them tightly to the rack, and repeats the process with the hind legs in the back. In aerobics class, the pig's pose is called Superman. The sow looks ready to take off, up, up into the air! The flesh is vibrant. The scents are fresh in the warm night air. The men twist and turn the pig on the spit, making sure that nothing wiggles.

As the sunlight seeps away, a chorus of driving machines joins the group. Headlights from a pickup truck cast long, brooding shadows on one side as an ATV winks in the opposite direction. Doused in mechanical lights, the truck-bed tableau has the look of battle surgery performed on a downed soldier.

Carefully, Patrick and Kevin flip the pig onto its back, readying it for the next step. An hour later, the belly bulges from two freshly sliced pineapples, a sack of sweet potatoes, and tropical fruit from cans as big as milking pails. The idea is to add moisture so the pig doesn't dry out as it roasts. I am dubious. But it's not my wedding feast, and it's not my pig. If it *had* been my pig, I would have tried an ancient Roman recipe called the "Trojan Hog," which involved a pig stuffed with "thrushes, udders, gnatsnappers, and many eggs." Oysters and scallops went down the hog's mouth, followed by booze and polenta. The hog gets roasted over firewood until cooked, then served belly up on a platter. This dish was so ruinously expensive that it was illegal to make. The loophole? It wasn't illegal to eat. When Christianity rolled around, gluttony got made into one of the Seven Deadly Sins, linking the high cost of good food to an offense against God. The result wasn't fewer hogs being killed but cheaper hot dogs.

Christy wanders by to check out the work. She's been out somewhere in the field, probably mowing the lawn. "Pat, are you peeing?" she exclaims in surprise.

Patrick looks down. "Nur," he mumbles. "That the pig!" Fruit juice is pouring out the butt end of the pig. Because of the angle, it looks exactly as if Patrick is taking a whizz.

Phsssttt, the yellow juice splats, puddling sweetly on the ground.

"So much for holding it in," another hunting buddy grumbles. His nickname is Smeg, as in *smegma*, otherwise known as "a white secretion of the sebaceous glands of the foreskin." It's not so much an insult as shorthand. Lumbering forward, Smeg jams in an orange potato the long way, using the tuber to block the hole. But it's too late; all the pale yellow liquid has run out the butt.

"Guess we made her nervous," Kevin jokes. He looks down at the bony old beagle curled up near his feet. "Right, Bobo?" Bobo is the grandfather of Patrick's beagle Beebee, which means that Kevin and Patrick are in-laws through their dogs.

Bobo's ears flick up. His brown eyes blink in agreement. Then he goes back to sleep.

The final step is closing the seam. The pig is as overstuffed as a duffle bag leaving for college. It takes a lot of strength to pull the two sides together. The skin is pliable yet tough. As darkness falls, a heated discussion ensues regarding whether it is better to use the staple method that worked for the spine, or to sew it together by pulling one long piece of wire through the sides. Patrick wants to staple. Kevin wants to sew. Kevin wins. He threads a long piece of wire in and out, using a classic overhand stitch, and tugs the length through once the threading awl has gone all the way up the neck. The sides pull neatly together. The seam is firm. There are no gaps.

Because it's taking a really long time to get through the prepping, Ruth drives an ATV down from the house to observe the goings-on in the dark. She arrives just in time to see the final stitch going in. "That's the same stuffing used in that *New Yorker* article about the pig roast," she remarks. Around the sewing circle, thick eyebrows raise. She adds hastily: "It got sent to Christy after someone heard she and Patrick were doing one for the wedding."

"Guess that means that pig roasts are trendy," I say.

"I guess," Ruth says dubiously. She stands around watching for a few minutes more, but it's just a bunch of guys sewing up dinner. Nothing she hasn't seen before. Abruptly, she climbs back into the ATV, swiftly backs it up and wheels it around, making the headlights careen wildly.

Still resting in the truck bed, the pig gets packed in lavish amounts of ice, and then wrapped in a blue tarp along with two large sides of beef. Finally, Patrick reaches down, lifts up the back of the truck, closes it with a loud thump, and hops out.

"That'll make it hard for the coyotes to jump in," Patrick says, as if saying it aloud made it true.

". . . coyotes?" I repeat in surprise. But they'd turned up their noses at the sick chicken!

"Sure," the men nod in unison, looking like a chorus line of bobble heads on the dashboard.

Darkness has fully fallen, and Christy has collapsed into a sleeping bag set up in a two-man tent by the truck. She and Patrick will be camping outside tonight, because the fire will have to be started soon. All the hunting buddies will be staying the night in tents and campers lining the other side of the field. Since no one's driving home, there'll be serious drinking tonight.

"We done here?" Kevin asks, giving the pig an experimental slap.

"Done!" Patrick agrees. And off they vanish into the woods, looking for the pony keg that Christy hid somewhere.

Day Three: 6:15 A.M., and the entire household is awake. John got up an hour earlier and vanished somewhere between the bathroom and the henhouse. It's too noisy for me to get back to sleep, so I stumble into the kitchen to see what's happening.

"They're up," Ruth says without preamble. "The coffee's on the roaster." She jerks her head down the hill, and resumes setting up the kitchen for the caterers.

I nod, pull on jeans, t-shirt, and a pair of hikers, and trundle down the hill to visit the pig. It's now on the roaster, and its skin is completely black as if it's been cooking for hours.

"Good morning!" I grog, waving at Patrick who is standing by the pig, and turning it slowly on the spit. He's wearing dry clothes but his hair is wet, which means he's been up at the house already and taken a shower.

"Got up at three," Patrick yawns by way of greeting. "Me and Kevin made the fire. It took a couple hours for the flames to die down and the coals to heat up proper." He pokes the coals with a stick, and throws on a fresh log for good measure.

"Is there still coffee?" I ask hopefully, gesturing at the camping pot resting on a gas grill that materialized in the middle of the night. In response, Patrick grabs a bottle labeled "Spray-on Stripper," and starts spritzing the pig with it. The air fills with the smell of apple juice. I take that as a Yes.

I grab a tin cup, wipe it off on my t-shirt, pour myself some hot coffee and take an experimental sip. It's muddy and good, because it's chilly out here. "So I guess you guys didn't get much sleep last night," I say, eyeing the blackened pig.

Patrick shrugs and spritzes again. "We were already up 'cause some coyotes came to visit."

I give him a skeptical look.

"I could hear 'em," Patrick declares staunchly, as he casts an affectionate look at the dog curled up next to the roaster. "Basel couldn't *'cause he's deaf!*" he hollers at Christy's pet. Cocooned in silence, Basel stares out at nothing with glazed eyes full of doggy love. "But he could smell 'em!" Patrick crows. "Coyotes had jumped up in the trailer. Baz and I went out to chase 'em off, but they took one look at us and scattered right quick."

"What about Christy?" I ask, looking over at the tent—so flimsy, now, when compared to the hunger of predators. "Was she scared?"

"Nur," Patrick replies. "She didn't wake up."

"First heard the 'yip! yip! yip!' next to my camper," Kevin comments, jumping into the conversation as he walks up from the other side of the field. He looks remarkably jaunty considering how little sleep he managed. "I was like, 'Shit! Them's coyotes out there!'" He looks down at the beagle trotting beside him. "I had to hold back Bobo. He was going crazy. Weren't you, Bobo?" he coos.

Hovering by Kevin's heels, Bobo looks up eagerly at the sound of his name, and his ears perk up as he awaits the command to run. When the command doesn't come, he trots forward, greets Basel, crawls under the belly of the roaster and curls up into a comfortable ball. It looks cozy under there. Bobo is a smart dog.

"Coyotes got the beef," Patrick tells Kevin, who has pulled up a lawn chair and is making himself comfortable in front of the roaster. Watching the meat turn slowly over a fire is clearly the best entertainment of the day.

"There's still plenty o' meat," Kevin says cheerfully. He points to a cooler resting under the shade of the elms. As it happens, he accidentally set it on top of the graves of two pet rabbits named Strawberry and Oak. "Been hunting pigs 'round Okeechobee," he explains. "I brought a couple of haunches for the grill."

Okeechobee is in Florida, a state with a wild hog problem. I know exactly where Kevin got his pig, because a friend and I once tried to go mountain biking in the area and accidentally wandered into the middle of a hog hunt. I'd thought we'd stumbled into the middle of an old-fashioned Revivalist tent meeting, because there were suddenly dozens of people sur-rounding us, giving off a certain festive air combined with religious zeal. Then a hard-faced man walked forward, blocked the path, and warned us, in a heavy Southern accent, that *we'd best be runnin' along now; they is here to hunt hogs and the situation weren't safe for us.* That's when I noticed that everyone was carrying rifles, including women and children, squinting all flinty-eyed and tough, brandishing weapons in one hand and pudding cups in the other.

We wheeled around and left the woods. Because if you've ever played with empty pudding cups, you know they're more addictive than crack.

From the other side of the field, Smeg rambles up with a camp fireplace, a rickety contraption that looks like a really big oil lamp.

"You need some coffee?" I ask him, jabbing my thumb towards the tin pot. "Patrick put some fresh on the roaster."

"Nah," he burps extravagantly, and holds up a can. "Already on beer."

Yesterday, Kevin tells us, he rubbed his boar haunches with his secret mix and topped them with barbecue sauce. Just in case that fails, there are three turkeys as backup.

One turkey is already roasting in a smoker by the garage. A second bird will be dunked in a moon rocket that's landed in the middle of the field. I half expect a little door to pop open and aliens to march out and declare, in tinny voices, "Greetings, earthlings! Take us to your leader!" But nothing happens, because the moon rocket is the turkey fryer.

"You're gonna love it," Kevin declares earnestly. "But ya gotta make sure they're all the way thawed before putting it in the deep fryer, or else,"—he chuckles—"boom!"

"Boom!" Smeg and Patrick echo with pleased expressions on their faces.

The third bird will be cooked inside the aluminum garbage can sitting behind the roaster. I am assured that the "garbage can" method produces a superior bird. Mostly, it seems to be another excuse to set a small bonfire and call it "cooking."

The sound of a loud buzzing interrupts the cooking chitchat. As we watch, shading eyes with one hand, a prop plane comes into focus. It comes closer . . . closer . . . flying very low until "What the—?" I start, nervous that the lost airplane is going to crash the party.

Patrick, Kevin, and Smeg tip their heads back and squint at the vehicle, now coming toward us at alarming speed.

"That Chris?" Kevin asks Patrick in a bored tone of voice.

"Yep," Patrick nods laconically.

Playfully the plane dips a wing as it zooms directly overhead, so close that we become infants reaching for a toy plane on a mobile hanging over a crib. For no particularly good reason, we all wave like idiots at the flying machine as our heads crane to watch it, invisibly tethered like sunflowers following the moving body in the sky. With a final swoop, the plane zooms away and vanishes into the clouds.

Slowly, the fields regain their quiet as sunbeams stuff my ears.

"He comin' later?" Kevin asks Patrick, though I have no idea why. It's like the bit about the tongue: Kevin seems to say aloud things that everybody already knows.

"Yep."

"Landin' here?" Still lounging in his lawn chair, Kevin points at the very long driveway between the road and the Big House.

Patrick looks out at the driveway and shakes his head sadly. "Nope."

"Didn't think so," says Kevin, and all is well in the world.

As the morning sun rises and the dew starts to dry, the campers on the other side of the driveway begin spewing out dogs needing to be walked. Since yesterday, campers have been arriving at sporadic intervals, driving up and parking in the field out front. Each camper is bigger and more elaborate than the last. Yesterday afternoon, the first to arrive were the hunting buddies who pitched pup tents and set up little campfires next to their pickups. Sometime during the wee hours of the morning, pop-ups staked their claim in the field. They were followed by station wagons hauling small Airstream campers, the ones that look like giant silver toasters on wheels. The newest campers are sparkling new RVs with kitchenettes and tinted windows. It's only ten campers so far, but the rate of fancification is astonishing. By the end of the day, I expect one to arrive with a built-in swimming pool and its own drive-in theater.

As we stand and watch the driveway, an enormous RV approaches the driveway, awkwardly maneuvers the sharp turn, and starts rolling at a painfully slow, indecisive pace up towards the Big House. This is exactly how an RV would look if it was being driven by a determined poodle.

I look at Patrick, who has become bored and resumed the more interesting work of turning the pig on the spit. "That's definitely not John," I joke.

"Nope."

"Where is he?"

"Out."

I look at Kevin, who clarifies Patrick's remarks by pointing at the RV, which is now lumbering alarmingly off the driveway, heading for that part of the field serving as an impromptu campground. In theory, it is trying to park, but I fear it will hit a groundhog hole and topple over, starting a domino reaction that will take the other RVs down. "Now *that's* a toy hauler," Kevin says appreciatively, as if this explains everything I need to know about John's whereabouts.

From this wealth of information, I deduce that John is out getting the chairs and the tables.

Kevin nods approvingly as two pickups roar up the driveway, swerve off onto the grass, and screech to a stop. "Oh, look," I exclaim. "John and Christy are here!" I dash over to help them unload, leaving Patrick to stand by the pig, periodically adding more logs to the fire as Smeg helps out by watching.

Six hours later, a few dozen banquet tables are set up and decorated, the flowers have been delivered, and the caterers have arrived, armed with chafing dishes for the buffet table under the Big Tent. They are two women in matching frilly aprons. Because this is not a church supper, the caterers have made all the potato salad. Because this is Maine, guests bring their special dishes anyway. By mid-afternoon, a small village has materialized on the front lawn, including all of John's aunts, uncles, siblings, and cousins, along with their respective kids, cats, and dogs. Some of the nieces are playing croquet, and all of the nephews are riding the ATVs. There's Norm the Neighbor, Keith the Hunting Buddy, and all the stubbly members of Patrick's rabbit club including Chris the Pilot, along with Susan the Ski Shop Babe, a languid brunette who can't seem to find the right man, Masumi the Japanese Widow, who looks like what Josie Packard from *Twin Peaks* would look like if she made it to old age, and Tracy the Horse Lady, a leggy blonde who had a high school crush on John and is now flirting energetically with him.

An excellent bluegrass band gets everyone dancing before dinner. A blubbering wreck, Christy is overcome by the onslaught of old friends, new relatives, and her big-haired mom, who is fluttering around with a dazed expression and a scented hanky, clearly wondering how she ended up outside in the dreaded sunshine without a parasol and a corset to keep her upright. I am making sure that Kevin's boar doesn't burn on the grill, and all the hunting buddies are standing around behind me, waiting for the meat, because that's what men do. Out of the corner of my eye, I spot a parade of women emerging from the Big House with serving bowls in their hands, prompting hungry guests to put dibs on seats as they begin to gather under the Big Tent.

As the parade of side dishes go by, wheels in Patrick's brain start to turn. If the bean-hole beans are done, surely the flying pig must be done too? "C'mon, Kevin!" he hollers across the lawn to his friend.

"C'mon, Bobo!" Kevin commands, and two men and a beagle set off to take the pig off the roaster. Heads swivel towards the better action. En masse, the hunting buddies adjust their John Deere caps and troop over to the other side of the field. I follow too, because it's the sort of job that requires an audience. Patrick produces a meat thermometer from his pocket, jabs it dramatically into the pig's thigh, and announces loudly, "Done!" Squaring their shoulders, he and Kevin take their places, one on each end, and one, two, three, hup! The pig comes off the roaster, and is carried with great ceremony to a waiting table set with serving platters and carving knifes.

But as soon as Patrick sets it down, bringing it low enough for me to take a good whiff, my nose sounds the alert.

"It needs to be cooked more," I say nicely.

"No, it durn't," Patrick insists, but not with much conviction because he can't get the knife to go in. He hacks away at the belly seam, yanking the wire threads apart, and then reaches in and unpacks the sweet potatoes. He scowls, because the tubers are still hard as rocks. "They're fine," he says defensively, as he chips off a few bits of charred meat, tosses them with a great rattling into a tray, and carries it off to the Big Tent to join the accidentally vegetarian buffet.

Don scowls as he pokes the underdone pig in disgust. Then he looks at me. "Next time we do a pig roast," he growls at me, "we're not letting Patrick be in charge of the pig." I look at him in surprise. It's the nicest thing he's said to me. And off he wanders to yell at the grandkids for riding the ATVs too fast around the old people.

Sighing, I grab the carving knife and whack off an entire haunch. "I'm taking this leg and I'm going to finish cooking it," I announce loudly to the startled foragers, grabbing my pig from the table, and marching back to Kevin's grill with my unladylike prize. I *will* grill it, I mutter to myself, and it will be falling off the bone once I'm done with it, and I'm not going to get married just to do a proper pig roast, even though John believes in the whole legally-wedded business because he's a lawyer *and* a Republican.

Still muttering to myself, I march straight back to the pig table, gather up a tray of sweet potatoes, and parade haughtily off with them. The hunting buddies swarm in to fill the void, still plucking at the underdone pig with calloused, optimistic hands. I'm going to put the sweet potatoes directly onto the embers in the fire pit dug for the bean-hole beans just because I want to be able to say to Ruth, when she asks me what happened to them: "They're in the bean-hole bean hole!" It shouldn't take them too long to cook. By the time my grilled haunch is done, I expect they will be ready too. (See "Microwave.")

It takes no time at all to bury the potatoes out back, say hello to the chickens, yell at the nephews, and circle back around to enjoy the sight of my two roasts, one wild boar, the other domestic sow. They look quite happy together, soaking in the slow, dry heat of the grill. Closing the lid, I pull up a lawn chair and sit down to guard them, doing my best to look large enough to discourage thieves. A few minutes later, John strolls up with fake grin on his face, a lawn chair in one hand, and a glass of lemonade in the other. Cheerfully, he plops down beside me, teasing: "Don't rush me!" mimicking my familiar complaint. The ruse is that he's helping me guard the meat, but he's really guarding me, because his brother will never forgive him if he lets me start dancing. The old timers have seen plenty of tween boys tearing around in ATVs, but they've never seen me trying to dance to a bluegrass band. It'll scare the bejeezus out of them, and the last thing that Patrick wants is an unholy mess at his party.

Holding hands, John and I sit contentedly on the lawn, watching the festivities from a sunny spot in my brain between Paris, France, and Paris, Maine. We look quite happy together, the Yankee and me, soaking in the warmth of the late summer sun beaming down on a wedding feast. All this activity is making me hungry, but Smeg snapped off the pig's ears this morning and gave them to me as a snack, and I'm allergic to lemonade. Because he can read my mind, John rises from his chair. When he returns, he's holding a tall glass of ice water. Solemnly, he hands it to me. Solemnly, I thank him for it.

One of the most famous miracles in the Bible is the one where Christ turns water into wine. He performs this miracle at a wedding, the subject of an immense painting by Paolo Veronese hanging in the Louvre. The *Feast of Cana*, 1563, is a masterpiece. It also happens to be the largest painting in the Louvre, but it might as well be textured wallpaper because the other painting in the salon is the Mona Lisa. She sucks all the air out of the room.

Whenever friends come to visit me in Paris, France, they insist on seeing her, but she's got a tiny head, hovers about ten feet off the ground, and stays behind velvet ropes and bulletproof glass. All you can see is glare. Durn't matter. There's always a mob struggling to be photographed with her. That's the power of staying a singleton with an inscrutable expression on your face while refusing to wear a wedding ring.

The Louvre's curators must have thought it would be hilarious to make a woman with no eyebrows stare forever at a wedding where the guest list was so exclusive that the son of God attended. Theoretically, the centerpiece at the Cana wedding was roast lamb, except the men were butchering the baby sheep at the party, right in front of the guests, who didn't seem the least bothered by the gruesome sight of limbs being whacked. The lamb wouldn't be properly roasted for hours, so the guests have already moved on to dessert . . . which is kind of like what's going on right in front of my face, because every time Baird and his cousins roar by on the ATVs, there is strawberry dribbling from their chins. The women under the Big Tent are so distracted by the potluck assortment of sweets that they forget all about the other food options, like, say, the three turkeys, which end up totally ignored in the pig debacle.

Today, alas, no water gets transformed into wine, but the caterers accidentally leave the stand-alone mixer to mindlessly whip cream, and so it gets turned into butter. To the immense delight of the flies, the underdone pig sits unloved and unprotected as the last of the men gives up trying to find a cooked bit and walks away, defeated. Seizing the opportunity, Goldie the Golden Retriever gnaws off a great chunk of the pork. She runs away as fast as a hunting dog can while slobbering over ten pounds of hard meat, her floppy ears and wagging tail signaling her ferocious glee. Wrapped around the knobby bone, her doggy smile matches the one on Mona Lisa's face.

"I have something important to say," John declares earnestly, as the daylight drains and the bluegrass band starts up again under peeking starlight. All the children have gone inside the Big House and passed out from exhaustion, and John has eaten three plates of roast beast and a pound of plain strawberries. "From now on," he says carefully, squeezing my hand, "you're in charge of the pig."

I look at him and reply, sweetly, "I think I already am."

The next morning, right after dawn, Christy comes up to the Big House to take a shower. "I gotta meet my mother for breakfast," she explains preemptively. I pour myself some coffee and peek outside. It's another gorgeous day, and a few hunting buddies are outside boiling quahogs by the Big Tent. It's unclear if they're just getting up or never went to bed.

"Did you guys get any sleep?" I ask Christy.

"Nope!" she admits, her expression slightly abashed. In the wee hours of a boozy night, Christy relates, Smeg tripped over a pile of firewood on his way to pick at the leftover pig, fell on his head, and dislocated his hip. His skin was so tough that the EMTs couldn't get the cortisone shot in. He got carted off to the hospital, and a doctor from Portland came up and put his hip back in.

"I slept through an ambulance?" I blurt in dismay.

"Uh huh!" Christy nods, and takes a grateful swig of coffee.

I shake my head glumly. "That's worse than sleeping through coyotes."

"What are you girls talking about?" John asks, yawning in flannel pajamas as he heads for the coffee.

"Smeg fell on his head," Christy tells him with an amused air, sucking down the dregs of her coffee before she heads out in her Jeep.

John snorts. "At least this time it wasn't Patrick."

This afternoon will be a lobster feed, so the plan involves driving to Portland to pick up some fresh lobster from a

seafood wholesaler. Through the window, I watch as another
RV clears out of the field. Already, the impromptu parking lot
is nearly empty.

"Get dressed, plumpkin!" John urges me cheerfully. "We
can sight in my rifle out back before the kids wake up!" This
time, it's a new .30–06 Savage with a cheap scope. He won it
a decade ago in a raffle. It's a good caliber for moose hunting, and once I get my hunting license, I can start entering the
moose lottery too. "We're going to run a patch through the
bore after groups of three, okay?"

It probably says something about our relationship that I
now know what he means.

Epilogue

For the next two weeks, I'm holing up on a writing fellowship in a summer house on a hefty tract of private land located on Shin Pond up north. It's Patten Pioneer Days this week, and the festivities are in full swing. The big event is the fireman's barbecue on Friday, followed by fireworks, and a spaghetti supper at the Methodist church. There will be traffic this weekend because of it. The town only has a few hundred residents, but this weekend, everyone comes back, including me and my dad, who is bringing his new girlfriend, and they are both staying with me ("in *separate* bedrooms," he repeats a hundred times, just to make sure I've understood.) He and Barbara met at the Senior Center over slabs of meatloaf, and they've been happily doddering away ever since. Strip away the externals, and the two of them are weirdly alike. On spindly legs they potter along, peeling oranges and marveling at the fresh air. They count their pills, worry about finding the bathroom at night, and they're starting Spanish language classes together.

"Why Spanish?" I ask them.

"Why not?" they reply, smiling.

As they sit outside on the porch, watching the golden eagle soar overhead and listening to the loons on the pond, I roast a chicken and set the table, then call them inside for supper. With happy smiles of anticipation, they wait for me to serve them, as my dad reads aloud the daily meditation from the *Upper Room* and says grace as we hold hands around the table. For dessert, they eat ice cream and play Scrabble together on the card table. Barbara wins every time. My dad doesn't mind.

The next day, we drive to Houlton so Dad can show Barbara where we used to live. The Town and Country shop is still there, and so is Cole's shoes. Ricker College is gone. The Elm Street Diner burned down and got rebuilt at a different spot in town, but it still sells whoopie pies the size of your head. The Christian Missionary Alliance Church is now the Church of Latter Day Saints. The old Congregational Church is in the same place, and so is the Methodist Church on the corner of School Street. The church and the library are still facing each other across a small park, a large statue of a civil war soldier marking the halfway point between them.

The old parsonage is a different color. I recognize it immediately, but it's the maple tree out front and the Jarvis's house next door that I really remember. Roy and Mary were skinny old folks who didn't have kids because they didn't like them. They retired in Houlton to get away from people, and Roy re-upholstered boats as a hobby that grew into a booming business. This was not the plan. So he sold it, and resumed his cantankerous routine, sitting on the front porch muttering about young whippersnappers and feeding us gingersnap cookies.

"They were Greek," my dad says randomly. "Jarvis is a Greek name."

My best friend from middle school still lives in Houlton, so Nancy and I hang out for a while and she updates me on all the gossip before we drive back to Patton and park near the Methodist church to attend the church supper. On the street, cars are lined up on both sides. The church supper is in full swing. As soon as we go through the door and enter the vestibule, the elderly woman taking tickets recognizes my dad immediately.

"Reverend Lee!" Sally exclaims in pleased surprise, moving her oxygen tank out of the way so she can hug him properly. "How nice to see you!" After they chit-chat for a while and he introduces Barbara, Sally turns to me with an expectant look on her face. "And which one are you?" she asks with characteristic Yankee bluntness.

"I'm the middle one," I say cheerfully.

She looks at me more closely, and her confused expression clears. "Oh yes!" she exclaims in recognition. "Why, you've hardly changed at all! Your sister was the pretty one." And her face lights up in pleasure because she actually remembers the three of us kids running around the church and going Christmas caroling in subzero temperatures.

I smile back, because she's correct: I'm just as short and stubborn as I was when I was ten. However, the next time one of the old parishioners asks me which one I am, I'm going to grin widely and say, "I'm the Ho!"

Thanks to my korma, it's finally true.

ACKNOWLEDGMENTS

I owe many people a great deal of gratitude for helping bring this work to fruition, including my staunch friends Nancy Ketch, Carol Abraczinskas, Rose Acker, Jennifer Morris, Jane Pollard, Kate Marsland, Anat Pollack, and Katherine Haskins. This book would not exist without Cordula Robinson, who accidentally helped me meet my great love John, who is the only conservative I've ever met who doesn't want me to agree with him. I'm indebted to the editors and staff at Travelers' Tales/Solas House, Inc. for their faith in this book and their willingness to bring it forth into the world. As always, I owe my family the greatest thanks, because they have to put up with my cooking. When this work started, both of my wonderful nieces, Sophie and Emily, were shorter than me. They are now both taller. Finally, to Baird, who for three years asked me relentlessly, "Is your book done yet?" I can now finally reply: "Yes."

Paula Young Lee is a cultural historian and backwoods cook. Her books include *Meat, Modernity, and the Rise of the Slaughterhouse* (ed.); *Game: A Global History*; and *The Birdcage of the Muses: Observing Animals at the 17th-century Ménagerie at Versailles*, forthcoming. Her research has been supported by fellowships from the National Endowment for the Humanities and other institutions. She splits her time between West Paris, Maine, and Wellesley, Massachusetts.